Ancient History for Teens

An Enthralling Journey Through Egypt, Greece, and Rome

© Copyright 2025 - All rights reserved.

The content contained within this book may not be reproduced, duplicated, or transmitted without direct written permission from the author or the publisher.

Under no circumstances will any blame or legal responsibility be held against the publisher, or author, for any damages, reparation, or monetary loss due to the information contained within this book, either directly or indirectly.

Legal Notice:

This book is copyright protected. It is only for personal use. You cannot amend, distribute, sell, use, quote, or paraphrase any part, or the content within this book, without the consent of the author or publisher.

Disclaimer Notice:

Please note the information contained within this document is for educational and entertainment purposes only. All effort has been executed to present accurate, up-to-date, reliable, and complete information. No warranties of any kind are declared or implied. Readers acknowledge that the author is not engaging in the rendering of legal, financial, medical, or professional advice. The content within this book has been derived from various sources. Please consult a licensed professional before attempting any techniques outlined in this book.

By reading this document, the reader agrees that under no circumstances is the author responsible for any losses, direct or indirect, that are incurred as a result of the use of the information contained within this document, including, but not limited to, errors, omissions, or inaccuracies.

Free limited time bonus

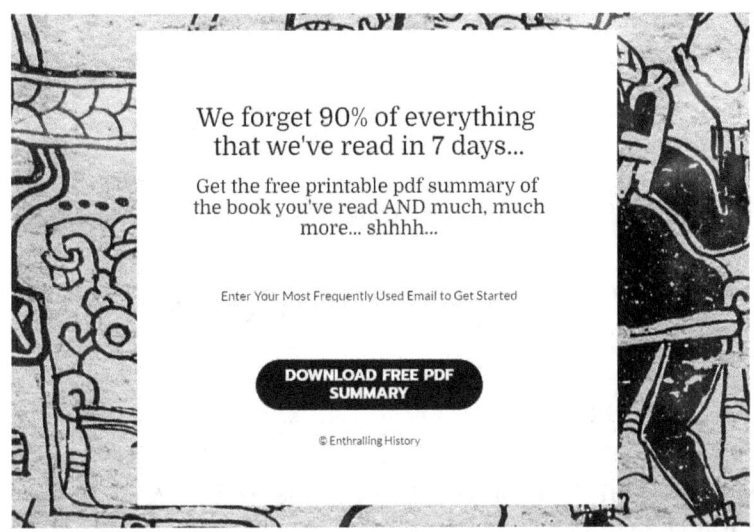

Stop for a moment. We have a free bonus set up for you. The problem is this: we forget 90% of everything that we read after 7 days. Crazy fact, right? Here's the solution: we've created a printable, 1-page pdf summary for this book that you're reading now. All you have to do to get your free pdf summary is to go to the following website:
https://livetolearn.lpages.co/enthrallinghistory/

Or, Scan the QR code!

Once you do, it will be intuitive. Enjoy, and thank you!

Table of Contents

PART 1: ANCIENT EGYPT FOR TEENS 1
    INTRODUCTION 3
    CHAPTER 1: THE RISE OF THE PHARAOHS: EGYPTIAN UNIFICATION 7
    CHAPTER 2: THE MIDDLE KINGDOM AND THE HYKSOS DYNASTY 19
    CHAPTER 3: ANCIENT EGYPTIAN SOCIETY AND CULTURE 32
    CHAPTER 4: ANCIENT EGYPTIAN ARCHITECTURE 44
    CHAPTER 5: THE AFTERLIFE: EXPLORING LIFE AFTER DEATH IN ANCIENT EGYPT 55
    CHAPTER 6: HATSHEPSUT: THE FEMALE PHARAOH 66
    CHAPTER 7: AKHENATEN: THE HERETIC 78
    CHAPTER 8: TUTANKHAMUN: A BOY AND HIS LEGACY 88
    CHAPTER 9: THE BATTLE OF KADESH 102
    CHAPTER 10: THE FALL OF THE NEW KINGDOM 114
    ANSWER KEY: ROUNDUP ACTIVITIES 123

PART 2: ANCIENT GREECE FOR TEENS 129
    INTRODUCTION 131
    CHAPTER 1: AN INTRODUCTION TO ANCIENT GREECE 133
    CHAPTER 2: GODS AND GODDESSES OF OLYMPUS 148
    CHAPTER 3: THE RISE OF ATHENS FROM CITY-STATE TO EMPIRE 159
    CHAPTER 4: BECOMING A SPARTAN 170

CHAPTER 5: THE PERSIAN WARS: MARATHON AND
THERMOPYLAE 180
CHAPTER 6: THE GOLDEN AGE OF ATHENS: ART,
PHILOSOPHY, AND DEMOCRACY 191
CHAPTER 7: THE PELOPONNESIAN WAR 202
CHAPTER 8: ALEXANDER THE GREAT 212
CHAPTER 9: THE HELLENISTIC AGE... 223
CHAPTER 10: GREEK SCIENCE AND TECHNOLOGY 235
ANSWER KEY FOR ROUND-UP ACTIVITIES 245
PART 3: ANCIENT ROME FOR TEENS 253
INTRODUCTION 255
CHAPTER 1: ROMULUS AND REMUS 257
CHAPTER 2: WHAT WAS THE ROMAN REPUBLIC? 269
CHAPTER 3: FROM REPUBLIC TO EMPIRE 280
CHAPTER 4: THE ROMAN ARMY 291
CHAPTER 5: PATRICIANS, PLEBIANS, AND SLAVES 301
CHAPTER 6: LEISURE, ENTERTAINMENT, AND ECONOMY 310
CHAPTER 7: KEY ACHIEVEMENTS OF ANCIENT ROME 320
CHAPTER 8: COLOSSAL FIGURES 329
CHAPTER 9: CONSTANTINE AND CHRISTIANITY 341
CHAPTER 10: THE FALL OF AN EMPIRE... 352
ROUNDUP ACTIVITIES ANSWER KEY 362
HERE'S ANOTHER BOOK BY ENTHRALLING HISTORY THAT
YOU MIGHT LIKE 367
FREE LIMITED TIME BONUS 368
BIBLIOGRAPHY 369
IMAGE SOURCES 375

Part 1: Ancient Egypt for Teens

An Enthralling Guide to Important Events and Rulers in Egyptian History

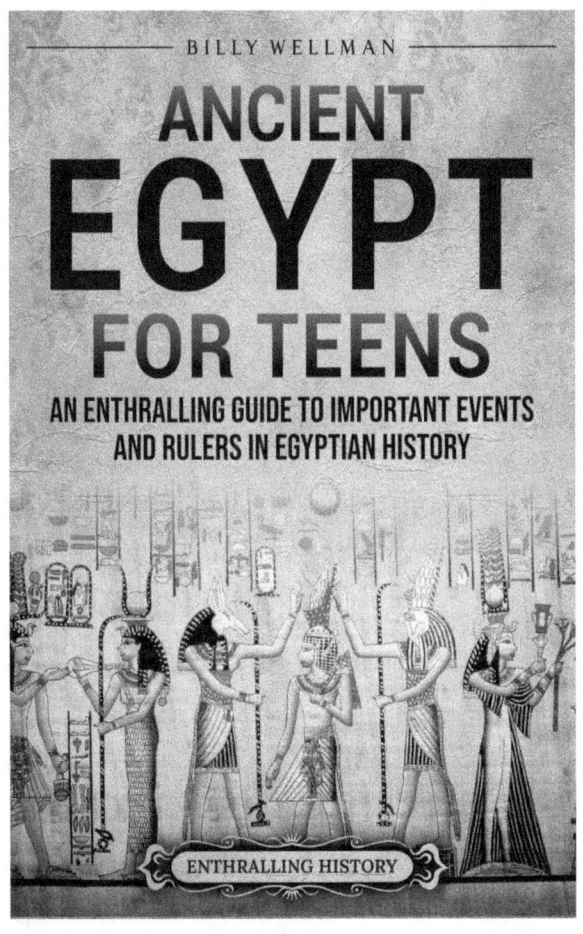

Introduction

What leaps to mind when thinking of ancient Egypt? Pharaohs? Pyramids? Mummies? All three are essential elements of its history, but there's so much more. This book unpacks the stories of Egypt's pharaohs and ordinary people. What was everyday life like? What was the dark side of the people's relationship with their kings? How did the world's longest river enrich Egypt? Did Egyptian hieroglyphics give birth to the world's first alphabet?

When diving into ancient Egypt's history, the problem of dates arises. What happened when? The ancient Egyptians didn't record dates the same way we do today. Instead, they measured time by the reigns of their kings. For instance, they would write a date like "the third year of Khufu." This leads to another question: when did Khufu reign? It all gets a bit confusing because, sometimes, more than one king ruled part of Egypt at the same time.

Did you know the Egyptians didn't call their kings "pharaohs" until around 1500 BCE in the New Kingdom? The Hebrew people used the title "pharaoh" for Egypt's kings because they wrote the Torah and the rest of the Tanakh (Old Testament) in the New Kingdom or later. The name stuck and is commonly used today, even for earlier kings.

In the third century BCE, an Egyptian priest named Manetho tried to organize ancient Egypt's thousands of years of history. He listed thirty **dynasties**. (A dynasty is when a series of kings and queens from the same family or ethnic group rule). In the 1800s CE, Egyptologists developed the idea of three golden ages: the Old Kingdom, the Middle Kingdom, and the New Kingdom. Egypt had powerful kings, unimaginable wealth, and stunning new technology in these kingdoms. Between these three golden ages, Egypt fell into "intermediate periods." Culture and economics suffered in these times of messy politics.

Scholars fiercely debate the dates for these three kingdoms and their dynasties. The dates in this book are a rough estimation and may be slightly different from other sources. Each of the three kingdoms and intermediate periods had several dynasties. Egypt was occasionally divided so that two or three dynasties ruled simultaneously.

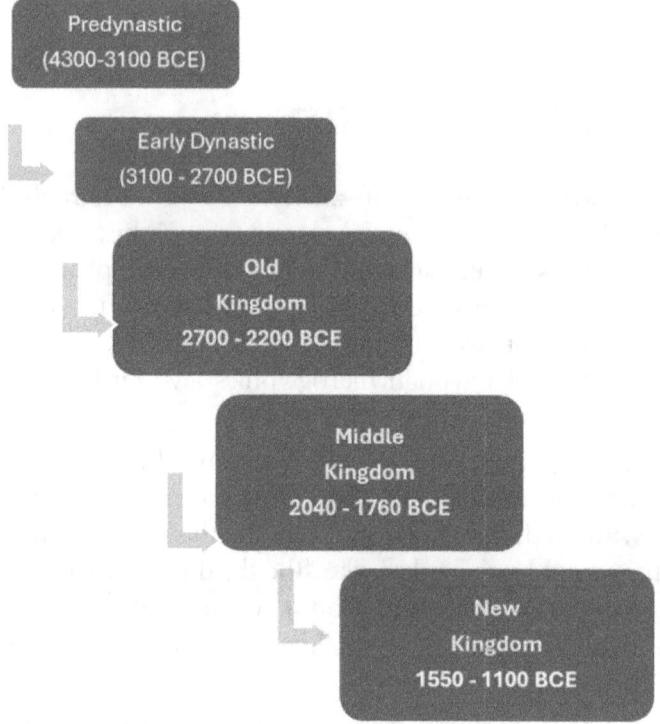

A flowchart of the dynastic periods[1]

This book begins with an overview of Egypt's Predynastic and Early Dynastic eras, when Egypt united and developed its hieroglyphic script. It then delves into the rise of Egypt's great kings who formed the *Old Kingdom*, the Age of the Pyramids. Did you know the Great Pyramid of Giza was the world's tallest structure for almost four millennia? How did they pull off such a fantastic feat 4,600 thousand years ago?

We will then dig into the ***Middle Kingdom***, a time of cultural flowering and reunification. One powerful king, Senusret, divided Egypt into three administrative regions. Little did he know that Egypt would split into two (possibly three) separate kingdoms within decades. You'll also learn the answers to the following questions: How did Queen Sobekneferu become Egypt's pharaoh, and what happened when she died without heirs? How did the foreign Hyksos grab power in Egypt? Who were they, and where were they from?

Next, the book explores Egyptian culture. Did the pharaohs really marry their sisters? Why were the ancient Egyptians so consumed with the afterlife? What were the mummies and pyramids all about? How did the Nile River and Egypt's climate affect its culture?

Did you know the Nile River flows ***north*** from Lake Victoria in Uganda? In ancient times, people called the land Upper Egypt and Lower Egypt. What's confusing is that Upper Egypt is in the south, and Lower Egypt is in the north. However, Upper Egypt is mountainous, and the Nile flows north from these highlands to Lower Egypt, the flat delta region.

Finally, we'll unwrap all the drama of the ***New Kingdom*** when Egypt pushed its borders north to Syria. What pharaoh turned Egypt's religion upside down? Who was the only god he worshiped? Was the child king, Tutankhamun, physically disabled? How did chariot technology help Ramesses II win the Battle of Kadesh despite being hopelessly outnumbered by the Hittites?

Ancient Egypt's story has intriguing twists and turns that will keep you turning the pages. But aside from being entertaining, what's the point of reading history? History unlocks secrets from the past, shedding light on why the world is the way it is today. History is all about change and how and why it happens. It inspires us to be agents of change for a better future. As we read the history of Ancient Egypt, we'll see how it passed through multiple transformations that sparked innovative technology and culture. On the other hand, the dark side of Egypt's history is a lesson in what *not* to do.

Now, let's jump back in time on a journey through ancient Egypt's spellbinding history.

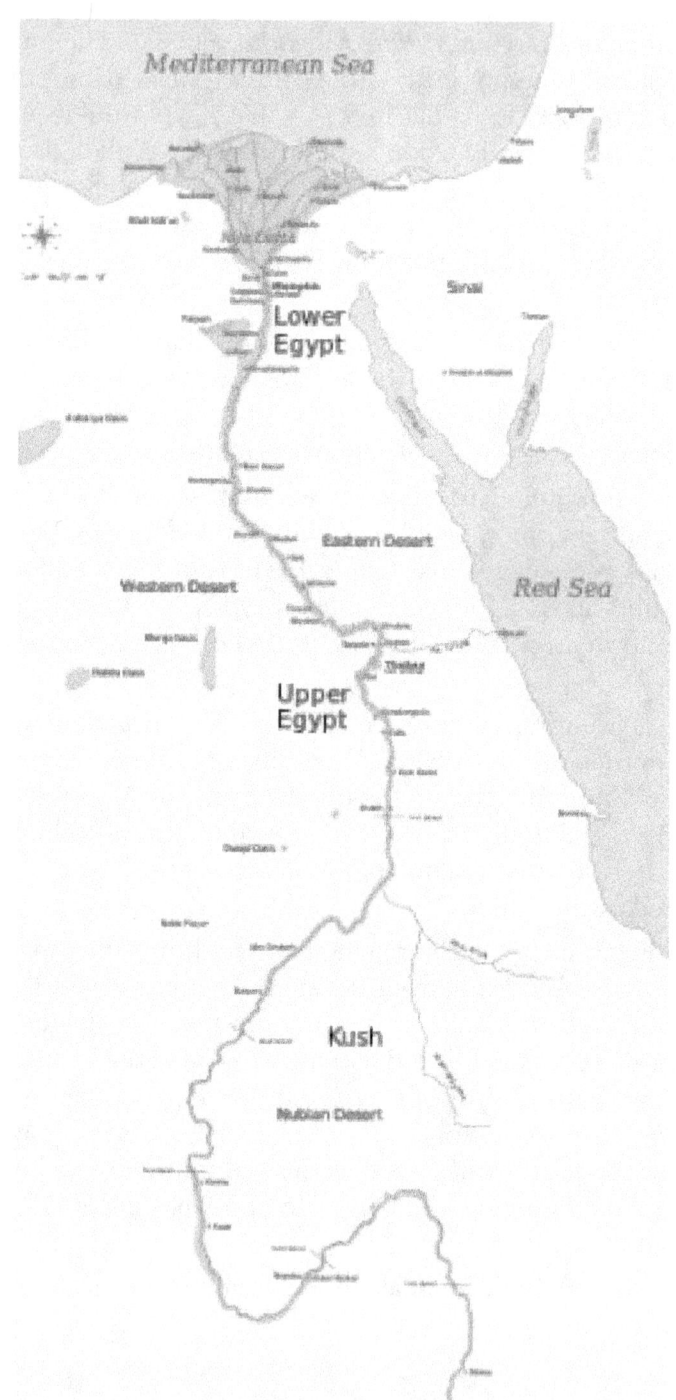

Upper and Lower Egypt

Chapter 1: The Rise of the Pharaohs: Egyptian Unification

King Djoser was in the depths of despair. The rain had stopped for seven years. Unimaginable suffering gripped Egypt. Children were wailing in hunger. No one seemed to know how to make it rain again. Djoser called for his advisor, Imhotep, an architect and priest of the sun god Ra.

"What should I do?" he asked Imhotep. "Who is the god of the Nile's headwaters? We need to ask him for help!"

"Let me travel upstream and find out," Imhotep said.

Imhotep returned to report, "I found a temple called Joy-of-Life. Khnum is its god. He opens and shuts the gates of the Nile."

Djoser made an offering of beer and oxen to Khnum. That night, Khnum visited Djoser in a dream.

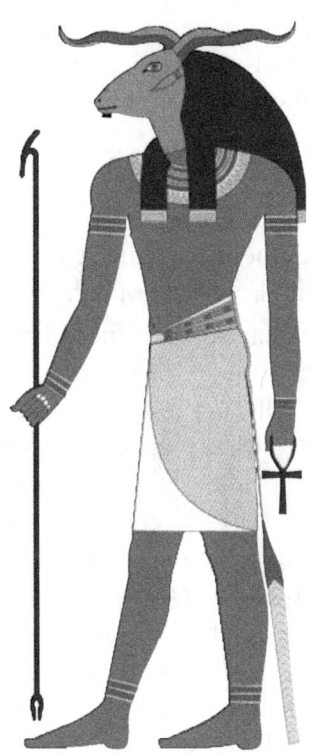

The ram-headed god Khnum'

"My temple on the island of Elephantine is falling down. I gave the Egyptians life through my river! Now, everyone has lost respect for me."

When he awoke, Djoser ordered the temple to be torn down. He built a beautiful new temple on its foundations. The famine ended, to everyone's relief.

The ruins of that temple to Khnum are still on Elephantine Island, 4,700 years later. The stone stela with this story was found on Seheil Island in the Nile, just south of Elephantine Island.

Predynastic Egypt (4300–3100 BCE)

Djoser was the first king of Egypt's Old Kingdom, but what happened before that? How did Egypt's early people live in the misty ages before they started to write? Archaeological evidence shows that in Predynastic Egypt, people built oval huts with mud-plastered walls and woven mats on the floor. They herded cattle, sheep, and goats and grew wheat and barley. They ground the grain into flour and formed a round, flat dough. Then they lit a fire inside a dome-shaped clay oven and let it burn until the walls got hot. After putting out the fire, they slapped the bread dough on the inside of the oven's walls, which baked the bread.

By 3400 BCE, ancient Egyptians were building houses from sunbaked bricks. Some homes were grander, with central courtyards. Egypt's early cities sprang up in the delta region. Xois was built, and people continually lived there for almost 3,800 years. Nekhen (Hierakonpolis) grew into a town of 5,000 people by 3400 BCE.

What about mummification? When did that start? Egyptians usually buried their dead in desert cemeteries, where the hot sand would naturally dry out and mummify the bodies. By 3350 BCE, Egyptians started wrapping their dead in linen cloth soaked in embalming agents like aromatic plant extract, gum, natural petroleum, and pine resin. By 3200 BCE, they began building large brick or limestone tombs with multiple rooms for burying family members.

Between 3400 and 3200 BCE, Egyptians began drawing pictographs in Abydos. These were simple pictures that could represent either the object in the image or another word with a similar sound as the object. These pictographs evolved into hieroglyphic writing. In the earliest stages of hieroglyphics, Egyptians didn't write sentences. They used the pictographs for labels and record keeping.

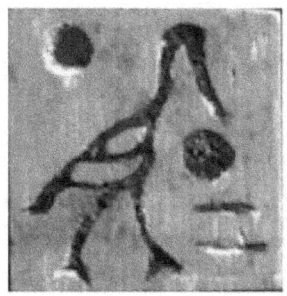  

Pictographs from Abydos[*]

Archaeological digs from this era show the Egyptians had brilliant blue beads made from the lapis lazuli stone. Yet, Egypt didn't have lapis lazuli, so where did it come from? The nearest source was Afghanistan, over 2,000 miles away! Southern Iraq was probably the middleman in long-distance trade, as Iraq's Ubaid culture had the same beads.

The Ubaid traded with both Egypt and Afghanistan in long and arduous journeys by donkey over the deserts. The humble donkey was the world's first transportation animal, domesticated from the wild African ass around 5000 BCE.

Other items made from lapis lazuli were cylinder seals. Egypt adopted these from southern Iraq around 3300 BCE. A cylinder seal was a stone cylinder about four inches long with carvings of tiny pictures on it. When the owner rolled it in soft clay, it left an impression of the image. The clay hardened, and the picture represented the owner's signature.

Egypt Unites! Early Dynastic Egypt (3100–2700 BCE)

Over the next four centuries, there was an explosion of culture as writing and stunning technological advances developed. For the first time, Upper and Lower Egypt united into one country. How did that happen? It was the work of Narmer, the first king of Egypt's unified state. With a central government and economy, Egypt could organize massive projects like building pyramids. This didn't happen until the Old Kingdom emerged, but Egypt's Early Dynastic era set the stage.

Drawing of the Narmer Palette[6]

"Stinging Catfish"

What do we know about Narmer, the first king of unified Egypt? The hieroglyphs for Narmer's name are the signs for "catfish" and "painful." The dates are fuzzy, but he ruled around 3100 BCE. He was probably Menes, a king mentioned by the historian Manetho. Egyptian kings had personal names and throne names, which can get confusing. Narmer, the "Stinging Catfish," unified Egypt and began its First Dynasty. Narmer was from Upper Egypt and conquered Lower Egypt, which was epic since Lower Egypt had developed earlier and was more powerful. Upper Egypt now had the upper hand.

The "Narmer Palette" is a two-foot-high stone slab. On carvings on one side, Narmer brandishes a mace, a club-like weapon. He grabs a kneeling captive by the hair, probably Lower Egypt's ruler. A falcon represents Horus, the king-making god. On the opposite side of the palette are two "serpopards," leopards with serpent necks. Their intertwining necks represent Upper and Lower Egypt's union.

Drawing of serpopards from the Narber Palette*

Narmer expanded Egypt's power into the Sinai Peninsula and Canaan (ancient Israel and Palestine). Artifacts found in Gaza and Israel have his name on them. His long reign ended when a hippopotamus killed him. (Yes, hippos are deadly animals. They kill about 500 people every year in Africa!)

Narmer's wife was the powerful Queen Neithhotep. Their son, Hor-Aha, was still a small child when Narmer died. Queen Neithhotep ruled Egypt until her son grew up and became the next king.

The MacGregor Plaque is an ivory tablet dating to about 2985 BCE from the tomb of King Den. In the writing on the tablet, Den boasts of making "the first strike to the east." What does he mean by "east?" Narmer had already pressed east as far as Canaan. Did he mean Mesopotamia (ancient Iraq)? We can't be sure, but the picture on the tablet shows him grasping the hair of an eastern king who wears his hair and beard braided in Mesopotamian style.

King Den and his eastern captive[7]

The Old Kingdom:
Age of the Pyramids (2700–2200 BCE)

After four centuries and two dynasties, a new era dawned for Egypt. The Old Kingdom was the first of Egypt's three golden ages. This age began when the first pyramid rose from the sand to dominate Egypt's landscape. The energy, manpower, and materials poured into building the pyramids in this era are mind-blowing. Dynasties three through six ruled Egypt in these glory days.

Djoser

As we said earlier, King Djoser began the Old Kingdom, the era of pyramids. He built the first pyramid and was the first king of the Third Dynasty. Ornate architecture blossomed under his reign. He extended Egypt past Libya's borders and took back the Sinai Peninsula, a valuable source of turquoise and copper. Upper and Lower Egypt had separated in the turmoil toward the end of the Early Dynastic period, but Djoser or his father brought the two back together. No sooner did Djoser become king than he jumped into multiple building projects like nothing ever seen before.

Mastabas: Pyramid Precursors

Before Djoser, Egyptian royals were buried in mastaba tombs, which had flat roofs and mudbrick walls that sloped in. A mastaba was rectangular and about twenty to thirty feet high. The dead person wasn't buried inside the mastaba but under it. A shaft went underground to a small burial room; another shaft descended to a second room next to the burial room. This room held things the dead person needed in the afterlife, like beer, clothing, food, and jewelry.

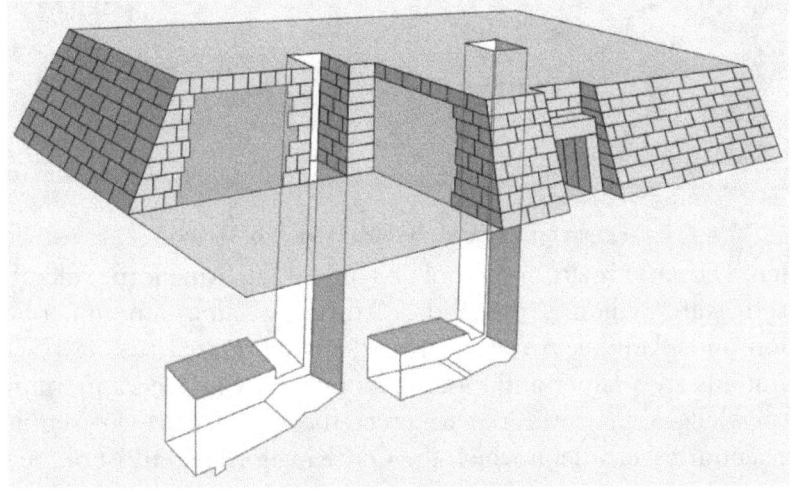

A mastaba*

The First Pyramid

Djoser had his tomb built like a mastaba, but instead of one layer, he wanted six layers. His architect, Imhotep, built each layer slightly smaller than the one underneath, forming steps. Instead of mud bricks, he used stone. The Step Pyramid of Djoser soared 204 feet high, the highest structure in the world up to that time. The Sumerians in ancient Iraq had been building ziggurats, similar to step pyramids, but none were yet this high.

Djoser's actual burial place was under the pyramid, as in the mastabas. His burial shaft descended ninety feet under the pyramid. Imhotep discouraged tomb robbers by building a maze of tunnels so that finding the royal burial vault was nearly impossible. Despite Imhotep's best efforts, ancient tomb robbers broke into Djoser's tomb and stole almost everything. All that was left was a mummified left foot.

Egypt's first pyramid, the Step Pyramid of Djoser

After Djoser's reign, most of Egypt's Old Kingdom rulers were obsessed with building pyramids. An astonishing amount of their attention and planning revolved around their eventual resting place. As the pyramids grew larger and more elaborate, they needed a monumental and knowledgeable workforce to erect them. This activity required a strong central government, which the Old Kingdom had most of the time.

Thousands of workers cut the stones at a quarry and transported them to the building sites. But Egypt didn't have the wheel until the Fifth Dynasty, so how did they move those hefty stones over long distances? They used gigantic sleds pulled through the sand. Workers ahead of the sled poured water on the sand, making it slippery. Most pyramids were near today's Cairo, stretching about forty miles along the Nile.

The First "True" Pyramids

The step pyramids were the "steppingstones" to the first "real" pyramids with smooth sides and a pointed top. King Sneferu of the Fourth Dynasty built the first three smooth-sided, pointy-top pyramids around 2500 BCE. His first pyramid was a disaster. The architects only used a rock foundation for the inner core. The outer layers lay on a sand foundation, which couldn't support the pyramid's weight. The pyramid collapsed in the final stage of construction, burying the workers underneath it.

Sneferu didn't give up. He built a pyramid at Dahshur. However, his architects were still figuring out how to get the angles of a true pyramid right. They erected the pyramid at a 55-degree angle, which worked fine until they were about halfway to the top. The pyramid began showing instability, so the builders switched to a flatter 43-degree angle. This made the Bent Pyramid appear bent at the top, hence the name. Dissatisfied, the architects immediately built the Red Pyramid entirely at a 43-degree angle. Its stones were a rusty red.

The Bent Pyramid[10]

Khufu, Builder of the Great Pyramid

Khufu was the next pharaoh after Sneferu and probably his son. He was remembered as an oppressive king who did not value the lives of his people. He pressed the Egyptians into forced labor to build his masterpiece, the world's highest pyramid of all time. Standing at about 481 feet high, the Great Pyramid was the highest building in the world for almost 4,000 years. It was also the largest pyramid until the Mesoamericans built the Cholula Pyramid in Mexico, beginning in the third century BCE. The Cholula Pyramid had a much larger base and volume, but the Great Pyramid was still higher.

The Westcar Papyrus, written in the seventeenth century BCE, tells five stories about magical happenings. The first story deals with a miracle performed by Imhotep during Djoser's reign. Khufu's son, Khafre, supposedly tells the second story, which happened in the earlier reign of King Nebka. According to the story, the king's chief priest discovered his wife was cheating on him. Her lover was sneaking into the priest's property to meet with her. To get revenge, the priest made a wax crocodile and used his magic to bring it to life. His servant threw it into the stream that his wife's lover crossed to visit her. The crocodile grabbed the man, pulled him to the bottom for seven days, then ate him.

Khufu's son, Baufra, tells the third story about his grandfather, King Sneferu. One day, the king was bored and had nothing to do, so he had twenty beautiful young women row him around the palace lake. One of the young ladies wore a necklace with a fish ornament, her favorite jewelry piece. When the necklace fell into the lake, she was hysterical.

"Don't worry. You can have any necklace in my treasury!" Sneferu said, trying to console her.

But the young woman only wanted her necklace at the bottom of the lake. Finally, the king's priest split the water so she could get her necklace, then returned the water to where it had been.

Khufu's son Hordjedef tells the fourth story about a magician named Dedi who claimed he could tame lions and reattach an animal's head that had been cut off. He also knew how many secret rooms were in the shrine of Thoth. Khufu called him to his court to test him out. "Here's a criminal," Khufu said. "We'll cut his head off, and you can put it back on."

"No. We can't kill a man. That isn't proper for dark magic. Bring some animals instead."

Khufu had his servants cut off the heads of a goose, a duck, and a bull. The magician successfully reattached them.

"Well done!" said Khufu. "Now, tell me, how many rooms are in the shrine of Thoth?"

"I don't actually know," Dedi admitted. "But I do know *where* they are. However, I can't tell you how to get into the rooms. The gods haven't given you access. The future king born from the woman Rededjet, wife of the priest of Ra, will have access to the rooms of the shrine."

The child of the priest and Rededjet who became a king was Userkaf, the first king of the Fifth Dynasty.

Dedi tells the fifth story, giving a prophecy about Rededjet and her triplets. The birth was dangerous, so the god Ra sent Isis and other deities to assist her. The three boys were safely delivered and came out of their mother with lapis lazuli crowns and gold covering their arms and legs.

The Old Kingdom Crumbles

The Egyptians' preoccupation with building pyramids led to the priests acquiring more power. Everyone was so consumed with the afterlife that they let the priests control things. They carried out the rituals for the dead and started calling the shots in Egypt. During the Fifth and Sixth dynasties, the kings gradually became weaker and more irrelevant. The solid central government began to melt away, and the cost of building elaborate pyramids bankrupted the country. Priests and *nomarchs* (governors) held dominance over local areas.

A horrendous drought and famine in the Sixth Dynasty devastated Egypt. The *4.2-kiloyear BP* event was one of human history's worst climate changes. (*Kiloyear* means a thousand years, and *BP* means "before present," so it happened about 4,200 years before the twentieth century CE.) It struck the Middle East, bringing cooler temperatures and only half the average rainfall. Drought, political woes, and financial disaster led to the fall of the Old Kingdom.

In the First Intermediate Period (2200-2040 BCE), each region of Egypt ruled itself. The Seventh through Tenth dynasties ruled this era, but not over the entire country. In these chaotic times, miscreants raided tombs, destroyed precious artwork, and broke up the statues of the earlier kings.

Roundup Activity: Who Am I?

Match the person with who they were or what they did. Check your answers in the back of the book.

1. Dedi — I was the first king of a unified Egypt. A hippo killed me.

2. Djoser — I was King Narmer's wife. After he died, I ruled Egypt until my son grew up.

3. Imhotep — I built Egypt's first pyramid and rescued Egypt from a famine.

4. Khnum — I was the god of the Nile's headwaters. I got angry when my temple fell into disrepair.

5. Khufu — I was Djoser's right-hand man. I was also an architect and priest of the sun god Ra.

6. Narmer — I was a Fourth Dynasty king who built three pyramids until I finally got it right.

7. Queen Neithhotep — I built Egypt's Great Pyramid, the highest in the world.

8. Rededjet — I was a magician who could reattach an animal's head that had been cut off.

9. Sneferu — I gave birth to triplets. One baby was Userkaf, the first king of the Fifth Dynasty.

Chapter 2: The Middle Kingdom and the Hyksos Dynasty

Egypt's Second Golden Age: The Middle Kingdom (2040-1760 BCE)

How was order restored to Egypt? Several cities were fighting for control of the country. The two strongest were Thebes in the south and Herakleopolis in the north. King Mentuhotep II of Thebes trounced Hierakonpolis, becoming the Middle Kingdom's first king. Once again, Egypt was united. It was a time of spectacular strides in culture. New painting and sculpture techniques in this golden age influenced the rest of Egypt's ancient history. The stability brought by powerful kings allowed trade to soar, enriching Egypt.

Mentuhotep's son and grandson ruled Egypt for several decades. Then, Amenemhat I came on the scene. He was King Mentuhotep IV's advisor and not from a royal family, yet he thought he could do a better job running Egypt. Somehow, he stole the throne

Mentuhotep II, the first king of the Middle Kingdom[11]

for himself. He moved Egypt's capital from Thebes to Iti-tawi, further south. Amenemhat I began Egypt's Twelfth Dynasty, which ruled Egypt for two centuries. This dynasty took Egypt to a peak of wealth and culture.

The Asian Invasion

People from *West Asia* or the *Levant* (Syria, Lebanon, and Canaan) had been moving to Egypt since the First Intermediate Period. What brought them to Egypt? Often, it was a lack of rain. The biblical book of Genesis says that a famine brought Abraham from Canaan to Egypt. He lived there briefly but fell out of favor with the Egyptian king over his wife, Sarah, who was also his half-sister. He ended up getting kicked out of Egypt. Like Abraham, other shepherds needed grass and fresh water for their sheep, cattle, and camels.

Egypt was friendly with Syria as far back as the Old Kingdom. The Syrian king Irkab-Damu of Ebla received gifts from Egypt's king. When he died around 2340 BCE, the gifts were buried with him in his tomb. Egypt had a trade colony in the coastal city of Byblos, Lebanon. Ships traveled back and forth from Byblos to Egypt in a thriving trade.

The Egyptians called the people from Syria, Lebanon, and Canaan "Aamu," which meant "*West Asians*."

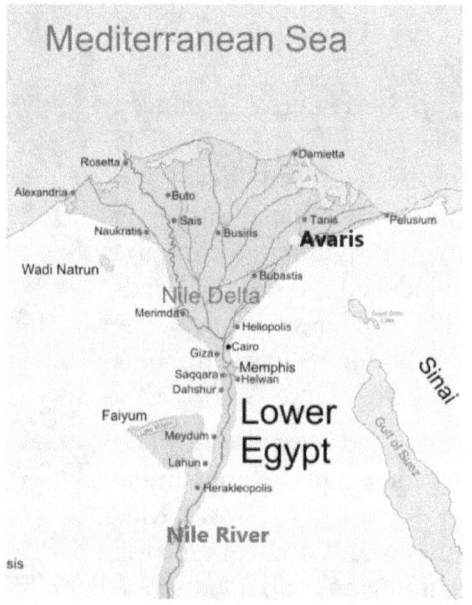

Avaris on the eastern Nile Delta[13]

Most West Asians who came to Egypt lived in the Nile Delta, where the Nile split into seven branches that spread out for 150 miles and emptied into the Mediterranean Sea. Egypt's Nile Delta usually remained relatively green even during a drought because the Nile's seven branches flooded yearly. This lush region of Egypt was great for the shepherds' flocks.

Many West Asians lived in Avaris, a city on the easternmost branch of the Nile close to the Mediterranean Sea. It was a key trade city with Byblos in Lebanon. Scientists did an isotope analysis of the skeletons buried in Avaris's cemeteries. Curiously, they found that 77 percent of the non-Egyptians were female. Why? Maybe women were brought in as enslaved people or wives. The Amorite women of Syria and Canaan were famous weavers.

The Phoenicians of Lebanon were the masters of the sea. Egypt imported Phoenician shipbuilders and sailors to build ships and sail Egyptian fleets. Cattle breeders, weavers, stone masons, artisans, and military men also found a warm welcome in Egypt. These migrants got new Egyptian names when they arrived but also kept their West Asian names. Some West Asians rose through the ranks to become governors or the pharaoh's advisors.

The book of Genesis says that Abraham's grandson Israel (Jacob) brought his clan of seventy people to live in Egypt. They joined his son Joseph in Egypt during a famine. Joseph was enslaved in Egypt until the king elevated him to second in command.

Based on the biblical timeline, Israel's family came to Egypt in the Middle Kingdom. A powerful governor named Khnumhotep II ruled Egypt's Oryx *nome* (province). His elaborate tomb has a painting of a family arriving from Canaan. The date on the painting is the sixth year of King Senusret II. It must have been an event of some importance to be painted on his tomb with a date.

A family from Canaan arrives with gifts for the Egyptian king.[13]

The Alphabet's Ancestor

Around 3,500 years ago, someone carved graffiti on a rock in the Sinai Peninsula near an Egyptian turquoise mine. When scholars found it in the early 1900s CE, they got excited. The writing was a form of Egyptian hieroglyphics. However, its words were in a Semitic language (spoken by West Asians), not Egyptian. The writer knew how to write Egyptian hieroglyphics but applied it to his own language. Scholars called this new form of writing "Proto-Sinaitic." It gave birth to the Phoenician alphabet of Lebanon.

Word	Proto-Sinaitic	Phoenician	Latin
'a*l*p ("ox")	🐂	✗	A
mem ("water")	∿	ϻ	M
'*en* ("eye")	👁	○	O

Proto-Sinaitic, Phoenician, and Latin alphabets compared[14]

"Beautiful Crocodile," Egypt's First Woman Pharaoh (1764–1760 BCE)

Sobekneferu stood at the deathbed of her half-brother and husband, Amenemhat IV. Who would rule Egypt now? They both came from a long line of strong and stable kings of Egypt. Sobekneferu's mother was the queen and official wife of their father, Amenemhat III. But Amenemhat IV's mother was a minor wife and not royalty. The only way to get the Egyptians to accept him as king was for Amenemhat IV to marry Sobekneferu. (Yes, Egyptian royalty commonly married their siblings to keep the sacred royal blood in the family.)

Amenemhat IV only reigned for nine years and then died without any children by his sister Sobekneferu. His minor wife huddled weeping in the corner with her two small sons. Sobekneferu glanced at them. The boys wouldn't be old enough to rule for years, and they weren't legitimate. They weren't born to a royal wife, nor was their father. There was only one thing to do. She would have to be the next pharaoh. Sobekneferu, whose name meant "Beautiful Crocodile," became Egypt's first woman pharaoh. Other women had ruled Egypt as regents while their sons grew up. However, Sobekneferu was the first woman ruler of Egypt who wasn't a regent. She had full royal titles.

During the reigns of Amenemhat IV and Sobekneferu, the West Asians were stirring up trouble in northeastern Egypt. They blocked the roads to the Sinai Peninsula. Egypt had turquoise and copper mines in the Sinai; now, they couldn't get to them.

Sobekneferu only ruled for about four years and died around 1760 BCE. Sobekneferu had no children, so she was the last pharaoh of Egypt's Twelfth Dynasty. The Middle Kingdom ended with her death around 1760 BCE.

The Chaotic Second Intermediate Period

A wobbly Thirteenth Dynasty continued to rule from Iti-tawi. These kings didn't control all of Egypt, just Upper Egypt. Few kings ruled for more than three years; some only ruled for a few months before a contender overthrew them. The first two kings were probably the sons of Amenemhat IV's non-royal wife. In these tumultuous times, royal blood had lost its importance. Most of the kings of this dynasty were not from royal families and were proud of it. The Thirteenth Dynasty struggled along for about 150 years.

Egypt's First Foreign Kings

Meanwhile, a rival Fourteenth Dynasty ruled the Nile Delta region. Its rulers were foreigners, but not the same West Asians as the Hyksos Fifteenth Dynasty. Who were they? They may have been Canaanites, as they had a warm trade relationship with Canaan. The kings of this dynasty didn't keep many written records, so we have to piece together what the archaeological record reveals.

The Fourteenth Dynasty ruled northeastern Egypt. At first, they fought the Thirteenth Dynasty in southern Egypt, but eventually, the two dynasties decided they needed to cooperate to survive. So, they formed a truce and traded with each other. The Fourteenth Dynasty allowed the folks in the Thirteenth Dynasty to sail up the Nile to the Mediterranean Sea. The Thirteenth Dynasty let the Fourteenth Dynasty people pass through their land to reach Nubia in the south. Unlike the Thirteenth Dynasty rulers, the Fourteenth Dynasty kings had long and stable reigns.

Another deadly famine rocked Egypt around 1700 BCE. The suffering was worse in the south, as the branches of the Nile provided irrigation for farms and herds in the north. But this drought lasted for fifty years. It eventually took its toll on the northern Fourteenth Dynasty, especially after an epidemic struck. People buried their dead in mass graves. Kings only ruled for months before they died of starvation, disease, or assassination.

The Hyksos Dynasty

Hyksos is Greek for the Egyptian word *Heka Khasut*, which means "foreign kings" or "shepherd kings." At first, the title seemed to be a generic catch-all phrase for foreign chieftains. It didn't mean a specific group of people. The Twelfth Dynasty governor Khnumhotep's tomb painting shows a man leading an ibex. The tomb inscription said he was "Abisha the Hyksos."

Abisha the Hyksos[16]

Later, the Egyptians used "Hyksos" for the West Asians that ruled Egypt's Fifteenth Dynasty. Their culture points to them being from Syria or Lebanon. The Egyptian historian Manetho said they were Phoenicians. Most likely, they were Amorites from the port city of Byblos in Lebanon. Avaris always had a warm relationship with Byblos, which the Amorites conquered in 2150 BCE.

The Hyksos did not leave any records telling how they conquered Egypt. The Egyptians' story was that the gods were angry at the Egyptians. Before the Egyptians knew what was happening, a swarm of foreigners had swept into Egypt from the east, catching the Egyptians by surprise. The crude foreigners burned down Egypt's cities, flattened its temples, and enslaved the people.

However, archaeologist Manfred Bietak, who spent decades unearthing the ruins of Avaris, says archaeology tells a different story. He says the Hyksos were in Egypt all along. Some lived in Avaris with the other West Asians; others lived throughout Egypt. They took advantage of the turmoil caused by the previously mentioned famine and epidemic. Over half of Egypt's population had died, destabilizing the Thirteenth Dynasty in the north and the Fourteenth Dynasty in the south.

Around 1650 BCE, the Hyksos conquered Memphis, making it the first capital of the new Fifteenth Dynasty. They elected their first king, Salatis. The Hyksos swiftly conquered the rest of Egypt and forced Upper and Lower Egypt to pay *tribute* (something like a tax). Salatis was concerned that the Assyrians of northern Iraq might invade, so he built fortresses along Egypt's northeastern border. He also stationed 240,000 troops there.

Salatis decided that Avaris would be a better capital as it was near the border and the Mediterranean Sea. Avaris grew to about 25,000 people, becoming Egypt's largest city of its day. The Egyptian king Kamose later described Avaris's busy and prosperous harbor. It had hundreds of ships filled with gold, silver, bronze axes, lapis lazuli, turquoise, incense, and expensive wood.

Around 1640 BCE, the Egyptians regrouped and formed an opposing kingdom, the Sixteenth Dynasty. The native Egyptians' capital was Thebes. At first, the Hyksos Fifteenth Dynasty and the Egyptian Sixteenth Dynasty were hostile. But they eventually became friendly, traded with each other, and permitted passage through their sections of the Nile. Around 1580 BCE, the Seventeenth Dynasty replaced the Sixteenth Dynasty at Thebes. Within decades, this dynasty grew strong enough to challenge the Hyksos.

Noisy Hippos

The humorous and probably fictional story, "The Quarrel of Apophis and Seqenenre," represents the growing tension between the Hyksos king Apepi (Apophis) and the Seventeenth Dynasty king Seqenenre. The Egyptian king was irritated that he had to pay tribute to Apepi. He found it appalling that Apepi spent so much time worshiping the god Seth (Baal) but ignored the other Egyptian gods. Meanwhile, Apepi was looking for a way to annoy Seqenenre even further. He wanted to test out the strength of Seqenenre's god, Amun-Ra.

Apepi called in his advisors and picked their brains.

"Hippos! Test him with hippos, O sovereign lord."

"Hippos?"

A hippo figurine from Egypt's late Middle Kingdom[16]

"Yes. Demand that Seqenenre remove the hippopotamuses from that canal outside Thebes. Tell him they're keeping us awake with their roaring."

Apepi snorted with laughter. Thebes was about 480 miles south of Avaris. No one in Avaris was hearing hippos at Thebes. Yet, he sent his ambassador to deliver the message to Seqenenre. At first, the Egyptian king sat in a stunned silence. Then he gathered his wits.

"Where are my manners? You must be starving! Here, have some of this delicious beef. And try this cake! Now, go back and tell Apepi I'll take care of the hippos."

As soon as the ambassador left, Seqenenre called his advisors. What should they do? No one could come up with an answer. But Apepi wasn't done goading Seqenenre. He called his ambassador to send another message.

At this juncture in the story, the ancient papyrus on which it was written is broken off. We don't find out what happened to the noisy hippos or who won the battle of wits. However, Thebes grew in strength and stopped paying tribute to Avaris. It even blocked the Hyksos trade routes to Nubia in the south. The two kings eventually warred against each other, and the Hyksos won. Seqenenre died a horrible death with multiple axe wounds to his face.

Ahmose Defeats the Hyksos

Seqenenre's son Kamose became king in his late teens, the last ruler of the Seventeenth Dynasty. Neither the Egyptians nor the Hyksos wanted to prolong the war. However, Kamose thought his war council was dropping the ball. He couldn't let the Hyksos get away with killing his father. And he was indignant that Thebes had to pay tribute to Avaris. Moreover, the Hyksos were blocking Egyptian ships from sailing up the Nile and into the Mediterranean.

"I'll take Apepi on, that Syrian prince with weak arms! I'll rip open his belly!" Kamose raged in his inscriptions.

He sailed his navy downstream to Avaris. "Look! I'm here! Everything you own is mine now! Is your heart stopping, you vile West Asian?"

Kamose raided the harbor and sank its ships but could not breach Avaris's high walls. However, he bragged about not losing a single man. Of course, he apparently didn't engage anyone in battle, so the Hyksos probably didn't lose any men either. At this point, Kamose made his younger brother Ahmose a co-ruler with him, although he was only ten. Kamose then marched south to fight the Nubians and died while still in his twenties.

Ahmose I came to the throne around 1550 BCE. His reign began Egypt's New Kingdom and its Eighteenth Dynasty. The war with the Hyksos paused until Ahmose grew up. In the meantime, his mother, Ahhotep, ruled Egypt as regent. Earlier, Kamose had captured some horses and chariots from the Hyksos. Ahmose used these as prototypes to build his own chariots to fight the Hyksos. This was the first time Egyptians used war chariots.

Pharaoh Ahmose defeats a Hyksos warrior. [17]

Ahmose defeated the Hyksos once and for all in his nineteenth year as king. One of the Egyptian commanders, whose name was also Ahmose, wrote an eyewitness account of the Egyptians chasing the Hyksos out of Egypt. He said they ran to the city of Sharuhen in Canaan. When the Egyptians tracked them down, they fought for three years. Finally, the Hyksos abandoned Sharuhen and ran to Syria. At this point, King Ahmose returned to Egypt, probably to avoid fight the Hyksos's allies in Syria.

The Hyksos Legacy

The Hyksos brought new war technology, enabling Egypt to dominate its neighbors in the New Kingdom. The Hyksos also introduced the first horses to Egypt. (The Egyptians hadn't even use animal-pulled carts until the Thirteenth Dynasty.) The Hyksos' spoke-wheeled chariots were fast and could turn on a dime.

The Egyptians had been using a simple bow from one piece of wood. The Hyksos brought the superior rounded composite bow to Egypt. This bow has several pieces glued together, making it more flexible. Arrows shot from a composite bow fly faster and farther and are more deadly.

The West Asian man on the left carries a composite bow and a duckbilled axe. The man on the right is playing a box lyre.[18]

Roundup Activity: What Happened When?

Look at the key events in ancient Egypt's Middle Kingdom and Second Intermediate Period. Number them (to the right of each sentence) in the order they happened. Check your answers in the back of the book.

1. Ahmose begins the New Kingdom and the Eighteenth Dynasty.
2. Ahmose conquered the Hyksos once and for all.
3. Amenemhat I usurped the throne and started the Twelfth Dynasty.
4. Mentuhotep II united Egypt again, beginning the Middle Kingdom.
5. Seqenenre was killed, and Kamose became king.
6. Sobekneferu, the "Beautiful Crocodile," died.
7. The Egyptians regrouped and formed the Sixteenth Dynasty.
8. The Hyksos conquered Memphis.
9. The Seventeenth Dynasty replaced the Sixteenth Dynasty at Thebes.

Chapter 3: Ancient Egyptian Society and Culture

In this chapter, we'll examine the daily lives of ordinary Egyptians. What kind of food did they eat? What was their clothing like? What was their religion, and how did they practice it? What was unique about Egyptian art? Why was the Nile more than just a river? And why did the Egyptians use a beetle-shaped seal to sign their names? Let's uncover the answers to these questions and more.

What Did the Ancient Egyptians Eat and Wear?

The ancient Egyptian's favorite drink was beer. They drank it every day. But Egyptian beer wasn't like our beer today. It was thick, like a milkshake, and they even used long straws to drink it. Beer was stored and served in jars with a narrow neck. The Egyptians made their beer by first baking bread dough made from emmer wheat until it was gooey in the middle. They crumbled the bread, mixed it with water, and let it sit. The yeast in the bread caused it to ferment. Even today, Egyptians drink home-brewed *bouza*, which is remarkably close to the ancient beer.

The main food in everyday Egyptian meals was barley or emmer wheat bread. Egyptians enjoyed vegetable side dishes like green onions, cucumber, celery, and lettuce. They loved fruit like melons, dates, figs, and grapes. The usual protein was stewed lentils, chickpeas, or beans. They also made cheese and ate eggs and fish. Meat was usually only eaten on special occasions. At weddings, festivals, and other special days,

Egyptians typically ate duck, geese, beef, mutton, and pork. Some of their stranger delicacies included mice and hedgehogs!

A West Asian man, apparently married to an Egyptian woman, drinks beer from a straw.[19]

Upper Egypt includes a section of the Sahara Desert, one of the world's hottest and dryest places. All of Egypt is hot, with an average summer temperature of 95 degrees Fahrenheit (35 degrees Celsius). Egyptian children under six usually wore nothing except anklets and bracelets. Workers and enslaved people sometimes wore nothing but a thong. Whether royal or ordinary, men usually only wore a lightweight, wraparound "kilt" or skirt called a ***shendyt***. The shendyt typically came to just above the knee; most were white. Women wore a straight sheath dress called a ***kalasiris***, sometimes with a shawl over the shoulders. Both men and women wore clothing made from lightweight, sheer linen.

Women usually wore their hair long, frequently in micro braids. The favorite length seemed to be several inches past the shoulders, but sometimes waist length. Men either wore their hair short or shaven. They rarely wore beards. If they did, it was a goatee. Boys had shaved heads except for one lock on the side. The West Asian men in Egypt typically wore a full beard and a "mushroom-shaped," chin-length hairstyle with a headband.

We usually think of Egyptians with black hair, but the examination of mummies shows some Egyptians (even before the Greeks took over) had naturally red or light-brown hair. They also liked to dye their hair red with henna. Most Egyptians had wavy or curly hair, although a small number had straight hair. Dramatic eye makeup was essential to both men and women. They wore eyeliner of kohl, a crystalized lead sulfide. Their green eye shadow was made of malachite, a copper carbonate.

Women lute players wearing head cones, braids, and collar necklaces[80]

Egyptians of all classes loved wearing jewelry. Most women wore elaborate headbands. Some women wore head cones filled with scented wax. Their body heat melted the wax slightly, releasing the scent. Women liked to wear bracelets, armbands, and huge earrings. Both men and women wore large collar necklaces. If a person was wealthy, their collar necklace was turquoise or gold. Ordinary people wore collar necklaces made with pottery beads.

What Was Their Social Structure Like?

Ancient Egyptian society was, ironically, like a pyramid. At the bottom were the farmers and enslaved people, who made up most of the population. Almost all farmers were serfs who didn't own the land they farmed. Wealthy landowners bought and sold land, but the serfs stayed with the land regardless of who owned it. The next layer up were merchants and artisans. The artisans were artists, stone carvers, perfume makers, weavers, jewelry makers, and carpenters.

A sculpture of a fifth-dynasty scribe at Giza[21]

The third highest level was military men (except for officers) and scribes. Until the New Kingdom, the king would call up the farmers and other men to fight as needed. Egypt formed a full-time army after the embarrassment of being defeated by the foreign Hyksos.

A scribe had to learn about 700 signs to write basic hieroglyphics. It took twelve years of schooling. They were in demand by royalty, merchants, and anyone else needing something written down. Most Egyptians did not know how to read and write.

The fourth layer was priests and nobles who owned large pieces of property. The Egyptians had thousands of gods and goddesses, so there were plenty of openings for priests and priestesses. Before a priest could enter the temple, he had to bathe in holy water and shave off his body hair. An essential priestly duty was embalming dead bodies before burial.

The fifth layer up was government officials and top military officers, often part of the king's family. The top official was the vizier or advisor to the king. He organized the other officials and served as the supreme court judge. Other important officials were the commander of the military and the chief treasurer. At the top of the pyramid was the king, or pharaoh. Unlike in Syria, where a king was considered the shepherd or father of his people, the Egyptians thought their king was like a god.

Since they were semi-divine, pharaohs were intermediaries between the people and the gods. The sacred duties of a pharaoh included ensuring rain and good harvests, defending the country from invaders, and acting as an impartial judge. The Egyptians obeyed their king without asking questions. In their minds, disobeying their king would bring disorder and poverty to Egypt.

What about women? What was their role in society? First and foremost, they were wives and mothers. Ordinary people usually married for love, although the pharaohs had to make politically strategic marriages. The Egyptians believed their spouse would be their husband or wife in the afterlife. Thus, they worked to make the relationship thrive. They didn't want to spend eternity in an unhappy marriage!

An Egyptian couple harvesting papyrus [22]

As wives and mothers, ordinary Egyptian women tended the children, kept the house clean, and prepared meals. They wove linen from flax. Farmers' wives helped their husbands in the fields. More well-to-do women supervised the household servants and maybe ran a business like perfume making. Egyptian women also served as priestesses to female deities. Compared to their West Asian neighbors, they had more rights. They could own and sell property, be witnesses in court, and associate with men they weren't related to. Egyptian women had the right to divorce their husbands and get a third of their property.

What Religious Beliefs Did the Ancient Egyptians Follow?

Most of the ancient Egyptians were *polytheistic* (worshiping multiple gods). Some were the state gods, revered by the king and his priests at the national temples. The ordinary people had local deities that they worshiped. Egyptians also believed in supernatural creatures like the griffin and the sphinx. The griffin had a lion's body and an eagle's head and wings; it was a protector. The sphinx had a human head and a lion's body, representing the sun god.

Among the most important Egyptian gods were Amun, Mut, and Khonsu. The Egyptians believed that Amun was the creator of the universe and merged him with Ra, the sun god. Amun's wife was Mut, the mother goddess. Her paintings and statues often showed her wearing a bright red dress with vulture wings and holding an **ankh**, a cross with a circle at the top that symbolized life. Khonsu, the god of the moon, was her son. He was the god of healing and fertility and the destroyer of demons.

The goddess Mut[28]

The Egyptian people's beliefs about their gods controlled how they lived and worked, their relationships with others, and their concept of life after death. Everyone was supposed to follow **ma 'at**, or living in harmony. The Egyptians believed their actions impacted others and determined their fate in the afterlife. They had to live in balance and cooperation with each other so the gods could maintain order in the cosmos. The Egyptians considered most of their gods to be kind friends.

Heka (magic) was real to the Egyptians. In their belief system, everything that happened, good or bad, had a supernatural cause. Heka was a personification of Amun-Ra. He controlled medicine and magic and could blind crocodiles. Heka was a cosmic force that could be good or evil; he could protect but also destroy. Egyptians believed they could manipulate Heka through their words, actions, and particular objects. They used magic for protection.

How Did the Nile River Impact Egyptian Society and Culture?

The Nile was infinitely more than just a river for the Egyptian people. If it weren't for the Nile, Egypt would be a dry and dusty desert. Actually, parts of it are. Cairo only gets one-half inch of rain a year! The only reason Cairo isn't a desert is because it's right on the Nile, where it flows into the Nile Delta. Most of ancient Egypt's major cities were on the Nile or its delta region.

Vast swathes of Egypt were rich farmland, thanks to the Nile. It poured life into the desert. The river flooded every year, covering the surrounding area with rich black silt. Egypt could grow enough grain to feed its people, with plenty left over to sell to other lands. For the Egyptians, life and wealth flowed from the Nile; it provided for virtually every aspect of life. It was the primary means of travel through Egypt. Tomb art from the Old Kingdom shows boats carrying cattle, wood, and vegetables down the Nile. The Egyptians buried their kings with ships near their tombs.

A boat model from Egypt's Twelfth Dynasty [24]

The Nile was home to many animals. Fish provided an essential source of protein for Egyptians. Hippos and crocodiles thrived in the Nile River. Elephants lived along the Nile until climate change increased desertification in the Early Dynastic Period. Gazelles, cheetahs, and the Egyptian wolf roamed the mountains and plains on the edge of the Nile's floodplains. Barbary lions were common in the Nile Valley until they were overhunted in the New Kingdom. A small remnant survived into modern times, but the Barbary lion is now extinct.

The Egyptians based their calendar on the Nile's annual cycle. It had three seasons. The season from July to November when the river overflowed its banks was Akhet. Peret was the season for farming, which ran from November to March. The harvest season was Shemu. The Egyptians methodically tracked and recorded the annual floods each year.

The ancient Egyptian fields were "basins" surrounded by earthen banks. Channels ran from the Nile to the fields. When the river flooded, the fields filled with water. The basins held the water for a month until the soil was thoroughly saturated and ready for planting. The fields were so soggy the farmers didn't need to water the crops at all at first. When the fields finally dried out, the Egyptians had an ingenuous system of dikes and irrigation canals to channel the river water to the fields.

Is the Nile really the world's longest river? The Amazon River is a strong contender. Current measurements say the Nile is 4,132 miles and the Amazon is 3,977. However, some scientists say the source of the Amazon is in northern Peru, not southern Peru. An international team of explorers is planning expeditions to find out. They hope they can settle the debate soon.

How Did Art Reflect Their Culture?

Did you know that most of the ancient Egyptian art we've discovered was never meant to be seen? These paintings, wall carvings, and statues were inside tombs. What was the point of spending all that time creating exquisite art and then hiding it away? The art was there for the dead people or the gods they wanted to please. Many carvings and paintings had symbols like scorpions, snakes, or weapons. These were to protect from evil in the afterlife.

The Egyptians believed that art was a way to communicate with the gods. Some of the tomb art depicted the pharaoh or other high-ranking person going about his or her life. It showed the person offering sacrifices, winning great battles, or relaxing with family. The ancient Egyptians hoped the tomb art would come to life and the dead person would do these things in the afterlife.

Almost all Egyptian paintings and statues had "captions" or inscriptions naming the people depicted and often what was happening. Statues had inscriptions on the back or at the base. Paintings and reliefs carved into rock usually had writing underneath explaining the scene. They were written in hieroglyphics, an art form in itself. This custom has been helpful to archaeologists as it gives them names and dates to piece together Egypt's history and influential people.

Nefu, a Fifth Dynasty official in the Old Kingdom, and his wife[35]

One aspect of ancient Egyptian art was that proportions reflected status. Statues of important men and their wives often depict the husband towering over the woman. Was he an exceptionally tall man, or was his wife very short? More likely, the artist used proportion to demonstrate the man's importance. The man is also usually painted in brilliant colors, while the woman is pale. These statues are endearing, as the couples show physical affection. In the sculptures of royal children with their parents, they look like little dolls compared to the adults' size. Paintings of the pharaohs with servants or military men often show the king twice the size of everyone else.

What Was a Scarab?

As we mentioned earlier, in the Predynastic era, Egyptians adopted the cylinder seal from the Sumerians of southern Iraq. In the Middle Kingdom, the Egyptians switched to one-inch oval "scarabs" to identify themselves in letters or business transactions. This type of seal was modeled after the scarab beetle.

The beetle side of a scarab seal on a ring [26]

The scarab beetle is also known as a "dung" beetle. It eats poop! If it finds some, it shapes it into balls and rolls them to its nest. Why would the Egyptians want to make seals in the shape of this beetle? To the Egyptians, the dung ball symbolized the world. When the beetle rolled his ball of poop along, he kept the world spinning on its axis. The ancient Egyptians also thought the sun entered the underworld each night when it set and resurrected each morning as a scarab beetle. The Egyptians considered this humble beetle highly significant in the cycle of life.

The top of the scarab seal was rounded and looked like the beetle. The bottom was flat, with hieroglyphics carved into it to identify the owner. Like the cylinder seals, the owner pressed his or her scarab into a little ball of clay. It hardened to form its owner's "signature." The Egyptians liked to wear the seal on a ring so it would always be handy when they needed to use it. Thousands of these Egyptian beetle seals or their impressions have been found in Egypt, Israel, Palestine, and Syria. They open a window to how engaged specific pharaohs were in trade or colonies in other countries. They're also fascinating examples of art on a tiny scale.

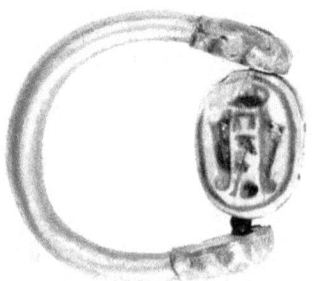

The back side of the scarab seal is pressed in clay. [27]

Roundup Activity: Fill in the Blank

Read the summary paragraph below. Fill in the blanks with the correct keyword. Check your answers in the back of the book.

The ancient Egyptians' favorite drink was _____, which they liked to drink through a straw. Because of the heat, they liked wearing lightweight clothing made from _____, which the ladies wove from flax. A scribe had to attend school for ____ years to learn all the hieroglyphic symbols. The Egyptians believed _____ was the creator of the universe. Egyptian artists used _____ to indicate the most important person in the painting or sculpture. The Egyptians thought the scarab beetle's dung ball represented the _____.

Chapter 4: Ancient Egyptian Architecture

When most people think of ancient Egyptian architecture, they picture the pyramids. Yet, the pyramids were mainly associated with the Old Kingdom. Ancient Egypt's palaces, temples, and other structures were also stunning. They showcased the imagination and incredible skill of Egypt's architects. Egypt's architecture displayed a pleasing balance of forms, reflecting the Egyptian's connection to their gods and their land.

King Khufu's solar ship [38]

The pyramids didn't stand out in the desert by themselves. A temple, a solar boat pit, and a palace often surrounded them. What is a solar boat? The Egyptians believed their king needed transportation in the afterlife. And when they thought of transportation, they thought of boats. After all, the Nile River was the primary means of getting from Upper to Lower Egypt. Several pyramids had a cedar-wood ship buried in a pit nearby. The ships were about 140 feet long with a cabin and oars. Some scholars think the king was transported to his tomb in the boat. However, the inscriptions at King Khufu's pyramid said that the solar ship carried his soul to the heavens.

How Were the Pyramids Built?

Many of Egypt's pyramids have lasted for 4,500 years! How did the Egyptians build them so well that they lasted so long? How did they build them without cranes and pullies and even the wheel? As we said, the Egyptians didn't have the wheel until the Fifth Dynasty, and the largest pyramid was erected in the Fourth Dynasty.

Did you know that the Great Pyramid had 2.3 *million* stone blocks? Each block weighed about 2.5 tons! To put that in perspective, that's about the weight of ten refrigerators. How did the workers get those blocks that high up in the air? Remember—the Great Pyramid was about 481 feet high. That's as high as a skyscraper with forty-eight stories. No wonder the Greek historian Herodotus put it on his list of the Seven Wonders of the Ancient World.

How could the workers complete such a massive feat in the lifetime of one king? It took a workforce of thousands of men. In 1992, NOVA produced a documentary called *This Old Pyramid*, in which they tried to replicate the effort of building even a small pyramid. They cheated a little. Those enormous blocks came in on flatbed trucks. However, the researchers were amazed that twelve men working barefoot in the eastern desert quarried 186 stones in 21 days. They didn't quite do everything the ancient way. They used an iron cable and winch to pull the stone out of the quarry. Still, the cutting and everything else was by hand.

Egyptologists Mark Lehner and Zahi Hawass did the math. Building the Great Pyramid in twenty years required 340 stones a day. How many men would it take to quarry those? Since the modern-day workers used iron tools and a winch, Hawass did his calculations based on thirty-two men instead of twelve. It took modern workers 21 days to deliver 186 stones, but the Great Pyramid needed 340 *daily*. They figured out that around 1,200 men could quarry 340 stones a day. The quarries for the core stones of the Giza pyramids were right there at Giza, so long-distance transportation wasn't an issue.

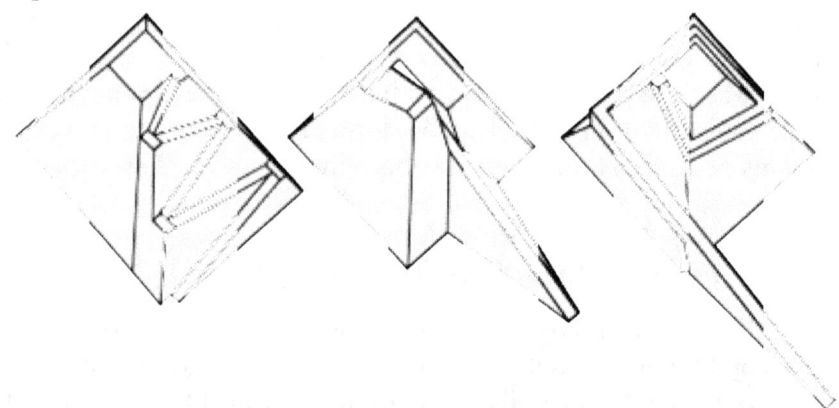

Three possible ramps were used to build the pyramids. The middle ramp is probably too steep. The zig-zag ramp on the left and the circular ramp on the right are more likely."

In their replication efforts, the *This Old Pyramid* team found twelve men could easily drag one colossal block on a giant sled over a slick surface. (Remember, they would wet down the sand to make it slippery.) The team estimated that it would take 1,200 men to cut stones in the quarry and around 2,000 men to drag them from the quarry to the pyramid. Once the stones arrived at the pyramid, a highly trained team cut them with great precision. They fit together so tightly a knife blade couldn't slide between two stones.

The NOVA experiment demonstrated what had to happen to carve a 2.5-ton block. Four to six men labored on one stone at a time. Two men worked with levers and a hard cobble under a block to pivot it around. Two to four people did the cutting. Researchers estimated it took about 5,000 men to do this job. They believe one team worked from each corner of the pyramid, and the middle of each face of the pyramid had another team.

The workers used the inclined plane (a sloping surface) to move the blocks up the pyramid on ramps. In addition to the granite blocks used in the pyramid's core, the outside had a layer of fine white limestone, polished so that it glistened in the sun. This limestone was quarried in Tura and shipped to Giza, about ten miles by way of the Nile.

Who Built the Pyramids?

Despite what you might have seen in old movies, it wasn't the Jews or any other foreign enslaved people who built the pyramids. The pyramids were built during the Old Kingdom. The Jews did not exist at that time since Abraham hadn't been born yet.

So, who were the thousands of men who built each of the massive pyramids? The Old Kingdom pyramids, including the Great Pyramid, were built by native Egyptians. The whole idea of a pyramid was to provide for the future afterlife of their king, who they believed became a god. From the Egyptians' perspective, their toil on the pyramids blessed Egypt and blessed their own future in the afterlife.

The most likely scenario was that a smaller crew of men worked year-round. From July to November, when the Nile overflowed its banks, the farmers didn't have much to do. Most were probably sent to work on the pyramids during those months. They worked in teams, and archaeologists have found where the teams signed their "tribal" names on the inner stones of the pyramids. One team called themselves the "Drunkards of Menkaure." They undoubtedly enjoyed a few rounds of beer when they finished the day's work! Other teams were named "Friends of Khufu" and "The Powerful Ones."

Pyramids at Giza[80]

Men working this hard needed a good protein source. Animal bones at the site and surviving records indicate cattle were brought in from the Nile

Delta region. Of course, sustaining this immense army of workers required another team of bakers and cooks to feed them. Archaeologists have unearthed bakeries that fed the workers at Giza.

They also found a cemetery where 600 people were buried. Archaeologists and doctors analyzed the skeletons of the workers in that cemetery, and they were Egyptians. Most of them died in their early thirties, and some died from accidents. Twelve of the workers had received treatment for earlier injuries to their hands or legs, where a stone had fallen on them. Amazingly, they lived for years after the treatment and must have continued working since they were buried right there.

What Was the Significance of the Pyramids?

The pyramids represented several aspects of ancient Egyptian culture. Egyptians believed in *ba*, which was a part of the soul. Only the king had a ba in the Old Kingdom, but later, everyone did. Ba appeared as a bird with a human head, representing the soul's flight after death. He could fly from Earth to the heavens, but he needed a landmark when he flew back to Earth. The pyramid guided him back to his mortal body.

Ba[81]

The Egyptians believed that the smooth sides and pointed peak of a pyramid guided the king's soul (ba) to the sun god Ra in the sky. The triangular sides represented the sun's rays. The Egyptians believed that ba left the body after death, but another aspect of the king's soul, **ka**, stayed in his mummified body. Thus, the priests would store goods he would need and bring more food from time to time. The pyramid was like a palace for the king's earth-bound ka.

The shape of the pyramids not only lifted one's eyes to the heavens but also had a practical side. The Egyptians intended their pyramids to endure forever. The smooth, polished, slanted sides allowed the little bit of rain that fell to run off quickly without eroding the structure. The pyramid shape also held up well to high winds.

Whenever merchant ships or ambassadors from other lands sailed down the Nile, they passed the majestic pyramids. The pyramids were a status symbol, showcasing Egypt's power and wealth. They spoke to the incredible workforce Egypt commanded and how the kings could unify tens of thousands of their citizens toward the single goal.

The Iconic Great Pyramid of Giza

The Pyramids of Giza are a cluster of pyramids built by several kings between 2600 and 2181 BCE. The Great Pyramid was built first. It was the largest of the group and the highest pyramid ever built in the world. King Khufu started its construction around 2550 BCE. When it was built, polished white limestone blocks encased all four sides of the pyramid. After earthquakes in 1356 CE, the Mamluk Sultanate stripped some of these casing stones off the pyramid and used them to repair buildings in Cairo. In the nineteenth century, the Ottoman governor Muhammad Ali Pasha took more outer stones to build Cairo's Alabaster Mosque. Almost all the casing stones are gone today. All that is left is the core structure, which is about 454 feet high, around 27 feet shorter than the original pyramid.

What's inside the Great Pyramid? It has three primary chambers. One is King Khufu's burial tomb. Another is the "Queen's Chamber," and the third is the Subterranean Chamber. The pyramid has numerous corridors snaking through its core and shafts going underground. Usually, the Egyptians painted the inner walls of their pyramids, but the Great Pyramid's inside is unpainted. Perhaps Khufu died before the artists had time to paint pictures on the walls. The only thing left on the inside walls is the graffiti of the work teams.

The workers cut the Subterranean Chamber into the bedrock about eighty-nine feet under the pyramid. This room was unfinished, again hinting that the pyramid was incomplete when Khufu died. What was the Subterranean Chamber used for? Scholars are uncertain. Some think it was meant to be Khufu's tomb, but plans changed when he died earlier than expected. Other scholars believe he may have changed his mind and wanted to be buried higher in the pyramid. The so-called Queen's Chamber may have also been intended for Khufu. At any rate, it appears that no one was buried there.

Granite slabs line the walls of the King's Chamber, Khufu's burial place. Over the millennia, robbers broke into the pyramid multiple times. The only thing left in Khufu's tomb is his granite sarcophagus, a stone coffin. The only reason the robbers left the sarcophagus was that it was too big to fit around the corner of the tight passage coming into the chamber. The ancient workers must have lowered Khufu's coffin into his chamber from above, then finished the roof of the chamber to seal it in.

Giza's Great Sphinx

Khufu's son, Khafre, built the second-largest pyramid at Giza. It seems higher than the Great Pyramid, but that's because it's on slightly higher ground with steeper sides. It stands 448 feet high compared to Khufu's (now) 454-foot pyramid. Khafre's pyramid still has some of its limestone casing. Grave robbers also raided Khafre's tomb and took his mummy and everything except his red granite sarcophagus.

When the Italian adventurer Giovanni Belzoni found the burial chamber in 1818 CE, he discovered writings in Arabic. They said that the tomb was opened during the reign of King Ali Muhammad, around 1200 CE. Weirdly, he found cattle bones in the burial chamber. Who put those there, when, and why? That mystery is unanswered.

The Great Sphinx of Giza[88]

Khafre's pyramid is famous for the hulking statue of a sphinx next to it, which has Khafre's head and the body of a lion. Over the millennia, the blowing desert sands covered the Great Sphinx until only its head stuck out. When archaeologists dug it out in the 1800s, they discovered that workers had never completed the lower part of the statue. It is 240 feet long and 66 feet high, as tall as a six-story building. Its artists carved the entire sculpture from one piece of limestone. The pigment on the ancient statue shows it was brightly painted in blue, yellow, and red when first erected. As artisans carved the sphinx statue, they used the blocks they chiseled off to build a temple in front of it. The Great Sphinx probably represented King Khafre offering sacrifices to his father, Khufu.

Why Did the Egyptians Stop Building Pyramids?

Pyramids built later in the Old Kingdom were smaller and of poorer quality. Egypt started running out of the wealth and manpower needed to create these extraordinary monuments. An intriguing detail of the later pyramids, beginning with that of King Unas, who died around 2345 BCE, was the inscriptions inside the pyramids. The walls were covered with the oldest known Egyptian religious texts. The purpose of these texts was to guide the king out of his tomb and into his new life with the gods.

The last sizeable pyramid was for Pepy II, who died around 2184 BCE. His pyramid was only 172 feet high. Shortly after his death, the Old Kingdom collapsed. Some Middle Kingdom kings and one New Kingdom pharaoh built pyramids, but they were much smaller.

The Hyksos Dynasty was infamous for blatant tomb robbing. They sold the stolen goods to the kings of Lebanon, who buried the stolen purloined treasures in their own graves.

What Other Astounding Architecture Did Ancient Egyptians Build?

In the Middle and New Kingdoms, the Egyptians focused on building temples rather than pyramids. Many of these temples have survived. They have incredible detail and beauty. One amazing example is the temple complex of Amun-Re and the Hypostyle Hall at Karnak near Thebes. The Egyptians built this temple in the Middle Kingdom and added to it in the New Kingdom. It was the worship center for Amun, his wife Mut, and the falcon-headed god of the military, Montu.

Painted columns at Luxor Temple[88]

The Karnak Temple Complex is one of the world's largest, with over twenty temples in its central worship area. A forest of 134 massive columns supported the roof of the Hypostyle Hall, a breathtaking open-air worship area. The roof in the hall's center was higher, with 69-foot columns. Over 600 sphinxes lined the 1.7-mile Avenue of the Sphinxes connecting the Karnak Temple with the Luxor Temple. The Luxor Temple featured a bright blue ceiling and brilliant red, gold, and sky blue columns.

Another spectacular architectural feature of ancient Egyptian temples was obelisks. These were towering rectangular stone pillars with a pointed top like a pyramid. Incredibly, they were carved from one huge stone. They served as the prototype for the Washington Monument in Washington, D.C. This striking architecture dates to the Predynastic Era in Egypt. The Egyptians built obelisks to honor an important king, a god, or a special event. The Egyptians often built a pair of obelisks together at the entrance to temples.

The Temple of Luxor entrance once had a second obelisk on the right.[84]

Roundup Activity: Build Your Own Pyramid!

Pretend you're an ancient Egyptian queen or king. Design and draw your pyramid. You can draw a sphinx by the pyramid with your face and a lion's body. If you want to get super creative, you can design the tunnels and chambers inside the pyramid. You might want to include landscape features nearby, like palm trees or the Nile River.

Chapter 5: The Afterlife: Exploring Life after Death in Ancient Egypt

As we explore the complex world of ancient Egyptian religion, we will first dive into the roles of gods and goddesses. What did the Egyptians believe about their deities? Who were Anubis, Ra, and Osiris, and how were they involved in the afterlife? What did the Egyptians think happened after they died? How did they prepare for the next life? What were mummies and the Book of the Dead all about? Let's unwrap the answers to these questions and more.

What Roles Did the Gods and Goddesses Play?

The ancient Egyptians believed in thousands of gods but had about thirty primary deities. They each had a specific role and special powers. For instance, the Egyptians believed some deities had the power to create. Others controlled the weather and the annual flooding of the Nile, which was crucial for growing enough food. Some gods protected people, animals, and even plants. Other gods cared for people after they died. Most towns and cities had a patron god who looked after the people there.

The Egyptians considered most of their gods friendly and helpful. However, they had several super scary gods. One of Egypt's cat goddesses was named Mafdet. She protected people from poisonous snakes but was also the goddess of executions. She was usually pictured as a woman with a cat head and snakes flowing down her back instead of hair. Ahti was a creepy goddess with a hippopotamus body and a wasp head. She was spiteful, harmful to children, and didn't seem to offer any benefit to humans. Another goddess with a hippo body was Taweret, the bizarre goddess of fertility, motherhood, and nursing infants. She had crocodile jaws, a hippopotamus body, a woman's breasts, and lion legs and claws.

Taweret, goddess of motherhood[85]

Amun was the Egyptian god of creation. He and eight of his children, grandchildren, and great-grandchildren formed the Ennead, the nine most powerful deities in Heliopolis, a key religious center near today's Cairo. Other places in Egypt had different groupings of the deities they considered the most important. The chief gods tended to change in importance over the thousands of years of ancient Egypt's history.

A favorite Egyptian goddess was Isis, the wife of Osiris and mother of Horus. She was first worshiped in the Nile Delta region, but eventually, almost everyone in Egypt honored her. The Egyptians believed that, in a sense, Isis was the mother of all the pharaohs because they thought their kings were earthly representations of Horus. One of her titles was Weret-Kekau, or "Great Magic." She was among the deities who made the Nile flood each year.

Isis with the New Kingdom Pharaoh Haremhab[86]

What Was the King's Role in Religion?

The Egyptians thought their king had godlike status, so he was the middleman between heaven and earth. Egypt had many priests, but the king was the head of both religion and the government. Thus, he worked to ensure harmony in his land and led religious ceremonies. The Egyptians knew their king was mortal and that he would die one day. However, as we said, they considered him the living representative of the god Horus. After he died, he became Osiris, the god of the underworld.

Parts of the Human Soul

As we mentioned in chapter four, the ancient Egyptians thought their souls had multiple parts. Ba was the personality or the person's true essence. This part of the soul left the body after death, and if all went well, the person continued existing in ba form in the underworld. A ren was a person's secret name, which needed to be remembered so the soul could continue to exist after death. Ka was another part of the soul that stayed on earth after the person died. As you may remember from our discussion of the pyramids, the ancient Egyptians left food and other things to keep this part of the soul fed and happy. The ib was the person's heart or morality. Shut was the person's shadow, a reflection of his or her personhood. Egyptian art sometimes showed the soul leaving the tomb in the form of a shadow.

What Offering Rites Did the Egyptians Follow?

The Egyptians believed they needed to honor their gods and goddesses, even the ones with bad tempers who looked like extraterrestrials. If the Egyptians kept the deities happy, life was smooth. If they got on their bad side, violence and destruction would hunt them down. Thus, priests and priestesses of every temple made offerings to the gods daily. These sacrifices included drink, food, ointment, and clothing for temple idols. They did not think the idols themselves were gods but visible representations of divine forces.

Before the priests approached the temple, they burned incense. Then, they broke a seal and untied the cords holding the door of the temple or shrine shut. The priests approached the god's image, kissed the ground before its feet, and raised their arms while singing hymns. They went down on their belly in front of the god's image, stretching their arms out on the ground. Finally, they anointed the idol with scented oil and burned incense before it.

Who Were Anubis, Ra, and Osiris?

Anubis, Ra, and Osiris were the Egyptian gods of the dead. The black jackal god Anubis was the god of mummification and funeral rites. He stood at the gates of the underworld with his scales. As dead souls approached, Anubis weighed their hearts with an ostrich feather on the other side of the scale. Which weighed more? A person who had lived a life of harmony and peace had a heart as light as a feather. This person could enter *Duat*, the underworld, with Anubis guiding their souls. However, Ammit, the "Devourer of the Dead," ate the people with hearts weighed down by disorder and constant arguments. She had a crocodile head, and her body was half lioness and half hippo.

Anubis weighs a heart as Ammit waits to eat those who don't measure up.[87]

The sun god Ra was one of ancient Egypt's most important deities. The Egyptians combined him with Amun, the creator. He traveled across the sky by day but passed through Duat at night. Every night in the underworld, he had to fight Apep, the serpent god of chaos. Apep wanted to keep Ra from rising again because the world would die without the sun. When Amun-Ra defeated Apep each night, he restored order and brought life and warmth back to the world as he sailed through the sky.

Amun-Ra fights the serpent Apep.[88]

Osiris was the god of fertility and agriculture. He got into an argument with his brother Set (Seth), who killed him and chopped him into pieces. Osiris was married to his sister, Isis. She went looking for her brother-husband and found the pieces of his body. She put them back together and wrapped him up in strips of cloth, forming the first mummy. Isis used her superpowers to bring Osiris back to life long enough to get pregnant with their son Horus. However, she couldn't keep him in the land of the living, so Osiris became the god of the underworld. He is portrayed with the green skin of a decomposing person.

How Did the Egyptians Prepare for the Afterlife?

Ancient Egyptians knew they wouldn't automatically enter Duat, the underworld. After they died, the Egyptians believed they had to fend off horrifying demons on their journey to the place of judgment. When they arrived, they first had to list all the sins they had *not* committed in their lifetime. If they passed that test, then Anubis weighed their hearts. The ones whose hearts were lighter than a feather began their journey to **Aaru**.

To get to Aaru, they had to pass through many gates guarded by frightening gods and demons. After they passed through the gates, they reached Aaru by boat. Aaru meant the "Field of Reeds," a lush place like the Nile Delta where they could grow plenty of food. Aaru had thousands of islands of reeds surrounded by water, so it was a wonderful place for hunting and fishing.

The ancient Egyptians knew they had to prepare in their lifetime for their eventual journey into the underworld. They needed certain things to protect and guide them to the place of judgment and through the gates to Aaru. Before they died, they collected magic amulets and writings from the Book of the Dead. **Amulets** were jewelry items they believed had special powers to protect and bring good luck. Most people had a **heart scarab** carved before they died, crafted with the same shape as the scarab seals. After death, it was placed on their chest before they were mummified. The scarab beetle represented the cycle of life and rebirth.

If they were lucky enough to make it to Aaru, the Egyptians thought they would have to work in the fields to grow food. Many Egyptians would bury **shabtis**, or little dolls, with them. These came to life when an incantation was spoken over them, and they did the work for the dead person in the afterlife. The rich buried hundreds of shabtis with them, ensuring they would never have to work.

What Was the Book of the Dead?

The Book of the Dead was a collection of writings about magic spells and other essential information a dead person would need on their way to Duat. The Egyptians thought they had a difficult journey to the afterworld when their souls left their bodies, and the Book of the Dead was their guidebook. They needed to know which incantations to chant to fight the demons. They also required directions for how to pass through the underworld and make sure they made it to Aaru.

These spells were written on papyrus scrolls, a paper-like material made from the reed-like papyrus plant that grew in water. Egyptians also used the Book of the Dead to guide their funeral practices in the New Kingdom. The Egyptian title meant "Coming Forth into the Day," reflecting the Egyptian belief that death was not the end but a transition to a new life.

Nauny (second on the left) stands in judgment before Osiris on his throne.[39]

Archaeologists found one of the papyrus scrolls in the Book of the Dead buried with Nauny, the chantress of Amun-Ra. A chantress was a priestess who sang or chanted songs and spells to the gods. Every day, she awakened the god in its temple by singing to it, then put it to sleep in the evening the same way. A chantress also served at funerals. She would sing the spells over the dead person to guide him or her to Duat. A chantress was usually a princess or from an upper-class family. Nauny was the king's daughter, and she died in her seventies.

The Book of the Dead scroll buried with Nauny was inside a wooden idol of Osiris. When unrolled, it was over seventeen feet long. The scroll was full of pictures and numerous magic spells for each part of the journey to Duat. In one image, Nauny stands before Anubis as he weighs her heart. Isis stands behind Nauny, and Osiris sits on a throne overseeing the judgment, wrapped up like a mummy. In front of him is a joint of beef that has been sacrificed as part of Nauny's funeral. A baboon sits on top of the scales, writing down the results. He is Thoth, the god of writing and wisdom. Did Nauny pass the test? Yes! Anubis reports to Osiris that her heart is a good witness.

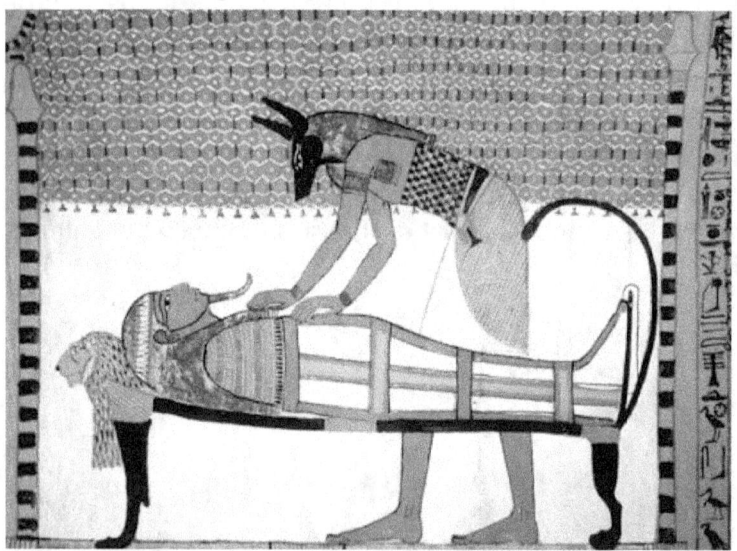

A priest representing Anubis prepares a mummy.[40]

Why and How Did They Mummify the Dead?

Because the ancient Egyptians believed the ka aspect of the soul continued to live in or near the person's body after they died, they embalmed the body so it would not decay. The god Anubis who weighed people's hearts was also the god of mummification. Special priests representing Anubis performed the embalming process. The first step in mummification was removing the person's body organs. The heart stayed in the body, but the brain was pulled out through the nose with hooks. The lungs, liver, stomach, and intestines were also removed.

These organs went into jars full of natron salt, which dried them out. Sometimes, the priests buried these jars with the mummies. Other times, they reinserted the dried organs into the body and sewed it up. They also covered the body in natron salt for seventy days to dry it. Once the body and organs dried out, the priests washed the body and rubbed oil over the skin. Next, they rubbed black resin over the whole body. After this, they wrapped the entire body in strips of linen, turning it into a mummy.

The priests decorated the mummy with jewelry and placed particular charms on the body to protect it. They usually put a mask over the head of royalty. When the mummy was ready to be buried, they placed it in a wooden coffin. If the dead person was royalty, a high official, or a priest, they set their coffin inside a massive stone sarcophagus. The coffin or sarcophagus then went into a tomb with things the person needed in the afterlife, like furniture, mirrors, clothing, food, drink, and games.

What Kind of Funerary Rites Did the Egyptians Follow for the Dead?

The ancient Egyptians thought tombs were portals through which the dead could travel between the land of the living and the underworld. Many pharaohs and distinguished Egyptians were buried on the Nile's west bank near Luxor in a place called the Valley of the Kings. A dramatic funerary rite that the Egyptians followed was sailing decorated funeral barges along this section of the Nile. They portrayed Ra's journey through the underworld at night and back into the sky during the day.

Burial of the New Kingdom scribe Hunefer. His wife and daughter mourn while a priest in an Anubis mask supports his mummified body. Other priests chant incantations.[41]

The priests held an important funerary rite after the dead person was mummified and just before he or she was buried. They gathered with the deceased person's family in front of the tomb for the "Opening of the Mouth" ceremony. In this ritual, a priest wore a jackal mask representing Anubis. He held the mummy in a standing position while the family mourned in front of the dead body. Meanwhile, other priests burned incense and offered the body food and clothing. Once this ceremony ended, the priests placed the mummy in the tomb's burial chamber.

Roundup Activity: Pop Quiz

Check your answers in the back of the book.

1. Who was the goddess of fertility and motherhood?
2. What did the ancient Egyptians believe happened to the ka part of the soul after death?
3. What was the role of the king in ancient Egyptian religion?
4. Why did the Egyptians consider Isis the "mother of the pharaohs"?
5. What god weighed the hearts of dead people?
6. Who was the god of the sun and one of the most important deities in ancient Egyptian religion?
7. How did Osiris become the god of the underworld?
8. Why did the ancient Egyptians bury shabti dolls with a dead person?
9. What was the purpose of the Book of the Dead?
10. What ceremony was held just before placing a mummy in its tomb?

Chapter 6: Hatshepsut: The Female Pharaoh

Of Egypt's handful of women kings, Hatshepsut stood out as one of the most powerful in ancient Egyptian history. Hatshepsut was among Egypt's greatest pharaohs, men or women. In her thirteen years as pharaoh, she restored wealth to Egypt and graced the land with breathtaking new monuments and artwork. Hatshepsut claimed to be a half-goddess, the daughter of Amun.

What Happened in the Early Years of the New Kingdom?

Who ruled Egypt's New Kingdom before Hatshepsut? Ahmose I, who successfully chased the Hyksos from Egypt to Syria, began the New Kingdom (1550-1100 BCE) and the Eighteenth Dynasty (1550-1292 BCE). He re-unified Egypt and made Thebes the capital of Egypt again.

Ahmose also regained command over Nubia (northern Sudan) to the south. The ancient Egyptians had always wanted access to Nubia's fantastically rich gold mines. Egypt's gold stores became legendary in the New Kingdom. A Mitanni king commented, "Gold occurs in Egypt like sand on the roads." Ahmose built the last pyramid in Egypt for a native ruler.

Amenhotep I became the next pharaoh at around age fourteen in 1526 BCE. He wasn't supposed to be king, but his older brothers died young. His mother, Ahmose-Nefertari, ruled as regent until he came of age. Amenhotep's court astronomer, Amenemheb, invented the first water clock. It was a stone vessel with sloping sides and a small hole at the bottom through which water dripped. The inside of the bowl had twelve lines marking the hours as the water slowly receded. Time could be measured by the sun during the daylight hours, but the water clock was useful at night. The priests needed to perform the necessary sacrifices at the right time.

Amenhotep I[a]

During Amenhotep I's reign, Egyptian doctors wrote the Ebers Papyrus, possibly copied from earlier texts. What was in this ancient medical book? For one, it had magic spells to cast out demons, as the ancient Egyptians believed evil spirits caused migraines and other medical problems. They often called these demons crocodiles in their spells.

However, exorcism wasn't the only treatment plan. The Ebers Papyrus described how to use herbal medicine for many conditions. It taught that the body has twenty-two vessels carrying blood, mucus, tears, and semen. Doctors believed that a blockage of any of these vessels caused disease. The ancient Egyptians also understood that the heart provided the body's blood supply. The Ebers Papyrus instructed doctors to take the patient's pulse to check the condition of the heart.

Ancient Egyptian doctors could diagnose cancer and diabetes, yet how they did it is unclear. The Ebers Papyrus also discussed mental illnesses like depression and dementia. It included methods of contraception and how to diagnose a pregnancy and gave instructions for setting broken bones and treating burns.

None of Amenhotep's children survived infancy, so Thutmose I became the next pharaoh. Thutmose was most likely Amenhotep's brother-in-law. His primary wife ("the Great Royal Wife") was also named Ahmose, so she may have been the daughter of Amenhotep and Ahmose-Nefertari. Thutmose arranged Ahmose-Nefertari's burial, not her son Amenhotep. She probably died after Amenhotep, and Thutmose was possibly her son-in-law. Thutmose's mother was Senseneb, a non-royal.

Thutmose I and his mother, Senseneb[48]

Thutmose I launched military campaigns in West Asia, conquering Canaan, Lebanon, and the kingdom of Qatna in Syria. He built a victory monument at Carchemish, on the border of today's Turkey and Syria. He also expanded Egypt's borders south to the Fourth Cataract of the Nile, in today's Sudan. His military conquests opened up robust trade and brought staggering riches to Egypt.

Thutmose I and Ahmose were the parents of Hatshepsut. They also had two sons and another daughter. The sons died before Thutmose did. Thutmose had a minor wife named Mutnofret, the mother of Thutmose II. Before he died, Thutmose arranged the marriage of Hatshepsut to her half-brother, Thutmose II. Hatshepsut was only twelve at the time. As the daughter of the "Great Royal Wife," Hatshepsut brought a higher level of royalty and credibility to Thutmose II.

Thutmose II's generals dealt with uprisings in Nubia, Canaan, and Syria. He did not seem to ride out to war himself, perhaps because he was too young. Thutmose II and his half-sister Hatshepsut had a daughter named Neferure, probably their only child. With a woman in his harem named Isis, Thutmose II had a son, Thutmose III. Thutmose II died around age thirty when Thutmose III, his only heir, was two years old.

How Did Hatshepsut Rise to Power?

Thutmose II's early death left a power vacuum in Egypt. Officially, Thutmose III was the next pharaoh, but who would rule as his regent while he grew up? His mother, Isis, was just a concubine in the harem. She wasn't royal, so she wouldn't do. Hatshepsut became the regent for her husband's son.

At first, she was a conventional regent, taking care of matters of state in his name. For the first few years, Thutmose III was clearly the only pharaoh of Egypt. But things took a dramatic turn in Thutmose III's seventh year as pharaoh. The boy was only nine or ten, still too young to rule independently. Suddenly, Hatshepsut began calling herself by a pharaoh's titles. She took the full powers of a king as a co-ruler with her step-son. Why? Did unbridled ambition drive Hatshepsut, or was something else at play?

Hatshepsut"

Some Egyptologists believe that someone threatened Thutmose's throne. Perhaps another branch of the family was making a move to snatch power. They might have argued that it would still be another decade before the boy was grown. Egypt needed an adult to deal with any crises. So, Hatshepsut may have stepped into the pharaoh's role to preserve the throne for her stepson. However, even when he came of age, she stayed on the throne. They co-ruled Egypt for fifteen years until Hatshepsut died.

Of course, Hatshepsut's power play shocked Egypt. She went to great lengths to defend her legitimacy to rule Egypt as a full pharaoh. She pointed out that she had more royal blood than anyone else in the family—and not just royal blood but divine blood as well! The custom in those days was for the pharaoh's wife or daughter to take the title "God's Wife of Amun." This title meant she was a priestess of the creator god. Hatshepsut assisted Amun's high priest by singing and dancing at rituals.

But then, Hatshepsut claimed that Amun was not just her spiritual husband but also her biological father. She said that before she was born, Amun took on an incarnation as Thutmose I. Amun found Hatshepsut's mother, Ahmose, asleep in her beautiful palace. The divine fragrance wafting off of Amun awakened Ahmose. When she saw the god, she thought he was her husband.

Ahmose's beauty aroused Amun, and he slept with her as the scent of perfume filled the palace. Afterward, he revealed his true identity.

As the daughter of Amun, the king of the gods, Hatshepsut elevated herself to half-divine status. No one else could compete or question her right to rule. Furthermore, Hatshepsut claimed that her father, the god Amun, had prophesied that she would rule Upper and Lower Egypt and all the foreign lands under Egypt's control.

To further cement her position as pharaoh, Hatshepsut went through a gender transition—at least her paintings and statues did. Since the Egyptians were adamant that their pharaoh should be a man, her images became more masculine. After she appointed herself co-pharaoh with Thutmose III, artwork showed her wearing men's clothing, with small breasts and a more muscular build. Sometimes, she had a beard or the shadow of a mustache over her lips.

Hatshepsut with a beard and male clothing[45]

Who Was Senenmut?

Hatshepsut knew that to keep power, she had to have supporters in key positions. Senenmut had been steward to Hatshepsut and her daughter, Neferure, and was a trusted friend. In the New Kingdom, a royal steward oversaw the pharaohs' land and was in charge of food for the palace. After becoming co-pharaoh with her stepson, Hatshepsut made Senenmut her chief minister and architect.

As chief architect, Senenmut was responsible for cutting and installing four pink granite obelisks in Hatshepsut's honor at the Temple of Karnak. They were the tallest in the world at that time, standing over ninety feet. Carving a single obelisk in one piece out of stone took seven months. One obelisk still stands today. Senenmut may also have been an astronomer. The oldest Egyptian star map is on the ceiling of his tomb.

Senenmut holding Princess Neferure on his lap"

What Did Hatshepsut Accomplish as Pharaoh?

Hatshepsut immediately set to work on building projects. She was so enthusiastic about building things that she accomplished more construction programs than any other pharaoh except Ramesses II. She sent military campaigns to Syria and Nubia, although her reign was mainly peaceful. Syria was Egypt's northern border through much of the New Kingdom, and the pharaohs often had to fight the Canaanites or Syrians to maintain that claim.

Hatshepsut falsely claimed that the Hyksos had destroyed Egyptian temples and burned down cities. She said she restored the damage. However, Ahmose had sent the Hyksos packing over seven decades earlier. None of the four kings before her mentioned devastation left by the Hyksos, nor does archaeology show this, except for a palace that burned in Avaris. And it was almost certainly a West Asian palace, not Egyptian.

Hatshepsut sent a sailing expedition of thousands of men down the Red Sea to Punt, also known as "God's Land." Where was Punt? Scholars have argued this question for centuries. It is well documented as an actual place, but apparently, the ancient inscribers assumed everyone knew where it was. Pictures of Punt painted by the Egyptians show houses built on stilts and surrounded by palm trees. The land had giraffes, leopards, baboons, and rhinos.

One clue is that the journey began by ship down the Red Sea. Another clue is what they got from Punt. The Egyptians traded for a treasure trove of gold, ebony, and myrrh. They also got wood from Punt—a rare resource in Egypt's desert lands—and electrum, a gold and silver alloy. A third clue is that they could also get there via the Nile (when they had friendly relations with Nubia), so Punt must have been somewhere in East Africa.

What Was Exceptional About Her Mortuary Temple at Deir el-Bahri?

Senenmut was the mastermind who designed Hatshepsut's mortuary temple on the Nile's west bank near Luxor. A mortuary temple was not a person's tomb. Instead, it was a place built near the tomb to worship the dead pharaoh and bring food and other offerings. Every day, priests performed rituals to honor the dead.

The mortuary temple designed by Senenmut was cut into the face of a cliff. The temple had reflecting pools, terraced gardens, and three layers of graceful colonnades. Sphinxes lined the walkways, and stone lions guarded the doorways. Everything was beautifully balanced and in harmony.

Hatshepsut's mortuary temple at the base of a cliff[v]

Did Thutmose III Continue Ruling after Hatshepsut Died?

Hatshepsut died in her late forties, around 1460 BCE, when Thutmose III was twenty-one. Thutmose ruled Egypt by himself for three more decades. Three months after Hatshepsut died, he led his first known military campaign to Megiddo in northern Canaan. Thutmose scored a jaw-dropping victory against a coalition of Canaanite and Syrian kings. It was the beginning of a stellar military career. Egypt's warrior king won at least seventeen campaigns and captured 350 cities.

Thutmose had to choose one of three possible routes as he approached Megiddo. His war council warned him not to take the narrow middle path, as it was slower and dangerous. But he chose that route anyway, riding his chariot in front until the pass became so narrow that his chariot couldn't fit through. The Egyptians took their chariots apart and carried them as they marched in single file. By taking the narrow path, they caught the Canaanites by surprise.

Thutmose III[a]

However, the Hurrians of the Mitanni Kingdom in Syria and Turkey were growing strong and overconfident. They made the mistake of raiding Egypt's territory in Syria. Thutmose III launched another surprise attack. His men carried boats inland and crossed the northern Euphrates River into Mitanni land. The Hurrians weren't expecting him to show up so suddenly and had no time to organize a defense. Their princes huddled fearfully in caves as the Egyptians laid waste to their cities.

Thutmose III had at least seven wives. Three wives were probably Syrian princesses, and their names were Menwi, Merti, and Menhet. They were buried together in a lavish tomb. They all seem to have died around the same time, perhaps of some epidemic. Another wife was

Merytre-Hatshepsut, an Egyptian noblewoman. She and Thutmose had six children, including Amenhotep II, who became the next pharaoh.

What Happened to Hatshepsut's Monuments and Images after Her Death?

What was the dynamic between Hatshepsut and Thutmose III? It's hard to tell. He was a child or teenager for most of her reign, and he left no inscriptions that said anything negative about Hatshepsut. Nevertheless, about twenty years after her death, he went to great lengths to erase her memory. Workers cut her images off walls and plastered over her name in places it appeared. Thutmose ordered her statues to be torn down, defaced, and buried in a pit.

However, he did not harm things hidden away in her tomb. He only focused on official records and what could be seen in public. He was so thorough that Hatshepsut was the forgotten pharaoh for thousands of years. No one knew she existed until the 1800s CE when Egyptologist Jean-François Champollion decoded the texts in her tomb.

Did Thutmose III resent that Hatshepsut had usurped his throne? Maybe, but he became the full pharaoh at age twenty-one, anyway. He had a long and successful career. Why wait twenty years after her death to remove her memory? Perhaps he wanted to ensure stability and order in Egypt's royal line. After all, pharaohs were supposed to be men, and the king was the earthly representation of the god Horus. Eliminating Hatshepsut from the record left a tidy, unbroken line of male kings, from Thutmose I to Thutmose II to Thutmose III.

Roundup Activity: Crossword

Check your answers in the back of the book.

Who or where?

Across
4. I co-ruled with Thutmose III
6. I was a god. Hatshepsut said I was her father
7. Where Thutmose II won his 1st great victory
8. My astronomer invented the water clock
9. Hatshepsut sent an expedition here

Down
1. I married Hatshepsut when she was 12
2. I co-ruled with Hatshepsut until she died
3. I chased the Hyksos out of Egypt
5. I was Hatshepshut's Chief Minister & architect

Chapter 7: Akhenaten: The Heretic

Akhenaten (1352-1334 BCE) broke the mold of what pharaohs were supposed to do. His real name was Amenhotep IV, but he changed it five years into his reign. His new name, Akhenaten, meant "effective for Aten." His name change represented a radical break in Egyptian religious beliefs. The Egyptian pharaoh was also the country's spiritual leader. Whatever he believed got imposed on everyone else. Akhenaten's goal was to reform Egyptian religion from the top down. Instead of worshiping many gods, he focused on only one: the Aten.

Did the ancient Egyptians always worship multiple gods? They may have been *monotheistic* (worshiping one god only) at the dawn of their civilization. Some scholars believe they only worshiped Amun, the creator, in their earliest days. Over time, they added more gods until they had dozens of primary deities and thousands of lesser gods. They happily followed this system for millennia.

And then, Akhenaten came onto the scene. By upending Egypt's religious system, he earned the title of *heretic*. A heretic believes and promotes things about religion that most people don't accept.

Who Might Have Influenced Akhenaten?

What happened in the seven decades between Thutmose III and Akhenaten? Were there any hints of religious change? Did other cultures influence Egypt's religion? The pharaohs married Nubian, Syrian, Hurrian, and Babylonian princesses. These people were also polytheistic, yet they did influence the Egyptians. For instance, the people of Byblos worshiped the goddess Baalat Gebal. The Egyptians who traded with Byblos also worshiped this goddess and sent gifts to her temple. They associated her with their goddess Hathor.

Pharaoh Merneptah and the sun god Ra [50]

The Israelites were the only known monotheistic people in the region. The first pharaoh to mention Israel in an inscription was the Nineteenth Dynasty Pharaoh Merneptah around 1208 BCE. On his victory monument, he bragged about clobbering the Hittites, Canaanites, Hurrians, and Israelites. The word he used for the Israelites was for a people, not a nation. Merneptah reigned when events in the Old Testament book of Judges unfolded. At that time, Israel was a loose confederation of twelve tribes living in Canaan, and they did not yet have a king.

Did Egyptian history say anything about the Israelites' exodus from Egypt, or was that just a myth? Obviously, such an event wouldn't have appeared on a victory monument. However, in the third century BCE,

Egyptian priest and historian Manetho wrote about it. He said the exodus happened when Amenophis was king. Manetho wrote in Greek, and Amenophis was the Greek word for Amenhotep. Four pharaohs had this name in the Eighteenth Dynasty. Of the four pharaohs named Amenophis (Amenhotep), the one that may best fit the biblical timeline is Amenhotep II (1427-1400 BCE).

However, his story takes a radical turn from what Moses wrote in the Torah. The Egyptian spin on the story was that Amenophis wanted to rid Egypt of people with leprosy and other undesirables. He forced 80,000 of them to work in the quarries. The lepers asked a renegade priest named Osarseph to be their leader. He later changed his name to Moses. He told them not to worship the Egyptian gods. Manetho said the lepers formed a coalition with the Hyksos, who had fled Egypt hundreds of years earlier.

Amenophis couldn't fight the coalition, so he escaped to Ethiopia while the lepers and Hyksos wreaked havoc in Egypt. Oddly, instead of dying of leprosy, the undesirables grew to hundreds of thousands. Eventually, Amenophis built up support and came back to Egypt. He drowned some of the lepers in the sea and drove the rest into the Sinai Desert. These people eventually settled in Judea and became the Jews.

At any rate, Akhenaten knew about the Israelites and their religion. Of course, the Israelites weren't very good monotheists. They kept straying into polytheism. Nevertheless, they could have put some ideas into Akhenaten's mind.

Was Amenhotep II the pharaoh during the Exodus?[61]

How Did Akhenaten's Family Influence Him?

Akhenaten's family dynamics became increasingly bizarre as he grew up. His father, Amenhotep III, became pharaoh as a child. He immediately married Tiye, his Great Royal Wife. Tiye was Akhenaten's mother, and she had several other children. She had unusual power for an Egyptian queen and helped her husband run the country. Artwork shows her as the same height as her husband, indicating they were equal partners in the marriage.

Amenhotep III also married two Babylonian princesses and the Hurrian princess Gilukhepa. Later, he married Gilukhepa's niece, Tadukhipa. Yet, he refused to give any of his daughters as brides to foreign kings. He didn't want foreigners to claim Egypt's throne via marriage. As Amenhotep III got older, things got really weird. He married two of his daughters and made them Great Royal Wives. Amenhotep III was the first pharaoh known to marry his children.

Like Hatshepsut, Amenhotep III claimed the god Amun was his biological father. The worship of Amun was quite popular at this time. The priests of Amun had almost equal standing with the royal family. By the time Akhenaten became pharaoh, the priests of Amun owned more land than he did.

Amenhotep III became increasingly interested in the Aten-tjehen, or the "Dazzling Sun Disk." (The Aten was the Sun Disk, or the visible sun—an aspect of the sun god Ra.) He promoted the solar cult—the worship of the sun—and even took the title "Sun Disk" for himself. Yet, he didn't worship the sun god exclusively. He also encouraged the worship of the moon, specifically the moon god Nebmaatre of Soleb, adopted from the Nubians. He believed that he was the moon god's living image on earth. In a sense, he thought he was the sun and the moon.

Akhenaten became pharaoh around 1352 BCE when his father died. He had a distinctive appearance. His face was long and thin, with high cheekbones, full lips, and an exceptionally pointed chin. Akhenaten's wife was the beautiful and elegant Nefertiti. They had six daughters together but no sons. Akhenaten had another wife named Kiya. This marriage was probably a love match, as an inscription called her "the king's greatly beloved wife."

Akhenaten (Amenhotep III)[58]

He also married his full sister, "The Younger Lady" (the name given to her mummy in recent years). Although it's unclear which sister she was, DNA analysis of her mummy shows she was the daughter of Amenhotep III and Tiye. It also proved she was the mother of the famous King Tutankhamun. Her mummy shows she shared her brother's unusual facial characteristics, including the long, pointy chin. She suffered a terrible wound that crushed her left cheek and jaw and killed her. Was it accidental, such as a kick from a horse, or was she the victim of violence, like from an axe blow? If so, who murdered her and why? We may never know.

How Did Akhenaten Focus on the Aten?

As we mentioned, Akhenaten's father had worshiped the Aten, but Akhenaten took it to the next level. At first, Akhenaten devoted his personal worship to the Aten but acknowledged that other gods existed and could be worshiped. Things began to change in the eighth year of his reign. By then, he had already changed his name from Amenhotep to Akhenaten.

Akhenaten next claimed to be the only human who could know and connect with the god. He said that the Aten was the only god who could be officially worshiped; however, no one except for him could worship the Aten. Everyone else had to worship Akhenaten as the Aten's living incarnation. He banned idols of any other gods and shut down the state temples of other deities. He even erased the name of Amun from Egypt's monuments. By suppressing Amun's worship, he reined in the power of Amun's priests, a threat to his kingship.

Akhenaten worships the Aten, portrayed as the sun's rays.[58]

The only image Akhenaten allowed was the sun with its rays. He taught that the image was only a representation of the Aten. No one could truly understand or portray the god. In Akhenaten's hymns and inscriptions, he spoke of the Aten as the supreme god. This loving and all-powerful creator maintained the universe. Egypt's priests had worshiped other gods in dark temples, but Akhenaten took worship outside, into the bright sunshine.

Why Did He Build a New Capital City?

When Akhenaten changed his name, he also built a new capital named after his god. Akhetaten meant "Horizon of the Aten." It was on the eastern side of the Nile River, about 250 miles north of the previous capital of Thebes. A break in the cliffs directly east of the city let in the first rays of the rising sun, bathing the city in its light and warmth. Today, it is called Amarna. No earlier city had existed on this site, as Akhenaten wanted his new city to have no former temples to any other god. The new capital represented a break from the old Egyptian gods and especially the priests of Amun. He wanted his capital to be completely dedicated to the Aten.

The new city was planned and built remarkably quickly, thanks to efficient new methods. The builders used smaller limestone blocks of standard size. Workers used mudbrick for many buildings; they could make the bricks quickly and then whitewash them. The city was ready for the royal family to move in within about three years. While workers built it, Akhenaten ordered new temples to the Aten built in Egypt's major cities, like Heliopolis and Memphis.

A magnificent open-air temple to the Aten stood in Akhetaten's center. The grand royal palace in the north overlooked the Nile. The entire city covered about eight miles, with land on the other side of the Nile used for farming.

Akhenaten built Akhetaten to honor his one god, yet the ordinary people weren't fans of monotheism. Archaeologists have dug up small idols in Akhetaten, like the hippopotamus goddess of childbirth. People only lived in Akhetaten for a few decades. After Akhenaten died, King Tutankhamun made Thebes the capital again. Akhetaten quickly became a ghost city covered by sand until a Jesuit priest rediscovered it in the 1700s CE.

Bust of Akhenaten⁴⁴

In the late 1800s CE, the **Amarna letters** were found in the city's ruins. These were a collection of clay tablets with the cuneiform writing used in the ancient Middle East. Although Egypt used papyrus for writing, the West Asians inscribed their writing on damp clay, which hardened into tablets. The nice thing about these tablets is that some lasted for thousands of years and left a historical record. The kings of Syria, Babylonia, Egypt, and other nations exchanged letters regularly. These letters found in the long-abandoned city opened a window into the relationships between the royalty of Egypt and West Asia.

The kings called each other brothers, sent gifts to each other, and planned the royal weddings of their children. They asked each other for help when needed, such as during an invasion or famine. When they had medical problems, one king would send the other his favorite doctor, medicine, or magician.

Sometimes, they wrote to complain. For instance, the Babylonian king Burna-Buriash II wrote to Akhenaten, "I was ill, and you never wrote me a get-well note!" His next grievance was far worse. Egypt controlled Canaan at the time, but the Babylonian merchants passing through Canaan to Egypt were being attacked. "You need to execute those bandits and pay me back for the money they stole!"

In Akhenaten's day, there were four "great powers" of the Middle East. They were the Egyptians, Babylonians, Hurrians, and Hittites. All four kingdoms wanted control of Syria, an important trade crossroads. The Hittite kingdom was between the Black Sea and the Mediterranean in western Turkey. When Akhenaten was busy building Akhetaten, the Hittites snatched Egypt's territory in Syria. For the rest of the Eighteenth Dynasty, the Egyptians and the Hittites were at each other's throats.

Did Akhenaten's Wife Nefertiti Co-Reign with Him?

Nefertiti was Akhenaten's Great Royal Wife, but was she more? Artwork shows her riding in a chariot. Two carvings show her with her hand raised, holding a weapon, about to violently strike an enemy. Another time, she is trampling the enemy. It's unlikely she actually went to war, so the artwork must be symbolic.

An iconic scene in ancient Egyptian art shows an Egyptian king holding a kneeling prisoner by the hair. The king holds a mace or some other weapon in the air, about to strike. This scene is repeated over and over throughout ancient Egypt's history. Some scholars suggest the scene doesn't always represent an actual event. It might show the continued power of the Egyptian monarch over the enemy.

Nefertiti[46]

This scene was always used for kings. Placing Queen Nefertiti in this scene is a vital clue that she became a co-pharaoh with her husband. Some historians believe that Akhenaten made her his co-pharaoh a few years before he died. Nefertiti's name disappeared from royal inscriptions in Akhenaten's twelfth year as king. Did she die, or did she get a promotion?

After Nefertiti "disappeared," Akhenaten suddenly had a co-pharaoh. The co-pharaoh's name was Neferneferuaten. She had the title "Akhet-en-hyes," which meant "effective for her husband." That must have meant this pharaoh was a woman and one of Akhenaten's wives. Neferneferuaten was almost certainly Nefertiti. She continued ruling for a year or two after Akhenaten died.

Roundup Activity: Two Truths and a Lie

Circle which of the three statements is <u>not</u> true. Check your answer in the back of the book.

- Akhenaten's wife was Nefertiti.
- Akhenaten promoted the worship of the moon god.
- Akhenaten built a new city devoted to the Aten.

Chapter 8: Tutankhamun: A Boy and His Legacy

If you asked someone to name an Egyptian pharaoh, chances are they'd say "King Tut!" A few might say Ramesses. Most people would not know the names of the other Egyptian kings unless they're addicted to the History Channel. What made Tutankhamun, who ruled from 1332 to 1323 BCE, so famous? What did he accomplish as Egypt's king?

The truth is that he didn't achieve nearly as much as some of the more obscure kings. After all, he was only eight or nine years old when he became pharaoh, and he died when he was only eighteen or nineteen. A regent ran Egypt for most of his reign. Yes, he (and his regent) accomplished significant changes in Egyptian culture. But Tutankhamun is more famous for his mummy than what he did while living.

What Was His Childhood Like?

Tut's father was Akhenaten, and his mother was one of Akhenaten's full sisters. This meant he only had one set of grandparents: Amenhotep III and Queen Tiye. Although DNA analysis reveals Tut's mother was his father's sister, it doesn't tell us which sister. Tiye had four or five daughters. When Tut was born, Akhenaten, the religious revolutionary, named him Tutankhaten, which meant "the living image of Aten," or "the life of Aten is perfect."

Tutankhaten was born toward the end of his father's reign when his stepmother Nefertiti was likely co-pharaoh. He had a wet nurse named

Maia. (Maia had her own baby but also breastfed Tutankhaten.) A carving of Tut as a teen shows him with Maia in an endearing scene. One of Maia's titles was "educator," which means she was also likely his tutor. She was also called "great one of the harem." Maia was probably a relative of Tutankhaten.

Tutankhamun and Maia[56]

Tutankhaten's birth mother must have died before he became pharaoh. No mention of her in his reign has been found. Typically, a pharaoh's mother appeared in artwork with her son and was a key influence. The fatal blow to her face, if murder, may have happened in the chaos surrounding Akhenaten's death. Her royal lineage and position as Akhenaten's wife made her a strong contender to the throne, a threat to Nefertiti and her son-in-law, Smenkhkare.

Tutankhaten was about seven when his father, Akhenaten, died. Two shadowy figures ruled Egypt for the next two years. One was Neferneferuaten, probably Nefertiti. The other was the mysterious Smenkhkare. His wife was Meritaten, a daughter of Akhenaten and Nefertiti. Smenkhkare may have been the son of Akhenaten's brother, Thutmose, who was the crown prince until his early death. Smenkhkare probably died after only ruling for a year.

This couple is probably Smenkhkare and his wife Meritaten.⁵⁷

Rise to Throne and Name Change

Either Neferneferuaten and Smenkhkare died, or Tutankhaten and his supporters grew strong enough to overthrow them. King Tut's reign marked the return to Egypt's polytheistic religion, with Amun the chief god again. Around age twelve, Tutankhaten took the new name of Tutankhamun, "living image of Amun." However, he still reverenced the Aten. He married his half-sister, the daughter of Akhenaten and Nefertiti. She was born Ankhesenpaaten, meaning "she lives for Aten." When Tut changed his name, she changed hers to Ankhesenamun, "she lives for Amun." Although they adopted Egypt's polytheism, they still reverenced the Aten, as a painting shows the couple bathed in the sun's rays.

Tutankhamun and his wife, Ankhesenamun[98]

Ankhesenamun was apparently Tutankhamun's only wife. The couple had no surviving children, but Ankhesenamun got pregnant at least twice. One female child died in the second trimester of pregnancy, and the other girl died shortly after she was born. Both girls were mummified and buried with their father.

Tutankhamun was too young to rule on his own, so who was his regent? His mother was probably dead by this time. The power behind the throne was Ay, whose wife Tey had been Nefertiti's wet nurse. During Akhenaten's reign, Ay was the overseer of the royal chariot horses. Ay and Horemheb, general of the armies, served as Tut's two closest advisors. Tutankhamun had a hot temper, and Horemheb wrote that he could calm the young king when he flew off the handle.

King Tutankhamun, the boy king[59]

Was Tutankhamun Physically Disabled?

Did Tutankhamun inherit any genetic defects from his parents' incestuous marriage? Remarkably, Tut didn't have the extremely long chin that both his mother and father had. However, an analysis of his mummy leads some scholars to say he was frail and deformed. In his tomb were 130 walking sticks, which some interpret to mean he couldn't walk on his own. His mummy appears to have a club foot or a foot that was twisted and turned in.

However, several Egyptologists and physicians point out that mummification could have caused the apparent club foot. They have seen other mummies whose tight wrappings have distorted the foot's shape. If King Tut had a club foot, the long bones in his leg would have shown signs of wear and distress, yet they were perfectly aligned. Moreover, the sandals in his tomb did not

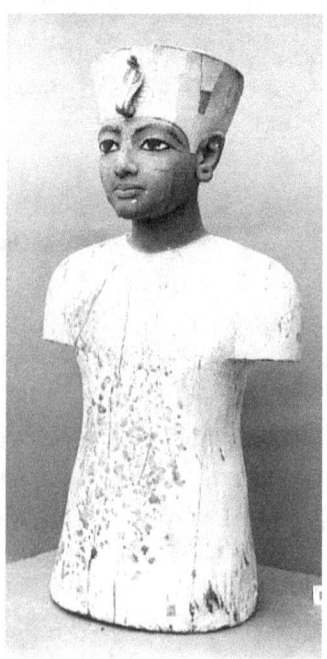

A wooden figure of King Tut[60]

show uneven wear. (Of course, they might have been a new pair). Scholars think the walking sticks were a status symbol, not an aid for walking.

What Did He Do as King?

Tutankhamun and his advisors restored the old polytheistic system in Egypt. During Tut's father's reign, the temples had fallen into ruin. The priests moaned that such neglect irritated the gods. "If we ask a god or goddess for advice, they won't listen!" King Tut rebuilt or restored the old temples and even built massive new temples.

About four years into his reign, when he would have been twelve or thirteen, his court left Akhetaten and moved to Memphis. The earlier kings of the Eighteenth Dynasty had ruled from Thebes, and it continued as Egypt's religious center. Yet, Memphis had a history as Egypt's capital stretching back to the Old Kingdom.

King Tutankhamun had to contend with the economic crisis that his father left behind. Akhenaten was so laser-focused on promoting the worship of the Aten that he ignored Egypt's foreign relations. The trade routes crumbled because bandits ran rampant. Tutankhamun worked to restore relationships with Egypt's old allies, like the Hurrians and Babylonians. Tut warred in Nubia, Canaan, and Syria, gaining back lost territory. Whether he actually led his armies is questionable. He would have been too young for most of his reign.

Tutankhamun as a sphinx, trampling the enemy[61]

How Did King Tut Die?

Tutankhamun died in his late teens. The cause of his death is a topic of fierce debate among Egyptologists. Some believe he might have died from a disability; however, it is doubtful that he was severely disabled. He did have a broken left thigh bone, which some scholars think might have happened in a chariot crash. The broken bone may have gotten infected (osteomyelitis). If untreated (and no one had antibiotics, then), osteomyelitis kills 20 percent of the people who have it.

King Tut's DNA indicated he had been sick multiple times with several strains of malaria. One strain of the mosquito-borne illness he had was Plasmodium falciparum, the most severe type of malaria that is often fatal. Malaria causes chills, fever, and headache, but the worst strain causes breathing issues, confusion, seizures, and coma. Even today, it kills over 400,000 people a year.

Another potential cause of death is an epidemic. The Egyptian military stationed in Syria had the bubonic plague or tularemia (rabbit fever) not long after Tutankhamun died. Both diseases are bacterial and have a 50 percent death rate without antibiotics.

Who Ruled after Tutankhamun Died?

Tutankhamun's death ended the Eighteenth Dynasty. Tut's advisor, Ay, became the next pharaoh and ruled from around 1323 to 1319 BCE. He oversaw Tutankhamun's funeral. Oddly, he even conducted the "Opening of the Mouth" ceremony. Usually, an important priest did this. Ay wore a leopard skin during the ceremony, which the high priest typically wore. Of course, the embalming process took seventy days. Ay would have been installed as pharaoh by the time the funeral took place, giving him priestly status.

Ay at Tutankhamun's funeral[62]

Tut's Queen and the Hittite Prince

Tutankhamun's wife, Ankhesenamun, found herself in an awkward position when her teenage husband suddenly died. Ay had taken the throne. He had some royal connections but no valid claim to the throne other than serving as Tutankhamun's advisor. He tried to fix the problem by forcing a marriage with Ankhesenamun. Not only was she Tut's wife, but she was also the daughter of Akhenaten and Nefertiti.

Ankhesenamun looked down her nose at the older man. She was far too royal to marry him! She could rule Egypt herself if she could find a royal husband. But who? In desperation, she wrote to Suppiluliuma I, the Hittite king: "My husband died, and I have no sons. I hear you have many sons. Could you send one of your sons to be my husband? They are trying to force me to marry a servant!"

Suppiluliuma was stunned when he received her letter. The Egyptians never allowed marriages of their royal women to foreign princes. Furthermore, royal women never negotiated their marriages. "I've never heard of such a thing!" Suppiluliuma gasped.

Yet, why not marry one of his sons to the Egyptian queen? His son could become Egypt's pharaoh. Suppiluliuma wondered if the letter was legitimate. He sent his chief advisor to Egypt to determine if the situation was as she described. The advisor returned with a second letter from the queen.

"Why do you doubt me? If what I said wasn't true, why would I send such shameful news to a foreign land? It's all still true. My husband died. I have no son. I refuse to marry a servant. I haven't written any other country, only to you! Send me one of your sons to be my husband, and he will be king of Egypt."

Finally, Suppiluliuma sent his son, Zannanza, to marry the Egyptian queen. But Ay must have gotten wind that he was coming because someone killed Zannanza before he arrived at the Egyptian queen's palace. Suppiluliuma was livid. He ordered his armies to attack the Egyptian lands in Syria and Canaan. The Hittites pulverized the Egyptians and brought hundreds of captives back to their land of Hatti. But Suppiluliuma didn't know that the plague was circulating around Syria. The captive Egyptian soldiers brought the plague with them to the Hittites, killing Suppiluliuma and his crown prince Arnuwanda and wiping out the Hittite military.

Suppiluliuma I, Hittite King from 1370–1330 BCE[68]

Horemheb Erases Tutankhamun

Horemheb ruled from 1319 to 1292 BCE. Although not royal, he had worked his way to power as the commander-in-chief of Egypt's army. King Tut sent him on diplomatic missions and made him his crown prince before he died. However, when Tutankhamun died, Horemheb was in Syria fighting the Hittites (and the plague). Taking advantage of his absence, Ay somehow elbowed his way into becoming the next pharaoh. Horemheb sat back and waited. Ay was elderly and probably wouldn't live long.

When Ay died four years later, Horemheb got his revenge. He shattered Ay's sarcophagus and erased his name and portraits from his tomb. He then wiped out the memory of Akhenaten, the heretic. Akhenaten had offended the gods and disrupted Egypt's harmony. Horemheb struck his name off royal documents and kings' lists. He flattened the city of Akhetaten and chiseled off Akhenaten's name from monuments throughout Egypt.

Horemheb continued his quest to rewrite history, erasing Neferneferuaten and Smenkhkare. After all, they were connected to Akhenaten. He even erased Tutankhamun, although the boy had named him his crown prince. However, Horemheb did not disturb Tutankhamun's tomb. Like Hatshepsut, Akhenaten and Tutankhamun became the forgotten pharaohs.

Discovery of Tut's Tomb by Howard Carter

In 1907 CE, Lord Carnarvon of Highclere Castle (where Downton Abbey was filmed) financed Howard Carter's quest to find King Tutankhamun's tomb. The forgotten king's existence had come to light when Akhetaten was unearthed at Amarna. After World War I interrupted his search for several years, Carter renewed his search in 1917. However, he found nothing, and Lord Carnarvon threatened to cut off his funding.

Carter returned to the Valley of the Kings, where a series of tombs had been carved into the hills. In November 1922, he removed debris in front of a large tomb. A boy bringing water to his workers tripped over a stone, but it wasn't just a random rock. It was a flight of steps leading underground to a doorway. Exhilarated, Carter telegrammed Lord Carnarvon. When Carnarvon arrived two weeks later, Carter chiseled a hole into the top of the door. He held a candle to the opening and peered inside.

"Can you see anything?"

"Yes! Wonderful things!"

King Tutankhamun's death mask"

Once they opened the tomb, they confirmed it belonged to King Tutankhamun. Instead of being carved into the hillside, like the surrounding tombs, it was cut into the valley floor. No one expected it to be there, including tomb robbers over the millennia. The tomb had been mostly untouched. Water had seeped in and damaged some of the items inside. Yet, unlike any other royal tomb in the Valley of the Kings, most of its treasures were undisturbed.

King Tutankhamun's mummy lay in a coffin nested inside two larger coffins. Covering his face was the spectacular gold death mask that has become iconic. It was solid gold inlaid with gemstones and weighed almost twenty-three pounds. A magic spell had been inscribed on the back of the mask to guide the king safely to the underworld. Thousands of other objects lay in the tomb, including a gilded throne, statues of King Tut, chariots, an alabaster lotus-shaped drinking vessel, furniture, baskets of fruit and meat, clothing, and cosmetics. Touchingly, King Tut's childhood toys had been buried with him.

What Myths Swirled Regarding His Tomb?

Newspaper headlines in 1922 announced a curse found at the entrance to Tutankhamun's tomb: "They who enter this sacred tomb shall be swiftly visited by the wings of death!" It turned out that this lurid inscription wasn't from ancient times. Neither was it on Tut's tomb. The journalists made it up to sell papers! Nevertheless, Lord Carnarvon died within months of blood poisoning, and the rumors resurfaced. Other team members mysteriously died, leaving some convinced that the tomb was cursed.

A shabti doll buried with Tut[65]

What Legacy Did King Tut Leave Behind?

Horemheb thought he had erased the memory of Akhenaten and Tutankhamun. However, the discovery of Akhetaten at Amarna shed light on Akhenaten's role as a religious revolutionary. Tutankhamun died as a teenager before workers completed his royal tomb. Consequently, he was buried in a borrowed tomb. His chief advisor, Ay, buried Tutankhamun in the tomb he had prepared for himself. Later, after serving as pharaoh, Ay was buried in the tomb meant for Tutankhamun.

The small, modest tomb where Tutankhamun lay escaped the attention of tomb robbers. After all, if no one knew he existed, why even look for his tomb?

King Tutankhamun's greatest legacy was the astounding treasures and records hidden with him for thousands of years. Although relatively insignificant as a pharaoh, Tutankhamun is the most well-known. Why? His tomb was opened in the modern day of newspapers and magazines. "Tutmania," the sensational news and photos of this astonishing find, circled the globe and continues to capture the imagination.

Roundup Activity: "Who Am I" Word Search

Find the answer to the questions below in the puzzle going up, down, forward, backward, and diagonally. Check your answers in the back of the book.

A	N	K	H	E	S	E	N	A	M	U	N	R
M	A	I	A	Q	P	O	N	M	L	K	O	J
E	I	H	G	F	E	D	C	B	A	E	V	M
N	E	T	A	N	E	H	K	A	Y	B	R	T
H	O	R	E	M	H	E	B	E	U	B	A	R
O	D	E	H	T	A	F	E	H	T	O	N	T
T	S	E	C	M	O	C	N	B	A	M	R	O
E	R	A	K	H	K	N	E	M	S	N	A	T
P	A	H	G	I	L	Y	E	H	T	D	C	N
I	A	H	T	U	I	R	T	E	H	T	D	N
I	A	Y	A	T	W	E	H	T	M	A	Y	I
I	S	U	P	P	I	L	U	L	I	U	M	A

1. I was King Tut's grandfather
2. I was King Tut's grandmother
3. I was Tut's father, the religious revolutionary
4. I was Tut's wet nurse and tutor
5. Neferneferuaten and I ruled Egypt just before King Tut
6. This was my new name after King Tut and I got married
7. I was King Tut's regent and the pharaoh after him
8. I was the Hittite king who died of the plague after capturing Egyptian soldiers
9. I became king after Ay and erased King Tut and his father from the records
10. I was the lord who financed Howard Carter's discovery of Tut's tomb

Chapter 9: The Battle of Kadesh

"He's coming! Ramesses is on his way! I saw a cloud of dust down in the valley," the shepherd reported, running down the mountain to join his companions.

"Iasmakh! Ride quickly to Kadesh. Let Muwatalli know they're approaching."

Iasmakh jumped on his horse and disappeared over a hill. Meanwhile, the other two shepherds moved under a tree near the road. When Pharaoh Ramesses II rode up with his hundreds of chariots, he saw an idyllic scene. Sheep and goats peacefully grazed on the hillside. Two shepherds were sipping goat milk in the shade by the Orontes River.

Ramesses reined his horses to a stop as his men breathed a sigh of relief. They had been riding for hours. The king stepped out of his chariot and nodded to his interpreter. They approached the shepherds, who stood up and bowed.

"Sire! Please! Sit down and rest here in the shade. You must be exhausted! Have some goat milk with honey."

"Thank you," Ramesses said, smiling. "But I won't rest until I reach Kadesh. How far is it?"

"Not far. A two-hour march."

"Where are Muwatalli and the Hittites?"

"Oh, they're nowhere near here!" the shepherds assured Ramesses. "King Muwatalli heard you were coming and fled to Aleppo. He's rounding up reinforcements. They say he was trembling with fear when he heard your army was on the way."

Ramesses grinned. "As he ought to be!"

The Egyptian commander-in-chief approached Ramesses. "Sire, the horses need water. And the foot soldiers need time to catch up."

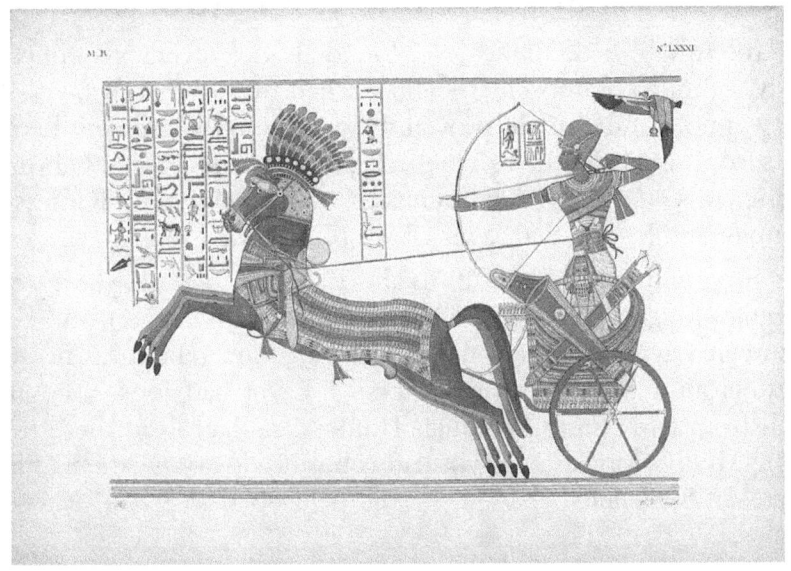

Ramesses stands in his two-horse chariot with the reins tied around his waist so he can fire an arrow.[66]

"Right. There's water here for the horses and men. We'll let everyone drink, then march on to Kadesh."

"With just the first unit? That's only 500 chariots and about 5,000 men! The other three units and chariots are far behind."

"Muwatalli's in Aleppo. He probably only left a small force in Kadesh. We'll ride ahead and set things straight in Kadesh. We need to reinstall our military there, or Muwatalli will retake the city when he gets reinforcements. The other units will catch up soon. We'll all spend the night at Kadesh."

Ramesses didn't know that Muwatalli had bribed the shepherds to give the Egyptians misinformation and keep him informed of their movement. The Hittites had *not* left the area and far outnumbered Ramesses's troops.

The 1274 BCE Battle of Kadesh (Qadesh) in Syria was one of the most significant military conflicts in ancient Egyptian history. What was the background behind this battle? Why were the Egyptians and Hittites fighting? What made Kadesh so pivotal? How did Ramesses almost get killed in the struggle, and who won? Let's jump into the thrilling story to discover what happened.

What Led Up to the Battle?

After Horemheb died, Ramesses I founded ancient Egypt's Nineteenth Dynasty, although he was elderly and reigned for less than two years. His family was not royal but had proved themselves in the military. Ramesses I had served as Horemheb's chief advisor. Because Horemheb had no surviving sons, he appointed Ramesses as his successor. Ramesses, in turn, appointed his son Seti as his crown prince.

For two centuries leading up to the Battle of Kadesh, the Egyptians and Hittites fought an on-again-off-again war. Syria, Lebanon, and Canaan lay between Egypt and Hatti, the Hittite kingdom. (Hatti was in western Turkey, around where Ankara is today.) Egypt had loosely controlled Canaan from early times, although Hittite clans had lived there from at least the Middle Kingdom. Egypt had robust trade arrangements with the city-states in Syria and Lebanon. It even held political power over several city-states.

During his reign, Akhenaten had given little attention to foreign affairs, and the Hittites had swarmed into Syria and Lebanon. Ramesses I sent his son Seti off to Canaan and Syria to take back the land Egypt had lost in the chaotic past half-century.

Seti I[47]

Seti I fought fiercely against the Hittites and recouped most of the lost territory in Canaan and Lebanon. After he conquered Lebanon, its chiefs sent yearly tribute of cedar wood. Seti also fought against a Libyan invasion of Egypt and subdued a rebellion in Nubia. When his father died, Seti ruled Egypt from around 1290 to 1279 BCE. He established military forts on the "Ways of Horus," a coastal road running through Gaza. He temporarily got control of Kadesh and the surrounding Amorite territory. However, it was so close to the Hittite kingdom that he could not hold it.

Meanwhile, Muwatalli II, the grandson of Suppiluliuma I, had become king of the Hittites. They were recovering from a fifty-year setback from the plague. Before getting struck down by the plague, Suppiluliuma I's goal was to control all of Syria west of the Euphrates.

The westernmost region of Turkey, on the coast of the Aegean Sea, was the land of Arzawa. Muwatalli's empire included Arzawa during his reign. Wilusa was a key city in Arzawa, and it paid tribute to the Hittites. Located on Turkey's northwestern coast, Wilusa was probably ancient Troy. Once thought to be mythological, scholars now believe Troy was a real place, based on Hittite records and archaeological finds at Wilusa. The Trojan War probably happened about seventy years after the Battle of Kadesh.

Sculpture of a young Ramesses II[68]

While Muwatalli grew in power, Seti I died, and his son, Ramesses II, became Egypt's pharaoh. He was the most commanding and dynamic of the New Kingdom pharaohs. Ramesses II became pharaoh when he was in his early twenties and ruled until he was in his nineties. He had many wives and around 100 children.

One of Ramesses II's first acts as pharaoh was pouncing on the infamous Sherden, one of the Sea Peoples. These were pirates who preyed on the ships sailing in the eastern Mediterranean Sea. No one is quite sure where the Sea Peoples came from. When Ramesses wrote about them, he didn't mention their homeland, almost as if he presumed everyone knew. However, he said they were in the league with the Hittites. Ramesses seemed to appreciate their fighting ability. Whenever he defeated a group of the Sea Peoples, he drafted them into his military.

Ramesses II, with his military under him[69]

What Were the Hittites and Egyptians Fighting Over?

The Hittites and Egyptians had competing interests in Syria, which lay on the Fertile Crescent's upper curve. The Fertile Crescent was an upside-down U-shaped trade highway with Syria as its pivotal center. From Syria, merchants followed the Euphrates River southeast through Assyria and Babylonia. They could also travel south through Lebanon and Canaan to Egypt or northwest to the Hittite region of Hatti and on to the fabulously wealthy Troy. Syria was a place where cultures mixed and mingled, one of the ancient world's most strategic trade hubs. It's no wonder that so many empires wanted control of Syria.

Fertile Crescent[70]

Syria had been on ancient Egypt's northern border for much of its history. Canaan had been a sort of buffer zone, protecting Egypt from invasions from the Assyrians, Mitanni, and other powerful nations.

Kadesh lay near the border between Lebanon and Syria. It was on the Orontes River, which connected some of ancient Syria's major cities, like Homs and Hama.

The Hittites had taken control of Kadesh, and Ramesses II was determined to get it back.

What Weapons and Military Men Did Each Side Have?

The Egyptians had about 20,000 men, but the Hittites had around 37,000. Muwatalli had convinced nineteen city-states in Syria and Turkey to join his side. The Hittite chariots numbered around 3,000, while the Egyptians had 2,000. With about 5,000 chariots altogether, it was the largest chariot battle in history.

The Hittites had been one of the earliest civilizations to use horse-drawn chariots with two spoked wheels. They had learned the skill of training chariot horses from the Hurrians. The Hittites had been riding chariots into battle for almost 400 years, far longer than the Egyptians.

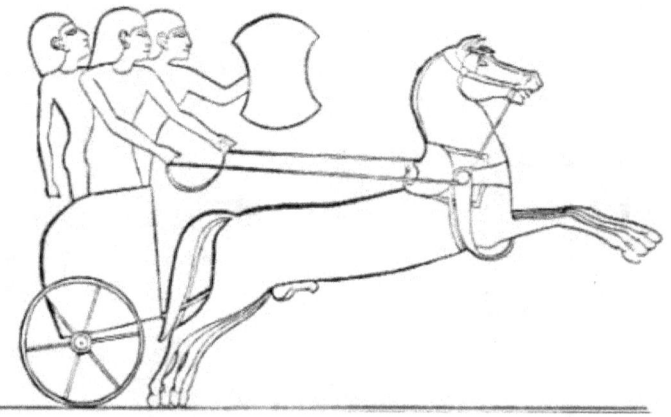

Hittite three-man, two-horse war chariot[71]

However, the Hittite chariots were heavier than the Egyptian chariots and held three men. One man was the driver, one carried a large shield to deflect arrows, and the third shot arrows or flung his spear at the enemy. The axle of the Hittite chariot was usually in the middle, allowing it to carry the extra weight of three men.

This made the Hittite chariots slower and clumsier than the Egyptian chariots. They used their chariots like battering rams, charging into lines of foot soldiers, crushing them and breaking their formation.

The Egyptians generally had two men in their chariots: a driver and an archer. Egyptian art typically showed the pharaoh in the chariot by himself with the reins tied around his waist. Egyptian chariots were mostly wood and lightweight. The axle was at the rear of the chariot, allowing for astounding maneuverability even at high speed. The men stood on a mesh of woven leather straps, which was lightweight and easier to balance when hitting bumps. The primary function of Egyptian chariots in battle was as moving platforms for shooting arrows or chasing down and trampling the enemy.

The Hittites were ahead of their day by using iron weapons. They had been smelting iron ore since 1400 BCE near the border of Syria. Their iron weapons were slightly harder and less likely to break than the bronze weapons used by the Egyptians. Even better, iron was cheap. It was readily available in Turkey and Syria. The Hittites could afford to outfit their entire army with iron weapons. The primary Hittite weapons were long spears, short daggers, and long, thin swords.

The Egyptians didn't have iron for another half-century. As mentioned, some of their weapons were bronze, an alloy of copper and tin. Copper was readily available in the Sinai Desert and along the Red Sea. But tin was more challenging to get and not readily available. The expense and rarity of tin made bronze weapons more expensive. Only the elite soldiers could carry them. Everyone else had to use copper, which was more brittle than iron and hard to sharpen.

In one image of Ramesses with his military, some soldiers carried long, pointed swords and round shields. These were the Sherden, the Sea People drafted by Ramesses II. He used them as his bodyguards in the Battle of Kadesh. In the painting, the Sherden wore longer skirts and distinctive helmets with horns and a ball at the top. Ramesses's Egyptian spearmen carried large, rectangular shields. No one seemed to wear body armor, except possibly some quilting in the chest area. Everyone wore sandals.

Ramesses II's soldiers[72]

What Happened in the Battle?

Ramesses II was so eager to capture Kadesh that he surged ahead with the Amun unit of his army, leaving the other three units far behind. They crossed the Orontes River and set up camp near Kadesh. But then, Ramesses received horrifying news. His scouts had captured two Hittite soldiers who were spying on the Egyptians. When Ramesses interrogated them, they told him, "Muwatalli is here! And he has more men than sand on the beach."

Ramesses whipped around and ordered several charioteers to race to the other divisions. "Tell them to come at full speed!"

He looked up and smiled to see his Ra division fording the river and working their way up the slope to his Amun division. But the Hittite army suddenly appeared from behind a small mountain. They charged the Ra division with their chariots, scattering them in all directions.

Ramesses wrote his version of how the battle went down in the Poem of Pentaur and other inscriptions. The Hittites confronted him with 37,000 troops and 3,000 chariots. With the Amun and Ra divisions, Ramesses only had about 10,000 men and 1,000 chariots. He was outnumbered more than three to one. And yet, despite his youthfulness, Ramesses was a veteran warrior. He had gone to war with his father from age fourteen.

Ramesses raced down the slope in his chariot, leading his men in a charge against the Hittite chariots that were coming between his two units. But he got too far ahead of his men, and the Hittite chariots circled him, cutting him off. Fortunately, Ramesses knew how to put the superior speed and maneuverability of his Egyptian chariot into play. He charged the Hittite line, time and time again, finally breaking through their lines. He was so fast and agile that the Hittite chariots couldn't compete.

He rejoined his men, but they were desperately outnumbered. When hope was almost lost, Ramesses saw his third unit, the Ptah division, arriving. He slumped in relief, then rubbed his hands in glee at the unfolding scene. Some of the Hittites had stopped at the Egyptian camp to plunder what they could find, leaving them trapped between the two sections of the Egyptian army.

Ramesses II continued to lead the Amun division in charges against the Hittites. His commanders led the Ra and Ptah divisions. The Ne'arin division finally arrived, yet the Egyptians were still outnumbered, almost two to one. Nevertheless, their chariots' speed and agility won the day. Curiously, Muwatalli II had a reserve force inside Kadesh, but he never called them out to join the battle. He may have decided that protecting the city was more important.

The Egyptians forced the Hittites and their allies to the banks of the river. Some jumped in and tried to swim away from their attackers, yet many drowned.

Ramesses forces the Hittites into the river.[78]

Who Won?

The victor depends on who was telling the story. Ramesses II went home and plastered paintings and inscriptions everywhere. He bragged of his spectacular victory against all odds. However, Muwatalli pointed out that he failed to take the city of Kadesh, where the Hittites had a substantial force. Ramesses II had neither the advanced siege engines to break through the high, thick walls nor the time to lay siege. He was far from home. Muwatalli could scrape up more allies and attack again. The Battle of Kadesh essentially ended in a draw. Ramesses won the land battle, but Muwatalli kept Kadesh.

Years later, Hattusili III, Muwatalli's brother, called Ramesses II out when he kept bragging about winning the Battle of Kadesh. About a decade had passed, and Hattusili was now the king of the Hittites. He and

Ramesses had a mostly friendly relationship, calling each other "brother." Ramesses sent a doctor to Hattusili with special herbs when he was ill.

Nevertheless, the relationship was occasionally strained. When his sister couldn't get pregnant, Hattusili again asked Ramesses for medical help. Ramesses scoffed, "She's over fifty years old! It's not the gods' will for her to have children. If the gods change their minds, I'll immediately send a doctor and a magician to cure her."

The Peace Treaty

Despite random awkward exchanges, Hattusili III and Ramesses II were savvy enough to know that peace between Egypt and the Hittites was better for both nations. Fifteen years after the Battle of Kadesh, the two kings signed the "Eternal Treaty." This was the first peace treaty in history. Ramesses II promised that he would never attack the land of Hatti or try to steal any of its territory. Likewise, Hattusili III swore never to attack Egypt or take possession of its territory.

Roundup Activity: Draw a Soldier (or Two)

Draw a soldier in the Battle of Kadesh. He could be Egyptian or Hittite, or you could draw both in conflict with each other. You can decide if your soldier is a charioteer or a foot soldier. What will he wear? What weapons will he use? Review the photos in this chapter or find some online for ideas.

Chapter 10: The Fall of the New Kingdom

The Nineteenth Dynasty only lasted twenty-three years after Ramesses II died. What happened? This chapter will unwrap how this brilliant dynasty that restored Egypt's strength crashed and burned. The Twentieth Dynasty rose to power at the New Kingdom's final flowering. The priests of Amun gradually overpowered the pharaohs until they ruled Middle and Upper Egypt.

From this point until the Roman conquest, foreigners ruled Egypt. Libyan pharaohs controlled Egypt in the Third Intermediate Period. Then, Cyrus the Great conquered most of the Middle East. His Persian descendants triumphed over Egypt and ruled it for centuries. When Alexander the Great arrived in Egypt, the Egyptians cheered him as their rescuer from Persian oppression. Macedonian pharaohs governed Egypt for the next three centuries. The last pharaoh fell to the Romans in 30 BCE.

What Happened in the Later Years of the Nineteenth Dynasty?

The Nineteenth Dynasty was the epoch of Ramesses II. It lasted about a century, and Ramesses II was its pharaoh for two-thirds of that time. Egypt prospered economically and grew in power and size under his energetic rule. Ramesses wanted to sear the memory of his epic reign in history for all time. He built more monuments than any other pharaoh. He even inscribed his name and accomplishments on other pharaohs' monuments.

Ramesses built a new capital city called Pi-Ramesses only a mile from the ruins of the old Hyksos capital of Avaris on the easternmost branch of the Nile River. It was a strategic location. Avaris had been Egypt's wealthiest trade city, and the Nile Delta was Egypt's most affluent agricultural area. From Pi-Ramesses, the Nile flowed north fifty miles and emptied into the Mediterranean Sea. The city was not only Ramesses' capital but also his navy base. It was close enough for his navy and merchant ships to easily sail in and out of the Mediterranean, yet it was far enough inland to protect against surprise attacks from the sea.

Pi-Ramesses was breathtakingly beautiful and luxurious. During the annual flooding of the Nile, it was a city of islands linked by canals. Over 300,000 people lived in the bustling urban center. Nevertheless, Pi-Ramesses's prime location had a downside. By moving his capital away from Thebes, Ramesses no longer had close oversight of the priests of Amun at Thebes, who had threatened the power of pharaohs for centuries.

Ramesses built his new city with four major temples at its four corners. One was to Amun, Egypt's chief god. One was to Wadjet, the Nile Delta's ancient winged cobra goddess. The third temple was to Astarte, a West Asian goddess introduced by the Hyksos. The fourth temple was to Set, the chief god of the Hyksos, who connected him with Baal. Set was Egyptian but had a bad reputation as the god of chaos, foreigners, and storms. What's worse, he murdered his brother, Osiris, and chopped his body into pieces.

A priest of Amun[74]

Why did Ramesses elevate Set and Astarte? The famed Egyptologist Manfred Bietak believes that some Hyksos remained in the Delta region and continued to influence its culture. Ramesses had West Asian heritage through the intermarriage of his male ancestors with Syrian princesses. Analysis of his mummy's hair roots showed he was a natural redhead. His enthusiastic embrace of Hyksos and West Asian gods created tension with Amun's priests.

After Ramesses II died in his early nineties, the Nineteenth Dynasty fell into steep decline. Ramesses had around fifty sons, but his twelve oldest sons died before him. This left the elderly Merneptah as Egypt's new pharaoh.

Merneptah sent grain when the city-state of Ugarit in northern Syria suffered a famine. Later, Ugarit's king wrote Merneptah in a panic after seeing ships off his coast, probably the infamous Sea Peoples that Ramesses II had hired earlier. Whoever they were, they sacked Ugarit and stripped its vineyards and food stores. The Sea Peoples attacked Egypt again during Merneptah's reign. He said they sailed to Egypt from the "northern sea," most likely somewhere on the north Aegean or Black Sea. This time, they didn't come just to raid and plunder but to find somewhere to live. Merneptah said they brought their families and household goods, traveling not only by sea but over land by wagons.

Twosret, the last pharaoh of the Nineteenth Dynasty[74]

Infighting among Merneptah's descendants marked the rest of the Nineteenth Dynasty. Merneptah's daughter, Twosret (Tausret), was the last pharaoh of this dynasty. The historian Manetho said that Troy fell during Twosret's reign, which was around 1191-1189 BCE. After Twosret's death, Egypt fell into anarchy and civil war.

The Sea Peoples Reappear in the Twentieth Dynasty

A pharaoh named Setnakht took power and began the Twentieth Dynasty, the last of the New Kingdom. This dynasty lasted for a little over a century with ten pharaohs. Setnakht may have been a distant relative of the Ramesses family. All the pharaohs of the Twentieth Dynasty had the name Ramesses except him.

In 1180 BCE, when Setnakht's son, Ramesses III, was pharaoh, the Sea Peoples reappeared. This time, they utterly devastated the Hittites and the Amorite kingdom of Amurru in Lebanon. Ramesses III said their attack in Lebanon was so vicious and complete that it was like no one had ever lived there. The Sea Peoples went inland to Syria to attack Kadesh and Carchemish.

After this, the Sea Peoples traveled south by sea and land. At this time, Canaan was still under Egypt's control. (Egypt's borders extended up the Mediterranean coast to Lebanon.) Ramesses III's charioteers were waiting for them and killed everyone who dared cross into Canaan. Ramesses III sent his archers to guard the coast from Lebanon to Egypt. They hid along the shoreline, waiting for the Sea Peoples' ships to come ashore for water or to plunder food from nearby villages. In those days, sailors also beached their ships at night. When the Sea Peoples' ships approached land, the Egyptian archers unleashed volleys of flaming arrows at their vessels.

Nevertheless, some of the Sea Peoples' ships made it to Egypt and tried to sail into the Nile, where they met their doom. Hails of arrows from the Egyptian troops along the banks darkened the sky. The Egyptian navy rammed the Sea Peoples' ships, sinking them, and the bodies of the dead floated ashore.

After this annihilation, the Sea Peoples never again attacked Egypt. Yet, the Sea Peoples had shattered trade in the Mediterranean. This supply chain disruption was one cause of the Late Bronze Age collapse that shattered Greece and the Middle East.

What Contributed to the New Kingdom's Fall?

Ramesses III's reign ended when one of his lesser wives, Tiye, led a coup d'etat to make her son Pentawer king. The conspirators slit Ramesses's throat, killing him. His crown prince, Ramesses IV, overcame the attackers and sentenced them to death by burning. After this, the Twentieth Dynasty limped along for about eight decades. The Greek historian Diodorus Siculus wrote that its pharaohs were lazy, addicted to luxury, and did nothing of historical note.

Another factor was climate change, which led to cooler weather and less rainfall. The Nile did not flood as high as usual, leading to crop failure and famine. Riots erupted in protest of the lack of food and inept and corrupt leadership.

Meanwhile, the priests of Amun at Thebes asserted their power over Upper Egypt. They controlled the economy and most of the shipping trade. For the next few centuries, Egypt was divided into two or three kingdoms, with Amun's priests ruling most of the land.

How Did the Persian Empire Take Egypt?

In 525 BCE, the Persian king Cambyses II conquered Egypt using cats as a secret weapon. At first, the Egyptians had held the Persians off with their chariots, archers, and catapults. But then the Persians deployed cats. Why cats? The Egyptian war goddess Bastet had a cat's head and a woman's body. No one dared offend her, and anyone who killed a cat was executed.

The Persians painted Bastet's image on their shields and released hundreds of cats on their front lines. This tactic paralyzed the Egyptians. They didn't dare fire missiles at the Persians for fear of killing a cat or hitting Bastet's image. Unhinged, the Egyptians fled, and the Persians won the war. Egypt had never been part of another nation's empire. For the next two centuries, the Egyptians revolted again and again. Each time, the Persians cruelly squelched the rebellion.

Cambyses II captures Pharaoh Psamtik III.[76]

What Happened When Alexander the Great Showed Up?

In 334 BCE, Alexander the Great marched into Asia with a massive coalition army of Macedonians and Greeks. He fought his way from Turkey to Gaza. However, the Egyptians welcomed him with open arms. They had detested Persian rule. The priests crowned Alexander as their new pharaoh.

Alexander built the gleaming new city of Alexandria at the mouth of the Nile. Its blend of Egyptian and Hellenistic (Greek) culture made it the ancient world's center of scientific and mathematical breakthroughs. When Alexander unexpectedly died at only thirty-two, his generals divided up his enormous three-continent empire. The Macedonian General Ptolemy took Egypt. His descendants ruled as pharaohs for three centuries in ancient Egypt's final dynasty.

Who Was the Last Pharaoh and How Did She Die?

Cleopatra VII was the last pharaoh of Egypt. When her father died in 51 BCE, she became pharaoh with her thirteen-year-old brother and husband, Ptolemy XIII. The two hated each other. Rome was on the brink of morphing into an empire and wanted Egypt. When Julius Caesar arrived in Egypt, Cleopatra joined forces with him against her brother, who died in the war. Cleopatra and Julius Caesar became lovers and had a son together named Caesarion. The relationship ended abruptly when Rome's senators stabbed Caesar to death in 44 BCE.

Cleopatra had been in Italy with Caesar but fled back to Egypt after his assassination. A few years later, Rome's new rising star, Mark Antony, met Cleopatra and fell under her spell. Rome's consul, Octavian (who became Caesar Augustus), was Antony's great rival. He went to war against Antony and Cleopatra, and the lovers lost and committed suicide in 30 BCE. At this point, Egypt became a province of the Roman Empire.

Cleopatra with her son Caesarion as a cupid[77]

What Is Ancient Egypt's Legacy?

Where do we start? Ancient Egypt continued to influence art, religion, and culture for millennia. They made revolutionary advancements in mathematics, science, and medicine that influenced Greek scholars in the days to come.

The Egyptians gave us the pyramids and obelisks, massive architecture that demanded advanced skills in quarrying and construction. They promoted harmony throughout society.

The ancient Egyptians developed irrigation systems that enabled them to produce bumper harvests and provide grain to the Roman Empire for centuries.

The ancient Egyptians took other civilizations' technology, like the chariot, to new heights. While the Middle East used heavy clay tablets to send letters or record data or literature, Egypt developed papyrus, an early type of paper. The hieroglyphics they wrote on that paper inspired the Proto-Sinaitic script, the ancestor of the alphabet we use today.

Roundup Activity: Multiple Choice

Underline the correct answer. Check your answers in the back of the book.

1. Who was the most famous pharaoh of the Nineteenth Dynasty?
    a. Amenhotep III
    b. Hatshepsut
    c. Ramesses II
    d. Tutankhamun
2. Who attacked Egypt but was defeated by Ramesses III?
    a. The Babylonians
    b. The Greeks
    c. The Hittites
    d. The Sea Peoples
3. What Persian king used cats as a secret weapon?
    a. Cambyses II
    b. Cyrus the Great
    c. Darius the Great
    d. Xerxes I
4. Who ruled Egypt after Alexander the Great died?
    a. The Libyans
    b. The Macedonian General Ptolemy and his descendants
    c. The Persians
    d. The Romans
5. Who was the last pharaoh of ancient Egypt before it fell to Rome?
    a. Cleopatra VII
    b. Hatshepsut
    c. Ramesses II
    d. King Tutankhamun

Answer Key: Roundup Activities

Chapter 1: Who Am I?

1. Dedi	I was the first king of a unified Egypt. A hippo killed me. **(6. Narmer)**
2. Djoser	I was King Narmer's wife. After he died, I ruled Egypt until my son grew up. **(7. Queen Neithhotep)**
3. Imhotep	I built Egypt's first pyramid and rescued Egypt from a famine. **(2. Djoser)**
4. Khnum	I was the god of the Nile. I got angry when my temple fell into disrepair. **(4. Khnum)**
5. Khufu	I was Djoser's right-hand man. I was also an architect and priest of the sun god Ra. **(3. Imhotep)**
6. Narmer	I was a Fourth Dynasty king who built three pyramids until I finally got it right. **(9. Sneferu)**
7. Queen Neithhotep	I built Egypt's Great Pyramid, the highest in the world. **(5. Khufu)**
8. Rededjet	I was a magician who could reattach an animal's head that had been cut off. **(1. Dedi)**
9. Sneferu	I gave birth to triplets. One baby was Userkaf, first king of the Fifth Dynasty. **(8. Rededjet)**

Chapter 2: What Happened When?

1. Ahmose begins the New Kingdom and the Eighteenth Dynasty. **(8)**
2. Ahmose conquered the Hyksos once and for all. **(9)**
3. Amenemhat I usurped the throne and started the Twelfth Dynasty. **(2)**
4. Mentuhotep II united Egypt again, beginning the Middle Kingdom. **(1)**
5. Seqenenre was killed, and Kamose became king. **(7)**
6. Sobekneferu, the "Beautiful Crocodile," died. **(3)**
7. The Egyptians regrouped and formed the Sixteenth Dynasty. **(5)**
8. The Hyksos conquered Memphis. **(4)**
9. The Seventeenth Dynasty replaced the Sixteenth Dynasty at Thebes. **(6)**

Chapter 3: Fill in the Blank

The ancient Egyptian's favorite drink was __beer__, which they liked to drink through a straw. Because of the heat, they liked wearing lightweight clothing made from __linen__, which the ladies wove from flax. A scribe had to attend school for __twelve__ years to learn all the hieroglyphic symbols. The Egyptians believed __Amun__ was the creator of the universe. Egyptian artists used __proportion__ to indicate the most important person in the painting or sculpture. The Egyptians thought the scarab beetle's dung ball represented the __world__.

Chapter 5: Pop Quiz

1. Who was the goddess of fertility and motherhood? **(Taweret)**
2. What did the ancient Egyptians believe happened to the ka part of the soul after death? **(They thought it stayed in or near the dead body.)**
3. What was the role of the king in ancient Egyptian religion? **(The king was the mediator between his people and the gods.)**
4. Why did the Egyptians consider Isis to be the "mother of the pharaohs"? **(She was the mother of Horus, and the Egyptians thought their pharaoh was the earthly representation of Horus.)**
5. What god weighed the hearts of dead people? **(Anubis)**

6. Who was the god of the sun and one of the most important deities in ancient Egyptian religion? **(Ra or Amun-Ra)**
7. How did Osiris become the god of the underworld? **(His brother Set killed him and chopped him into pieces. His wife Isis put him back together but couldn't keep him alive, so he became the god of the dead.)**
8. Why did the ancient Egyptians bury the shabtis dolls with a dead person? **(They thought these dolls became people who did the work for them in the afterlife.)**
9. What was the purpose of the Book of the Dead? **(It had magic spells and instructions for the journey to Duat.)**
10. What ceremony was held just before placing a mummy in its tomb? **(The Opening of the Mouth)**

Chapter 6: Crossword
Who or where?

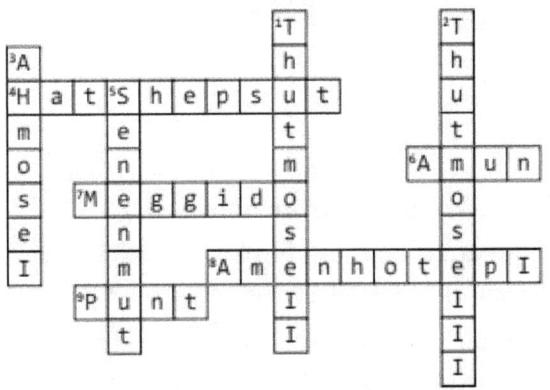

Across
4. I co-ruled with Thutmose III
6. I was a god. Hatshepsut said I was her father
7. Where Thutmose II won his 1st great victory
8. My astronomer invented the water clock
9. Hatshepsut sent an expedition here

Down
1. I married Hatshepsut when she was 12
2. I co-ruled with Hatshepsut until she died
3. I chased the Hyksos out of Egypt
5. I was Hatshepshut's Chief Minister & architect

Chapter 7: Two Truths and a Lie
- Akhenaten promoted the worship of the moon god.

Chapter 8: Word Search

A	N	K	H	E	S	E	N	A	M	U	N
M	A	I	A							O	
E										V	
N	E	T	A	N	E	H	K	A		R	
H	O	R	E	M	H	E	B			A	
O										N	
T										R	
E	R	A	K	H	K	N	E	M	S	A	
P				Y						C	
I			I								
I			T							Y	
I	S	U	P	P	I	L	U	L	I	U	M	A

1. I was King Tut's grandfather (Amenhotep III)
2. I was King Tut's grandmother (Tiye)
3. I was Tut's father, the religious revolutionary (Akhenaten)
4. I was Tut's wet nurse and tutor (Maia)
5. Neferneferuaten and I ruled Egypt just before King Tut (Smenkhkare)
6. This was my new name after King Tut and I got married (Ankhesenamun)
7. I was King Tut's regent and the pharaoh after him (Ay)
8. I was the Hittite king who died of the plague after capturing Egyptian soldiers (Suppiluliuma)
9. I became king after Ay and erased King Tut and his father from the records (Horemheb)
10. I was the lord who financed Howard Carter's discovery of Tut's tomb (Carnarvon)

Chapter 10: Multiple Choice

1. Who was the most famous pharaoh of the Nineteenth Dynasty?
    c. Ramesses II
2. Who attacked Egypt but was defeated by Ramesses III?
    d. The Sea Peoples
3. What Persian king used cats as a secret weapon?
    a. Cambyses II
4. Who ruled Egypt after Alexander the Great died?
    b. The Macedonian General Ptolemy and his descendants
5. Who was the last pharaoh of ancient Egypt before it fell to Rome?
    a. Cleopatra VII

Part 2: Ancient Greece for Teens

An Enthralling Guide to Major Events and Figures in Greek History

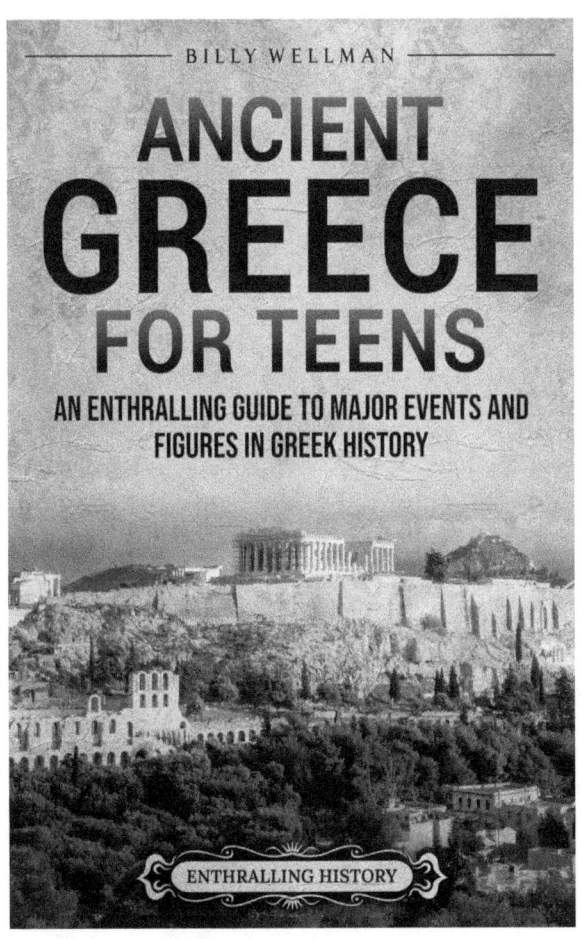

Introduction

When you think of ancient Greece, what comes to mind? Great philosophers like Socrates and Plato? Majestic temples with stately pillars and marble statues? People wearing long, flowy garments? The birth of democracy? Ancient Greece was all that and so much more!

Ancient Greece was never a united country. Southern Greece did form an alliance to send the Persians packing, but it didn't create a central government. The Greeks briefly united under Alexander the Great, but Sparta wasn't on board. Ancient Greece was a group of powerful, independent city-states that loved to fight each other. When they weren't killing each other, the ancient Greeks did some pretty awesome things.

The Greeks wrote epic poetry, built colonies around the Mediterranean Sea, and invented the Olympic Games. Once every four years, they stopped fighting each other to run races in their birthday suits. Yes, clothing was optional. And let's not forget about philosophy! Some of it was a little crazy, but it was still impressive. The Greek pursuit of wisdom influenced how we think and do government today. They came up with the idea of democracy and forged ahead in science. Leucippus and Democritus figured out that constantly moving atoms form all matter. How could they know that?

The ancient Greek civilizations were famous for rising to astonishing heights until everything came crashing down. But they never stayed down. They would rise from the ashes, dust themselves off, and dash back into the fray, more brilliant than ever. When Xerxes marched on Greece with his enormous army, the Greeks held the line. And we mean that literally.

Six thousand Spartans held off the Persians for three days, sacrificing themselves to give southern Greece time to organize a defense.

The purpose of this book is to take you on an entertaining and enlightening journey through the history of ancient Greece. Don't ever think history is just a bunch of dry facts and dates to memorize. History is the story of people. Some were geniuses, and some were stupid beyond belief. Most were a little bit of both. On this journey, we'll learn what made the Greeks exceptional. This book will bring their stories to life with all their flaws and inconceivable victories.

What's the point of reading history? Some folks do it for fun; they find it fascinating. And it is, but that's not the only reason. When we understand the past, it helps us realize why things are the way they are today. For instance, why do most of today's governments have a senate and elected leaders? It all started in ancient Athens. History also teaches us the **catalysts for change.** What causes change? What speeds it up?

Let's travel back in time to unpack the astounding story of the ancient Greeks. Follow the jaw-dropping journey of their stunning inventions, discoveries, art, architecture, philosophy, religion, wars, and politics.

Chapter 1: An Introduction to Ancient Greece

This chapter will discuss Greece's spectacular physical features and walk the reader through a basic timeline. Next, it will explore ancient Greece's culture, focusing on the Archaic Age. Finally, it will unwrap ancient Greece's lasting legacy.

Geography

Greece is a land of enchanting beauty surrounded by sparkling seas. Steep, craggy hills and mountains cover 80 percent of Greece's mainland and islands. The mountains presented a problem. As Greece's population grew, it became harder to feed the people. The Greeks used **terraced farming**, carving a series of flat ledges on the hillsides to plant more crops. Yet, even with these terraces running up the hillsides, only one-fifth of the land could grow barley, grapevines, and olive trees.

Although the ancient Greeks grazed sheep and goats on the mountains and higher hills, the lack of land wasn't the farmers' only challenge. Greece gets almost no rain in the summer. Back then, agriculture depended on rainfall and snow in the winter, but that was unpredictable. Crop failure happened a lot. The farmers lost their grain crops about every four years. Deforestation and overgrazing made matters worse.

Beginning in the Archaic Age, Greece started sending some of its people away to feed those who remained. These colonists sailed to distant shores around the Mediterranean. They grew crops in fertile lands and then shipped grain back to Greece. So, it's fair to say that ancient Greece wasn't simply the land of modern Greece. It was an empire of colonies stretching from modern-day Spain to the west and Russia to the east.

A vineyard growing on terraces on a steep hillside[78]

Greece is surrounded by the Ionian Sea to the west, the Aegean to the east, and the Mediterranean to the south. The entire country is one gigantic peninsula, and multiple smaller peninsulas stretch out like tentacles on an octopus. And then, there are the islands. Did you know that Greece has six thousand islands? Greece's early Cycladic people thrived on the islands in the Aegean Sea as fishermen and traders. They went spearfishing for tuna in primitive boats. Then, they began building ships with fifty rowers, which meant they could do deep-sea fishing. They could also sail to other lands. Greece became one of the world's premier sea traders.

Some of Greece's mountains are active volcanoes. Lava cooled to form obsidian, a black, razor-sharp glass. Obsidian was a hot trade item. Ancient people used obsidian for spears, arrowheads, knives, and other tools. Greece's islands were also rich in copper, iron, gold, silver, and marble. Greece exported minerals, wine, wool, olives, and exquisite ceramics.

Living near a volcano could be a nightmare. Around 1600 BCE, a volcano on the island of Thera erupted. It was disastrous. Ten million tons of rock and ash shot twenty miles (thirty-five kilometers) into the air. Its VEI (volcanic explosivity index) was a seven. The highest VEI is an eight, but that has not happened in about twenty-seven thousand years. The Minoan eruption at Thera was like several atomic bombs exploding at once.

Fortunately, earthquakes and other signs must have warned the people living on Thera that something big was about to happen. Most folks must have sailed to safety before the eruption since few bodies were found. Two hundred feet (sixty meters) of pumice and ash buried anyone who didn't get away in time. The volcano caused a gigantic tsunami that flooded Crete's northern coast, almost 70 miles (110 kilometers) away. The tsunami washed away their splendid cities. Pumice even showered down on Egypt, which was 800 miles (1,287 kilometers) away.

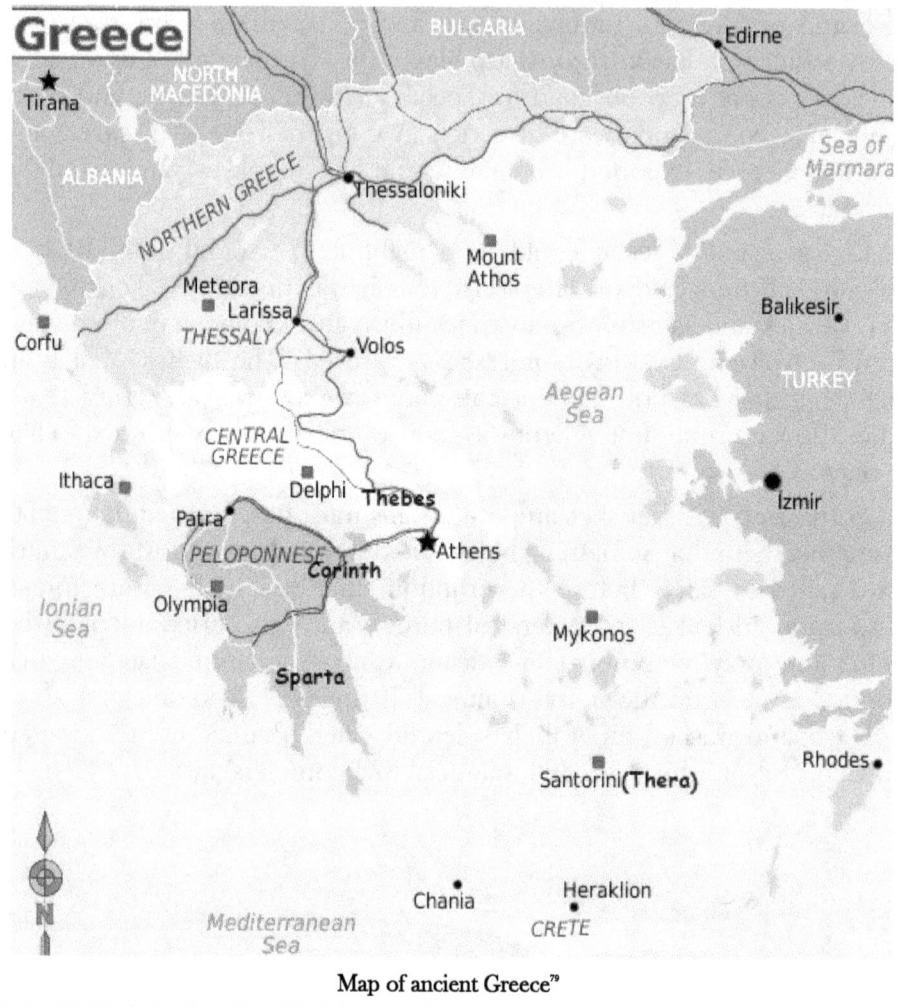

Map of ancient Greece[79]

Timeline

Bronze Age (began about 3200 BCE in Greece)

- Minoans settled the island of Crete around 3500 BCE.
    - 2100 BCE: Minoans' great leap forward into a complex civilization
        - Constructed Europe's first cities and palaces
        - Built the world's first navy
        - Ruled the Aegean and Mediterranean Seas
        - Developed Europe's first writing system, Cretan

         hieroglyphics
- 1800 BCE: Minoans developed Linear A writing with a phonetic alphabet
- 1700 BCE: Earthquakes destroyed most cities in Crete, but they were rebuilt.
- 1600 BCE: Minoan eruption on the island of Thera
- Carved marble figurines of women with long necks and no lower legs
- Buried their dead in tombs, which was advanced for this era in Greece

Myceneans, a rising power around 1700 BCE

- Thrived in southern Greece's Peloponnesian Peninsula and southern mainland
    - Seafaring traders and pirates
    - Built bridges, complex irrigation systems, and colossal walls.
  - 1420 BCE: Invaded Crete. Destroyed most cities but restored Knossos
  - Coexisted with Minoans on Crete until the Bronze Age collapse
  - 1400 BCE: Athens became a Mycenean city.
  - Adapted Linear B writing system from the Minoan's Linear A
  - 1200 BCE: The "mythical" Trojan War began when Myceneans attacked Troy in northwestern Turkey.
- **Bronze Age Collapse (beginning 1200 BCE)**
  - Many cultures fell in Greece, the Middle East, and North Africa.
  - Minoan, Cycladic, and Mycenean civilizations all collapsed.
  - Most Greek cities fell except Athens; much of Greece's population died.
  - Greece lost its writing system for three hundred years.
  - Causes?

- Environmental catastrophes, such as drought, volcanoes, and earthquakes
- The "Sea Peoples," mysterious pirates who attacked coastal cities and crushed sea trade

The Dark Ages (1200–900 BCE)

Geometric Civilization (900–776 BCE)

- Produced ceramics with geometric designs
- The population grew, and cities were built again.
- Greeks began smelting iron in high-heat furnaces.
- 900 BCE: The Dorians rebuilt Sparta

Archaic Period (776–500 BCE)

- 776 BCE: The first Olympic Games launched the Archaic period
- 770 BCE: A fresh writing system began, loosely based on the Phoenician alphabet
  - Over half the letters are in our alphabet today.
  - Greeks began writing epic poetry.
    - Homer wrote the *Iliad* and the *Odyssey*.
    - Hesiod wrote *Theogony* and *Works and Days*.
- 750–550 BCE: Greek city-states established colonies around the Mediterranean, Aegean, Ionian, and Black Seas.
- 650 BCE: Sparta crushed the Messenian revolt.
- 621 BCE: Draco wrote the first written law code for Athens.
- 594 BCE: Solon wrote the first constitution for Athens.
- 580 BCE: The Punic Wars began; they continued on and off through the classical and Hellenistic ages.
- 550 BCE: Sparta established the Peloponnesian League with Corinth, Elis, and Tegea.
- 547 BCE: Wars with the Persian Empire began and continued for over a century.
- 508 BCE: Cleisthenes brought democratic reform to Athens.

Sprinters in the Olympics; notice the new Greek writing system above the runners.⁸⁰

Classical Period (480–356 BCE)

- Golden Age of Athens (480-404 BCE)
- Greek coalition scored a great victory over the Persians.
    - 480 BCE: Battle of Thermopylae - Spartans against a massive Persian army
    - 479 BCE: Greek coalition trounced Persians in the naval Battle of Mycale.
- 477 BCE: Greek city-states formed the Delian League.
    - Kept the Persians out of the Aegean Sea for fifteen years
    - Rid seas of Dolopian pirates preying on Greek merchant ships
    - 460 BCE: Greece suffered a great loss when defending Egypt from Persia.
- 460-445 BCE: First Peloponnesian War between Sparta and Athens began.
- 451 BCE: Final face-off between Greece and Persia at Cyprus
    - Greeks crushed the Persian fleet.
    - Thirty-year Peace of Calais

- 431–404 BCE: Second Peloponnesian War
    - 430 BCE: Plague struck Athens, killing one-third of the population.
    - 404 BCE: Athens finally surrendered to Sparta.
- 399 BCE: Socrates was forced to commit suicide.
- 395-386 BCE: Corinthian Wars between Sparta and an alliance of Corinth, Thebes, Athens, Argos, and Boeotia
- 387 BCE: Persians formed King's Peace with Sparta, Athens, Argos, Corinth, and Thebes.
- 379 BCE: Thebes rose to power.
    - 375 BCE: Thebes defeated Sparta at the Battle of Tegyra.
    - 371 BCE: Battle of Leuctra: Thebes pulverized the Spartan forces.
    - Thebes invaded Thessaly and Macedon, taking young Prince Philip II hostage.

Macedonian-Greek Conquest of the Persian Empire (356–323 BCE)

- Philip II of Macedonia
    - 359 BCE: Became king of Macedonia
    - 358-340 BCE: Conquered Thrace and other lands north of Greece
    - 352 BCE: Became ruler for life of Thessaly in northern Greece
    - 338 BCE: Won Battle of Chaeronea and gained control of all Greece except Sparta
    - 337 BCE: All Greek city-states (except Sparta) formed the League of Corinth.
        - Goal: A coordinated Macedonian-Greek conquest of the Persian Empire
        - An advance force of ten thousand men sent to Ionia (western coast of Turkey)
    - 336 BCE: Philip was murdered by his ex-lover and bodyguard.

- Alexander the Great
    - 336 BCE: Became king of Macedonia, Thrace, and Greece after his father's death
    - 336-335: Reunited League of Corinth after Thrace, Athens, Thebes, and Thessaly pulled out
    - 334 BCE: Marched into Turkey with an army of forty thousand men
    - 334-333 BCE: Conquered western Turkey
    - 332 BCE: Took control of Lebanon, Syria, Judea, Gaza, and Egypt
    - 331 BCE: Fought Persian King Darius in Iraq and won
        - Darius fled; one of his governors then killed him.
        - Alexander then ruled the former Persian-Achaemenid Empire.
    - 330-324 BCE: Alexander conquered central Asia
        - Fell in love and married Roxana, daughter of a Bactrian chieftain
        - Explored Indian subcontinent
    - 323 BCE: Alexander became ill and died unexpectedly at age thirty-two.

The Hellenistic Age (323–27 BCE)

- 323-281 BCE: Wars of the Diadochi (Alexander's generals) were fought for control of the empire.
    - The empire was divided into several regions.
    - Seleucus, the last general, was killed in 281 BCE.
- The Hellenistic age blended Greek culture with Asian and Egyptian elements.
- 222 BCE: Sparta lost the Battle of Sellasia against Macedon; most male Spartans were killed.
- 215-205 BCE: First Macedonian War; Greek Aetolian League allied with Rome against Macedon
- 146 BCE: Rome conquered the Greek Achaean League at the Battle of Corinth.

- - Rome then dominated mainland Greece.
  - Greeks still ruled Egypt and western Turkey.
- 89–85 BCE: First Mithridatic War; Rome against Greek-controlled western Turkey
  - King Mithridates of Pontus (Turkey) took control of most of Greece.
  - 87 BCE: Rome's consul, Sulla, marched on Greece.
  - 86 BCE: Athens resisted but fell to Rome.

Culture

Greece's earliest known authors were Hesiod and Homer. They both wrote *epic poetry*, long poems that tell a story. The men and women in epic poems went on grand adventures. The stories usually involved the gods. Hesiod and Homer wrote at the very end of the Greek Dark Ages using Greece's new alphabet. Greece lost its earlier writing systems during the Dark Ages, which were mainly used for record-keeping, not literature.

Greek mythology says the hero Cadmus brought the Phoenician alphabet to Greece. The Greeks modified it for their own language, and it became the ancestor of the alphabet we use today.

Hesiod and Homer introduced literature to Greece. Their stories probably came from ancient tales retold by people for centuries. Homer wrote the *Iliad* and the *Odyssey* about the Trojan War and Odysseus's long journey home after the war.

Hesiod claimed to be a shepherd who met the nine Muses, goddesses of the arts, literature, and science. The Muses morphed Hesiod into a brilliant poet. In his poem, *Works and Days*, he told the story of creation, the great flood, and the five ages of man. The first age was the *Golden Age*, when the god Cronus created people. Everyone was good and got along with each other. No one knew pain or sadness. They ate fruit and vegetables and did not have to work hard.

A scene from a vase of three Muses playing a harp and lyres.[81]

It all fell apart when the god Zeus overthrew Cronus, which began the *Silver Age*. Now, folks had to work hard. They fought and quarreled with each other, but they still lived long lives, at least to the age of one hundred. Next came the **Bronze Age**, when people switched from being vegetarians to meat eaters. These warlike people were so corrupt, cruel, and violent that Zeus killed everyone in a flood.

Zeus kept one family alive, though. He noticed that Deucalion, his wife Pyrrha, and their son Hellen were honest and peaceful. Before opening the floodgates of heaven, Zeus told Deucalion to build an ark, fill it with food, and go inside. Then, the rain poured down, flooding everything and drowning all the violent people. Nine days later, the rain stopped. The ark rested on Mount Parnassus. Deucalion and his family came out on dry land and made a sacrifice to Zeus. Hellen's three sons formed the Achaean, Aeolian, and Dorian tribes, which repopulated Greece.

These three tribes began the next era, the Age of Heroes, when the Trojan War happened. The last age was the Iron Age, when Hesiod lived. He said the people of his age were brutal and self-absorbed. They were always tired and depressed. Hesiod warned that if folks didn't change, Zeus would also destroy this age.

The Lion Gate at Mycenae was built almost 3,300 years ago.[83]

During the "Age of Heroes," the city of Mycenae in southern Greece was the center of the Mycenaean civilization. Some of its massive twenty-foot-thick walls, built around 1250 BCE, still stand today. The stones in the walls were colossal. In later days, the Greeks looked at these boulders and decided that, even working together, humans could not have possibly lifted them. "Only the Cyclopes could do this!" they exclaimed. The Cyclopes were mythical one-eyed, man-eating giants. Mycenae's gate has a twenty-ton lintel supported by two ten-foot boulders. It is called the Lion Gate after the carving of two lions over the lintel. Even today, people look at this structure and wonder how ancient humans got those stones up there.

As mentioned earlier, the Greeks established colonies around the Mediterranean, Aegean, Ionian, and Black Seas. These seas were the communication highways of the ancient world. How did this cultural mingling influence art and culture? People learned from each other by sharing ideas about painting, sculptures, pottery, and metalwork. The

Greek colonies opened schools that trained students to blend Greek ideas with Middle Eastern and Egyptian art. These schools taught things like making ceramics, carving ivory, cutting gems, and crafting jewelry and metalwork.

The Greek cities around the ancient world held competitions. Who could build the grandest and most elegant temples? **Lyric poetry** became popular in the Archaic age. These were short poems about emotions and romance sung to the playing of the *lyre* (something like a small harp). Greece's leading art centers were Corinth, Athens, and Sparta. The Corinthians painted silhouettes of plants and animals. Athenian vases had mythological scenes. The Spartans produced exquisite ivory carvings.

An amphora vase from Corinth with a silhouetted lion.[88]

Archaic Greece's philosophers made great leaps forward in many areas. Thales of Miletus, the "Father of Science," learned to predict solar eclipses. He explained a circle's diameter and the equal base angles of an isosceles triangle. The ancient Greeks believed that the god Atlas held the world on his shoulders. Thales's student Anaximander shocked everyone when he said the world was floating free in the universe. Anaximander's student, Anaximenes, taught that planets were not the same as stars. He figured this out by observing their movements over time.

Pythagoras said the earth wasn't flat but a sphere, like a ball. He developed the Pythagorean theorem for a ninety-degree triangle ($a^2 + b^2 = c^2$). Heraclitus of Ephesus talked about the *logos*. He said it was an invisible force that directed the universe. People must be in harmony with *logos* to understand reality.

Legacy

The Greek politician and commander Pericles said, "What you leave behind is not what is engraved in stone monuments, but what is woven into the lives of others." The legacy of the ancient Greeks is undoubtedly woven into our lives today. We owe an outstanding debt to them for their ideas and discoveries in art, architecture, philosophy, astronomy, medicine, and mathematics. When the Greeks exchanged ideas and knowledge around the Mediterranean and Asia, they birthed scholars who surged forward in science, math, and medicine. They took knowledge in many fields to new heights.

Greece influenced Roman religion, politics, philosophy, arts, and science. Today, this fusion of cultures is called the classical civilization or the Greco-Roman culture. This Greco-Roman culture impacted the Renaissance scholars and artists of western Europe. Greek artists portrayed the human form realistically in their sculptures, mosaics, and paintings, and the Renaissance artists copied this style. The majestic pillars that are the hallmarks of ancient Greek architecture still grace government buildings, churches, and mansions today. Ancient Athens and other Greek city-states pioneered democracy, which left its stamp on multiple nations today.

Round-up Activity: Timeline Game – What Happened When?

How well do you remember the order of key events in ancient Greece's history? Number these pivotal events in ancient Greece's history in the correct order.

( ) A catastrophic volcanic eruption wipes out all life on the island of Thera.
( ) A horrible plague kills one-third of Athens's population.
( ) Battle of Corinth: Rome conquers the Greek Achaean League.
( ) Cleisthenes brings democratic reform to Athens.
( ) First Olympic Games.
( ) The Greek Dark Ages.
( ) Minoans develop Greece's first writing system, Linear A.
( ) The Greek League of Corinth forms to invade the Persian Empire under Alexander.
( ) The Greeks unite to crush the Persian fleet in the naval Battle of Mycale.
( ) When Alexander the Great dies, his generals fight for control in the Wars of the Diadochi.

Check out the answer key at the end of the book, just before the bibliography. How well did you do?

Chapter 2: Gods and Goddesses of Olympus

Intrigue swirled around an unbelievably beautiful young woman named Helen. In the *Iliad* and the *Odyssey*, Homer said she was the daughter of the god Zeus and Queen Leda of Sparta. Greece's unmarried princes and kings gathered in Sparta bearing gifts. Each man hoped to make Helen his bride. Of course, Helen had no say in the matter. It was up to the man she called father: Tyndareus, Leda's husband and Sparta's king.

Sweat dripped from King Tyndareus's brow. Who should he choose? No matter what man he picked, everyone else would be angry. What if they attacked Sparta?

Odysseus, the cunning prince of Ithaca, came to the rescue. He was one of the few men in Greece not interested in marrying Helen. He was madly in love with Penelope, the daughter of Sparta's other king, Icarius. Yes, Sparta had two kings; we'll get into that later. Odysseus told Tyndareus he would help him with his Helen problem if he would put a good word in for Odysseus with Icarius. The two men agreed, and Odysseus gave his advice.

"All the men who want to marry Helen must swear a sacred oath. They must vow to defend Helen's marriage to whomever you choose. They must swear that no matter what, they will not attack you or the man you select as her husband. Furthermore, if anyone steals Helen from the husband you choose, all the others must vow to bring her back."

"Was this the face that launched a thousand ships? Sweet Helen, make me immortal with a kiss!"
- Christopher Marlowe."

Tyndareus had everyone swear the oath, and they sacrificed a horse to seal the deal. Tyndareus chose Menelaus, prince of Mycenae, as Helen's husband. Helen had secretly hoped he'd pick Menelaus, so she breathed a sigh of relief. Menelaus and Helen married. They had several children and lived happily together for ten years. Tyndareus convinced his co-king, Icarius, to give his daughter Penelope in marriage to Odysseus. Everything was rosy for the two young couples until the goddess Aphrodite interfered.

It all started with a beauty contest for the prize of a golden apple. The goddesses Hera, Athena, and Aphrodite asked Zeus to decide which of them was the most beautiful. Zeus wasn't about to get involved in that messy affair, so he asked Paris to judge the contest. Paris was the prince of Troy, which was located in northwestern Turkey. He jumped at the chance. Three gorgeous goddesses—what could possibly go wrong?

Each of the goddesses offered a bribe to Paris. Hera said he could rule Europe and Asia if he chose her. Athena bribed him with superhuman warrior skills. Aphrodite promised him the love of Helen, the world's most beautiful woman. She forgot to tell him that Helen was already married, though. Paris chose Aphrodite as the most beautiful goddess, and she helped him steal Helen from Menelaus. Was Helen kidnapped, or did she go willingly? No one is quite sure. But Menelaus was hellbent on getting his wife back, and that was how the Trojan War began.

The Greeks were *polytheistic*, which means they worshiped many gods. However, their gods were like ordinary humans but with superpowers. They cheated on their spouses, lied, stole, quarreled, and tricked humans. They might intervene to help the humans they liked, but they could just as easily make someone's life miserable. Their erratic and selfish behavior irritated the Greek philosopher Socrates. "How can we expect people to be good if the gods aren't?" he ranted.

Who Were the Twelve Olympians?

The highest mountain in Greece is Mount Olympus. The ancient Greeks thought it was the home of the most important gods, the Twelve Olympians. They were Zeus, Hera, Aphrodite, Apollo, Ares, Artemis, Athena, Demeter, Hephaistos, Hermes, Poseidon, and Dionysus. Some lists have Hestia, the goddess of the hearth, instead of Dionysus. What were the roles and attributes of these twelve gods?

Zeus (or maybe Poseidon).[85]

Zeus was the king of the gods. He was the storm god, which was incredibly important in a land desperate for rainfall. He was responsible for ensuring that the gods and humans lived orderly lives. That didn't always pan out, especially since Zeus wasn't particularly orderly himself. Maybe it stemmed from his childhood trauma. His father, Cronus, ate his brothers and sisters. Zeus survived because his mother, Rhea, hid him on the island of Crete.

When Zeus grew up, he confronted his father and made him vomit up his siblings. He married his sister **Hera**, but that proved problematic. Hera was insanely jealous because Zeus would shapeshift into other forms to seduce women who were unaware of his true identity.

Hera, queen of the gods, took her wrath out on her husband's lovers and their children. For instance, she turned Callisto into a bear. Heracles (Hercules in Roman myths) was an illegitimate son of Zeus. Hera sent snakes to kill him when he was a baby. When that failed, and he grew up, she made Heracles insane. He killed his wife and children. In the Trojan War, Hera supported the Greeks because Prince Paris of Troy chose Aphrodite over her in the beauty contest.

Hera forced **Aphrodite**, the goddess of love and war, to marry her son, **Hephaistos** (known as Hephaestus in Roman mythology). He was the disabled god of crafts and volcanos. Hera abandoned him at birth, but he still became one of the Twelve Olympians. Aphrodite was unfaithful. Homer wrote that Hephaistos divorced her and demanded back the bride price he had paid at the wedding.

Red-on-black pottery with Dionysus walking and Hephaistos riding a donkey.[86]

151

Aphrodite mischievously used her powers to make the gods fall in love with human females. But her magic came back to haunt her when she saw a Trojan prince, Anchises, playing his lyre while tending his cattle. She draped herself in golden robes and revealed herself to Anchises, who fell under her spell. Aphrodite gave birth to Aeneas, who was raised as a prince in Troy. She guarded him through the Trojan War, saving him from being killed several times. After Troy fell, Aeneas traveled to Italy, and his descendants founded Rome.

Everyone loved **Apollo**, the god of the sun, music, archery, and healing. Well, maybe the Greeks didn't love him so much during the Trojan War since he supported Troy. Apollo saved the lives of Aeneas and his cousin Hector several times. He struck the Greeks with the plague and sent Paris's arrow into Achilles's heel, killing the great warrior. But after the war, the Greeks resumed their adoring worship of this handsome young god. He frequently appeared on Greek coins.

Ares was the unpopular god of war. He would get angry over trivial things and was always looking for a fight. Ares and Aphrodite had a fling, but Aphrodite's husband, Hephaistos, found out. Hephaistos designed a golden net that wrapped around the couple when they were in bed. He called the rest of the gods to witness the couple's infidelity. The gods encircled the bed, roaring with laughter at the embarrassed twosome. Hephaistos finally released them, and they slunk off in shame.

Artemis was the goddess of nature, wild animals, and hunting. Although she was a virgin, she was the deity of fertility and childbirth. When she was a little girl, her father Zeus asked what he could give her as a gift. She asked for all the mountains in the world because that was where she wanted to spend her time. Artemis healed Aphrodite's son, Aeneas, when he was wounded in the Trojan War. When Agamemnon, King of Mycenae, killed a deer in her sacred grove, she demanded the sacrifice of his daughter. If he refused, Artemis would stop the wind, and he wouldn't be able to sail to Troy. Agamemnon prepared to sacrifice the girl, but Artemis took pity at the last minute and made her a priestess in her temple.

Artemis is in the Bible. The apostle Paul was traveling through the Greek colonies on the western coast of Turkey. He stayed in Ephesus for two years, discussing the Christian faith in the city's lecture hall every day. Extraordinary miracles occurred through Paul in Ephesus, where Artemis was the patron goddess. The silversmiths got riled up because no one was buying statues of Artemis anymore. "He says that man-made gods are no gods at all!" The silversmiths led a protest, where a crowd shouted for two hours, "Great is Artemis of the Ephesians!"

Athena.[87]

Athena was the goddess of war, wisdom, and crafts. She was intelligent, brave, and a brilliant problem solver. Athena was the patron goddess of Athens, her namesake. Like Artemis, she was a virgin who didn't get involved in messy affairs. Hesiod said that Zeus swallowed his first wife, Metis, while she was pregnant. He was terrified that she would give birth to a son who would overthrow him, just as he had done to his father, Cronus. Athena burst through her father's head as a grown woman wearing armor. Despite splitting her father's skull open, she was Zeus's favorite child.

Athena helped the Greeks break into Troy by giving Odysseus the idea of using the Trojan Horse. Thirty-two Greek warriors hid inside an enormous wooden horse while the rest of the Greeks sailed away. They didn't go too far, though. The Trojans thought the Greeks had abandoned the war and brought the horse inside. That night, the warriors inside the horse crept out and opened the city gates for the other Greeks.

Demeter was Zeus's sister. She was an earth goddess who helped farmers and ensured the earth's fertility. She had two children with Zeus: Persephone and Iacchus. She got involved with a mortal man named Iasion, and Zeus killed him with a thunderbolt.

Hades, the god of the underworld, fell in love with Demeter's daughter Persephone and kidnapped her. Zeus wasn't interested in rescuing his daughter, so Demeter cursed the land, causing the rain to stop and all crops to die. Zeus finally commanded Hades to release Persephone. While she was in the underworld, she had eaten a pomegranate seed, so she had to return to the underworld for several months each year.

Hermes was the creative and playful god of wealth, livestock, gamblers, thieves, and travel. With his winged sandals, he could travel quickly between the world of humans and the world of gods. He served as the gods' messenger. Hermes also guided souls to the River Styx in their journey to the underworld. He introduced the alphabet, fire, panpipes, the lyre, and dice to humans. He was always up to mischief. He stole Apollo's cattle, but Apollo let him keep them in exchange for Hermes's lyre. Hermes supported the Greeks in the Trojan War and assisted Odysseus on his long journey home by helping him escape the sorceress Circe.

Poseidon was the god of rivers, seas, floods, earthquakes, and horses. Although he often brought destruction, he was seen as the protector of sailors. Poseidon lived under the ocean in a golden mansion. He was the father of the one-eyed Cyclopes, the winged horse Pegasus, and Charybdis, the sea monster that created whirlpools to sink ships so she could eat them.

Poseidon had a crush on Princess Scylla. His jealous wife, Amphitrite, turned her into a monster with six snake heads. Scylla ate sailors, including six of Odysseus's friends.

Dionysus was the god of wine, insanity, theater, and festivals. Dancers at festivals dedicated to Dionysus got into such a frenzy that they entered an altered state. King Midas of Phrygia rescued Dionysus's friend, so the god granted him a wish. Midas wished that everything he touched would be turned to gold. That became problematic when he couldn't eat because his food turned to gold. Worst yet, when he hugged his daughter, the little girl turned to gold. To his relief, Dionysus reversed the wish.

How Did the Ancient Greeks Worship Their Gods?

The ancient Greeks honored their gods by pouring out wine. They also sacrificed animals, such as bulls, sheep, goats, pigs, and geese. They sacrificed animals in the courtyard of a temple. The priests examined the animals' intestines to see into the future. They burned some of the bones and fat on the altar, and everyone ate the rest of the meat.

Ancient Greeks gave **votive offerings** to thank the gods for answering a prayer. They also made votive offerings when making a vow. A votive offering could be any number of things, including small images of the god, figurines of people praying, weapons, vases, or jewelry. The temples became storehouses for a vast number of votive offerings. Greek temples were usually within a walled sanctuary with gardens, fountains, statues, sacred trees, and altars.

The Oracle of Delphi advising a visiting king.[88]

Both men and women served as priests. Generally, goddesses had priestesses, and the male deities had male priests. Certain places, like Delphi, had a female *oracle*. The Oracle of Delphi was a priestess called Pythia. She would sit on a stool straddling a crevice from which fumes wafted up. Greek myth said the fumes were from the rotting body of the Python monster killed by Apollo. As she breathed in the fumes of the decaying dragon, she entered into a trance and could then answer the questions of those seeking advice.

Festivals were an essential part of the ancient Greek religion. The Olympic Games were one of these festivals. After sacrificing a hundred bulls to Zeus, everyone sat down to enjoy a grand barbeque. Only men could compete in the games. Married women could not attend. Maybe their husbands didn't want them to see the other naked men in the races. Single girls could attend. They had their own athletic competitions to honor Hera. The young women athletes wore short tunics with their hair loosely flowing down their backs.

Who Won the Trojan War? Did It Really Happen?

King Menelaus of Sparta wanted to get his wife back from Prince Paris of Troy. He reminded the other Greek kings of the oath they had sworn to defend his marriage. However, the other kings were hesitant. Troy was a powerful walled city guarded by fierce warriors. All the Greek city-states would need to send ships and soldiers if they had any hope of winning. They knew the war would come at great cost. And yet, taking control of Troy meant controlling the Dardanelles, a narrow strait in western Turkey that ran from the Aegean Sea to the Sea of Marmara. From there, ships could sail into the Black Sea. Controlling the Dardanelles meant gaining unimaginable wealth from trade.

For many years, most people considered the Trojan War a myth. Yet, the ancient Greek historians spoke of it as a historical fact, describing the city of Troy in detail and dating the war to around 1200 BCE. Recent evidence suggests the war really did happen. Homer said another name for Troy was Wilusa. The Hittites lived in western Turkey. Their records named Wilusa as a city in their empire. The Hittite chronicles speak of a prince named Alaksandu, which Homer said was another name for Paris.

In 1870, an amateur archaeologist named Heinrich Schliemann teamed up with Charles Maclaren and Frank Calvert to explore an archaeological site called Hissarlik at the southern end of the Dardanelles. Civilizations would build on top of the same site, and this site had nine layers of civilization. One layer had a dome and other architecture that matched Homer's description of Troy. This layer was suddenly destroyed around 1180 BCE, about the same time the Greeks said that Troy fell. Most scholars agree this city was ancient Troy.

Homer's *Iliad* says that King Agamemnon of Mycenae led an alliance of the Greek city-states against Troy. Agamemnon was the brother of Menelaus, who wanted Helen back. The Greeks sailed one thousand ships to Troy and fought for ten years. The Greek forces finally got inside the walls. They killed most of the Trojan warriors and burned down the city. Probably the only winner was King Menelaus, who got Helen back. But he and everyone else lost many dear friends in the fierce fighting. The Greeks crushed Troy, but it was a bitter victory. After being away for a decade, they returned home to find their wives with other men and their cities in chaos.

Menelaus and his dead friend Patroclus.[89]

Round-up Activity: Who's Who?

Match each of the Twelve Olympians with their description. Check your answers using the answer key at the back of the book.

1. Aphrodite
2. Apollo
3. Ares
4. Artemis
5. Athena
6. Demeter
7. Dionysus
8. Hephaistos
9. Hera
10. Hermes
11. Poseidon
12. Zeus

A. King of the gods and of rain
B. Queen of the gods and vengeful wife of Zeus
C. Goddess of love and mother of Aeneas
D. The disabled god of crafts and volcanoes
E. God of the sun, music, archery, and healing
F. God of war and one of Aphrodite's lovers
G. Goddess of nature, wild animals, and hunting
H. Goddess of wisdom who split open Zeus's head
I. Goddess of farmers and the earth's fertility
J. The messenger god with winged sandals
K. God of the seas and father of the Cyclopes
L. God of wine, insanity, theater, and festivals

Chapter 3: The Rise of Athens from City-State to Empire

The thriving Mycenaean civilization was a distant memory. The few surviving people lived in small villages, where they farmed, herded animals, and fished. Greece lingered in its Dark Ages for three centuries, from around 1200 to 900 BCE. Because the Greeks lost their writing system, it's hard to know what happened.

The Bronze Age Collapse

It wasn't only Greece that crashed during the Bronze Age collapse. Several other civilizations in western Asia suddenly fell. Why did people abandon these cities? What caused so many people to die? Although the Greeks did not leave a written record, the Egyptians and Syrians did. Additionally, archaeologists can explore the ruins of ancient cities for clues like earthquake damage or destruction by an invader.

Scientists can also study core samples from lake, river, and sea bottoms. Low pollen counts mean a lack of rainfall killed off plants. Stalagmites in caves are formed by water seeping down. Scientists can analyze stalagmites for their mineral content, which tells them about oxygen and carbon levels. Tree rings show how much rain fell each year and what the temperatures were.

The Bronze Age collapse was the perfect storm of environmental disasters and invasions. A deadly drought struck the area that is Israel and Palestine today. Greece suffered an "earthquake storm" from 1225 to

1175 BCE along a weakened fault line. The earthquakes toppled cities and caused tsunamis that flooded coastal areas. King Musili II of the Hittites wrote of a terrible plague that caused many people to get sick and die for over twenty years.

Remember, this was at the very end of the Trojan War. The ten-year war had emptied the treasuries of the Greek cities and killed many of its young men. There weren't enough husbands for the young women. Greeks usually didn't practice **polygamy** (marriage to more than one person). Fewer married couples meant fewer children and smaller populations. Some kings returned to find someone challenging their right to rule. Leadership struggles probably toppled some cities.

Lastly, the mysterious Sea Peoples invaded Greece, Egypt, Syria, and the Hittite Empire. They were savage pirates who raided cities around the eastern Mediterranean Sea. They stole food and burned cities down. Since they ruled the seas, they broke down the sea trade on which Greece and other civilizations depended.

One Egyptian pharaoh wrote that the Sea Peoples came from the "northern seas." The Egyptians said they traveled south in wagons with their families and possessions. Could these Sea Peoples be survivors from Troy looking for a place to resettle? Another theory is that once Troy fell, no one was there to guard the link from the Black Sea to the Mediterranean Sea. The Sea Peoples could have come from what is today's Ukraine or Russia. They might have been displaced by some catastrophe, such as climate change from a volcanic eruption.

Rising from the Ashes

Around 900 BCE, Greece began crawling out of its slump. Trade picked up, and the population doubled quickly. Restored ancient cities rose into cultural centers. The Greeks developed smelting technology, which allowed them to make iron weapons and tools. In 776 BCE, Greece celebrated its first Olympic Games, beginning the **Archaic period** (776-500 BCE). The Greeks started writing again with a new alphabet. Greece shone brighter than ever before.

Athens was the only major city in Greece that survived the Dark Ages. Once the threat from the Sea Peoples faded, Athens became the chief trade hub in Greece. It took control of the entire Attica Peninsula, ruling its towns and cities in a mini-empire. As Athens grew wealthy, it helped bring wealth to the rest of Greece.

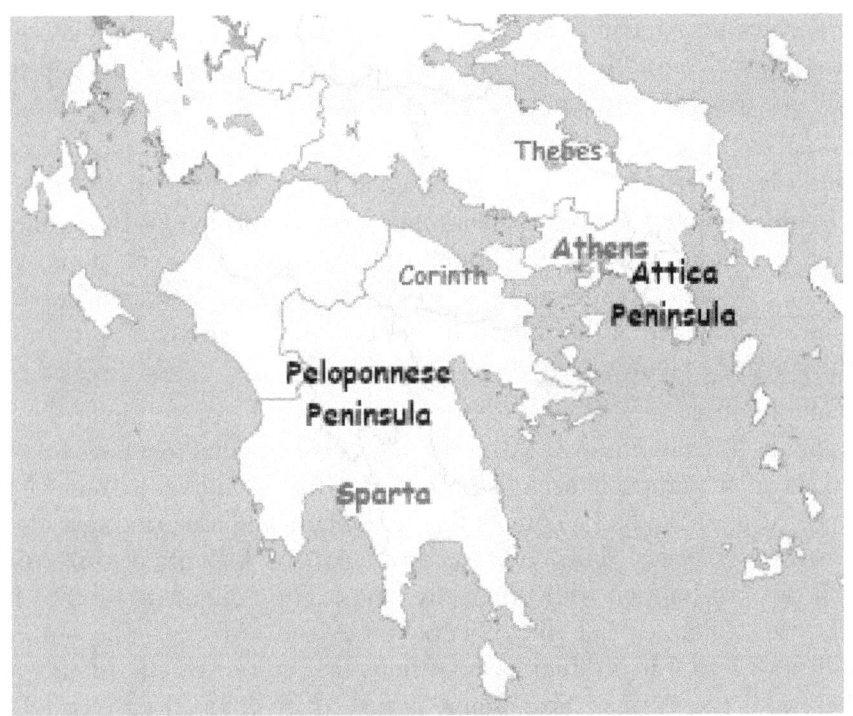

Ancient southern Greece.[90]

City-states

In Greece's Archaic era, various regions formed *city-states*. A city-state was a sizeable ruling city that controlled the smaller cities, towns, villages, and farmland surrounding it. It was like a small country.

Ancient Greece had no central government. Each city-state was independent. An interesting aspect was that each city-state did its own thing. Some had kings, some had a council of ruling elders, some had tyrants, and some began experimenting with democracy. Many of the city-states cycled through several types of government. As Greece rebounded, it grew to include over one thousand city-states. Athens, Sparta, and Corinth were the leading three city-states.

An Empire of Colonies: "Frogs around a Pond"

The city-states sent out expeditions to colonize new territories. They settled in northern Greece, Turkey's islands, and southern Italy. So many Greeks lived in southern Italy that it was nicknamed *Magna Graecia* (Great Greece). There were many colonies spread around the

Mediterranean, stretching as far as Spain and France. The Greeks sailed to the Black Sea and founded colonies around its shores. Plato said they were "like frogs around a pond."

Most of the colonies were independent of the city-state that sent the expeditions there. However, they had great loyalty to their mother city. If the main city-state fell under attack, they would send troops to defend it. By the end of the Archaic era, about 40 percent of the Greek population lived in colonies outside of Greece. There were around five hundred colonies. They sent athletes back to Greece every four years to compete in the Olympic Games.

Unlike other city-states, Athens continued to control its colonies, making it a true empire. Athens had governmental centers for the colonies in a particular area. For instance, the island of Samos in the eastern Aegean Sea had a council that made laws and collected taxes from the nearby colonies. The colonists from Athens kept their citizenship, which did not happen with other city-states. The Athenian colonies had their own militaries, but the officers came from Athens. The colonies could not go to war on their own. Athens first colonized the islands and coastline of the Aegean Sea. Later, it spread its colonial empire to the Black Sea, southern Italy, and Sicily.

The Rocky Path to Democracy

Athens had kings in the Mycenean era and the Dark Ages. The kings led a council of nobles who owned land. In the early Archaic period, Athens had three **archontes** (rulers). One was in charge of the government, one oversaw the military, and one led religion. An assembly of aristocratic male citizens (the *Ecclesia*) elected these three men from the nobility.

An attempted overthrow rocked Athens in 632 BCE. An Olympic athlete named Cylon tried to grab power. Cylon wanted to become Athens's tyrant, but he wasn't sure how to do it. So, he visited the Oracle of Delphi and asked her advice. The Oracle was sometimes cryptic in what she told people. The Oracle told Cylon to take power in Athens during a feast for Zeus. Cylon mulled this over. A feast for Zeus? Did she mean the Olympic Games?

Temple of Athena Nike in Athens.⁹¹

Cylon must have gotten the wrong festival because his attempt to take Athens did not go well. The Athenians fought hard to defend their city. Cylon escaped, but his soldiers hid out in the Temple of Athena. The temple was sacred ground, and the Athenians could not touch the men as long as they were in the temple. The soldiers had nothing to eat or drink. After a few days, they were desperate.

The Athenians promised Cylon's troops they wouldn't kill them if they surrendered. So, they laid down their weapons and came out. However, the Athenians broke their word and stoned them to death. By doing this, Athens's leaders broke the sacred "law of suppliants" (a **suppliant** is someone seeking mercy or forgiveness). Athens's leaders had to go into exile, and a curse followed them because they defiled Athena's temple.

The Athenians decided that part of the problem was that they didn't have any written laws. The rich rulers were constantly changing the laws to suit their needs. Sometimes, they pretended a particular law didn't exist. If they had written laws, it would clear matters up. So, in 621 BCE, they approached a nobleman named Draco and asked him to write down the laws. Draco didn't make up new laws for Athens. He just wrote down the unwritten laws that everyone was supposed to follow.

Draco's punishments for breaking laws were harsh. He ordered the death penalty for almost everything, even for something as trivial as stealing a cabbage. People who couldn't pay their debts became slaves. His harsh laws gave us the word **draconian**, which means something inhumane or unusually cruel.

On a positive note, Draco gave all Athenians equal legal rights. It didn't matter if they were aristocrats or commoners, wealthy or poor. The same laws applied to everyone. Previously, only wealthy landowners could vote or hold political positions. Now, military men could vote and serve in minor political positions. Draco paved the way for democracy to take root in Athens.

Solon.[23]

Nevertheless, the Athenians worried about the death penalty. In 594 BCE, they approached Solon, a poet and philosopher, and asked him to write a constitution. Solon got rid of Draco's law code. In Solon's opinion, the unrest in Athens was caused by the oppression of the poor and middle classes.

Solon started by "shaking off" the crushing debt that kept people down. The aristocrats had been seizing land from farmers if a lousy harvest kept them from paying their debt. Some people put themselves or their children up as security when taking out a loan. If they couldn't pay in time, they or their children became slaves. Solon canceled all debts. He freed those who had been enslaved because they were behind on their payments.

Solon's constitution divided the Athenians into four classes. Most people were in the lower class, and some got to vote for the first time. The four classes each sent one hundred men to the four-hundred-man council. All levels of society had equal representation. The city now had a balance of power. Back then, though, only the men were represented. Women couldn't vote in Greece until 1952 CE. It still wasn't a true democracy because even most men couldn't vote. Yet, it was a giant step in the right direction.

Solon made other reforms. He felt that marriages should be based on love, not on the money or property a man could get from his bride's **dowry** (gifts that were given to a spouse). Solon banned dowries. He also banned gossip and hate speech. Solon improved the court system by allowing poor people to have someone to defend them. Many of the judges were corrupt. Now, people could appeal to the four-hundred-man council if they didn't like a judge's ruling.

The lower classes loved Solon's constitution because it gave them more rights. But Solon knew it created enemies among the rich and powerful. He skipped town as soon as he finished the constitution and didn't return for ten years. When he came back, he was horrified to see Athens in **anarchy** (lawlessness and disorder because of the government's breakdown). The council had not elected an **archon** (political leader) in two years.

Tyrant Takeover

What's worse, Solon's cousin Peisistratus made himself a tyrant of Athens. What is a tyrant? When we hear that word today, we think of a power-hungry, oppressive ruler. Back then, a tyrant wasn't the enemy of freedom. A tyrant came into power outside of the usual way. A tyrant wasn't a hereditary king. A council didn't' select him, and he wasn't elected. Tyrants were **usurpers** who grabbed political power by force.

A tyrant was not necessarily evil. Yes, he had absolute power. He did not necessarily follow the laws of a city-state. But tyrants could improve the lives of ordinary people. A tyrant kept his position by keeping the people happy. Tyrants did things like build roads, bridges, and water systems. They created jobs for farmers and soldiers who had lost their land.

Peisistratus developed an army out of the lower classes. Solon might have doubted his cunning cousin, but Peisistratus proved to be a fair and generous ruler. His family had silver and gold mines in Macedonia, and he used his income to buy back the farmers' land. He repaired and enhanced Athens's **infrastructure** (public works like roads, sewers, and bridges). He taught the farmers how to make a profit by exporting wine and olive oil.

Peisistratus ruled Athens for five years until his enemies became powerful enough to banish him. A man named Megakles said he would help Peisistratus get back into power if he married his daughter. Megakles dreamed of having a grandson who ruled Athens. The two men agreed to the deal, but they faced a challenge. How would they get the Athenians on board, especially the rich and powerful?

They found a tall, beautiful young woman to help them with their plan. She dressed like the goddess Athena and rode in a fine chariot into Athens. "Peisistratus is the greatest of men! I want him to rule Athens!" The Athenians thought she really was the goddess and obeyed her. Peisistratus was in power again but only for a brief time. He married Megakles's daughter but refused to sleep with her. He didn't want her to have sons that would challenge his sons from his first marriage.

Peisistratus and the fake Athena.[98]

An angry Megakles drove Peisistratus out of Athens again. Peisistratus languished in exile for ten years. He used the money from his mines in Macedonia to hire **mercenaries** (soldiers who fought for another city-state or country for money). He allied with several other Greek city-states and retook Athens in 546 BCE. This time, he ruled for almost two decades until he died.

During his third reign, Peisistratus launched significant reforms. He taxed the rich landowners 10 percent of their income. This money funded loans for poor farmers. He transformed the farming system in the Attica Peninsula, making it highly productive. Athens dominated trade around the Mediterranean and Black Seas. Peisistratus rebuilt Athena's temple and developed Athens into a destination for festivals and theater.

Groundbreaking Democratic Reforms

After Peisistratus died, Athens descended into disorder again. The Spartans overthrew Athens, but the Athenians were able to get rid of them. They made Megakles's son, Cleisthenes, their new leader.

Cleisthenes wasted no time turning Athens's politics around. He reorganized the entire Attica Peninsula into ten tribes, each of which included people from the three different geographical regions around

Athens, ensuring a more balanced distribution of political power. The tribes had representatives from the city of Athens, the coastal towns, and the farm villages. Each tribe sent fifty men to serve on the council for one year. Only the five hundred men on the council could vote, but they represented all levels of society. This early form of democracy continued into Greece's classical period.

Round-up Activity: Word Search

There are ten key words/phrases hidden in the puzzle. Read the definitions below to figure out the key word, then find it in the puzzle. The answer key is at the back of the book.

E	S	P	A	L	L	O	C	E	G	A	E	Z	N	O	R	B
T	I	N	I	N	F	R	A	S	T	R	U	C	T	U	R	E
A	E	M	C	A	W	X	A	N	Y	M	A	G	Y	L	O	P
T	R	L	E	I	V	Y	E	L	A	R	O	U	D	S	W	L
S	A	K	A	N	U	A	R	L	G	R	F	N	R	Y	O	L
Y	N	J	R	O	T	Z	S	Y	A	E	C	D	O	E	T	I
T	E	I	G	C	S	H	R	C	U	E	U	H	W	T	R	T
I	C	H	A	A	R	W	I	O	T	N	A	R	Y	T	D	S
C	R	G	N	R	O	I	Y	O	O	H	O	A	E	W	S	U
D	E	R	G	D	Q	S	R	L	Y	A	Y	L	H	H	A	O
C	M	E	A	O	P	T	O	D	O	V	E	L	T	A	R	Y
B	A	Y	M	W	T	S	R	N	L	G	D	U	M	I	E	A

1. The sudden fall of multiple civilizations in the eastern Mediterranean around 1200 BCE
2. Marriage to more than one person
3. One large independent city ruling over towns and villages in the surrounding area
4. "Great Greece" region of southern Italy
5. An absolute ruler who comes to power outside the usual channels
6. Something inhumane or unusually cruel
7. Money or property a bride brings into a marriage
8. Disorder because of governmental breakdown
9. Public works like roads, bridges, and sewers
10. Soldiers who are paid to fight for another city-state or country

Chapter 4: Becoming a Spartan

The Spartans always marched to a different drum. When everyone else in Greece was doing one thing, they took an alternative path. For instance, Athens was progressive in its politics, and its citizens were always eager to discuss the latest ideas. The Spartans weren't big fans of change. They liked to keep things the way they were. Philosophy was for weaker people. They focused on building muscular bodies and iron wills.

Everything in Sparta revolved around the military. Fighting was a sacred job. Warriors were glorified as the core of Spartan society. Children did not belong to their parents but to the state. Every boy was considered a future soldier. Parents brought their newborn babies to the council, called the Gerousia, to evaluate their health and strength. If a baby didn't pass the inspection, it would be placed on a mountain to die.

Peculiar Politics

While other cities experimented with democracy and tyrants, Sparta stuck with its system of two kings. Why two kings? Well, Sparta started out with one king, whom they believed was descended from the hero Heracles. In Sparta's early days, lightning struck and killed King Aristodemus. He left identical twin baby sons. Which one should be king? The babies looked so much alike that no one could tell them apart. Even their mother claimed she couldn't be sure which was born first. The elders traveled to Delphi to ask the Oracle what to do. She said to make both of them kings, and that's what they did.

From that point on, Sparta kept the two-king system. This came in handy when Sparta was at war. One king could lead the army as commander in chief, while the other stayed in Sparta and kept things running smoothly. The system also provided a system of **checks and balances**. Neither king held complete power. Each contributed his own ideas, so the rule was more balanced. If one king's action plan was not a good move, the other king could "check" or block it.

Sparta had a ruling council, as most of Greece's cities did, but everyone on Sparta's council was at least sixty years old. All the younger men were off fighting battles. Sparta's council of twenty-eight elderly men was an **oligarchy** (a small group of people running political affairs). The two kings served on the council as the only ones under sixty. The kings took turns leading the troops in battles and serving as priests and judges.

Schooling Sparta's Soldiers

All Spartan men served full time in the military beginning at age twenty. They retired at age sixty. At the tender age of seven, Spartan boys left home to join the **agoge** training system, where they lived in dormitories with other boys. In the agoge, they trained in military skills, hunting, reading, writing, singing, and dancing. The boys learned to tolerate pain and live simple "Spartan" lives with plain food and no frills.

The Spartan training had three levels. From age seven to twelve, the boys trained in the first level, the **paides**. They then joined the **paidiskoi** for the rest of their teen years. Initiation into the paidiskoi was harsh, but it prepared the boys for military campaigns. The boys only had a red cloak to wear. They slept outside on mats they made from reeds. They had to scavenge food from the fields or steal from somewhere. If they were caught, they received a whipping. The boys were also ritually flogged each year in the Temple of Artemis to test their endurance and resistance to pain. Some boys died from the abuse.

The third level was the **hebontes**. These young men would range from age twenty to thirty. At this level, the Spartan trainees received hazing from their instructors and the older military men. If they showed any weakness, they were singled out. They lived in military barracks until they were thirty. They ate small and simple meals. Being overweight was considered unpatriotic since it kept a person from fighting well. The young soldiers drank diluted wine, but getting drunk was forbidden. The training was about discipline in all areas. A young man had to complete his training in the agoge to become a citizen.

A bronze figurine of a young Spartan soldier reclining while eating. He is probably eating a bowl of black bean soup, a typical simple meal. ⁹⁴

Warfare Tactics Taught to Spartan Boys

Sparta was Greece's leading military power. The other city-states trained their young men in the art of war, but they didn't have a full-time army. The soldiers were farmers, craftsmen, merchants, or administrators when they weren't fighting battles. However, Sparta's men trained for thirteen years before fighting their first battle, and then they trained for another decade. Their only job was serving in the military.

What military skills did they learn in the agoge? They learned hand-to-hand combat, sword fighting, and spear maneuvers. They also studied formation skills. In the Archaic era, Greek armies began using a ***phalanx formation***. The soldiers lined up side by side. There were about one hundred men in a row. Each man held his shield in his left hand so it slightly overlapped the shield of the man next to him. It was like a solid wall of shields.

The soldiers were called ***hoplites***. They wore bronze helmets, breastplates, and shin guards. In their right hands, they carried seven-foot spears. The typical Greek phalanx was eight men deep. The soldiers in the front row held their spears horizontally to spear the enemy. When the commander yelled, "Charge!" the warriors screamed and ran toward the enemy. The men in the back rows rested their shields on the backs of the men in front of them, pushing them along. It was like a massive bulldozer with spears sticking out.

Phalanx formation.⁹⁵

The Spartan warriors put their own spin on the Greek phalanx formation with the ***othismos tactic***. This formation only had four rows instead of eight, but it was much wider. This allowed them to get around the sides of the enemy phalanx. Another thing the Spartans did was slowly and steadily march toward the enemy rather than screaming and running at them. The incredibly disciplined Spartan troops held their formation, chanting their battle hymns to the tune of the pipers. It was a threatening sight, and it scared their enemies. Many times, the enemy soldiers fled in fear when the Spartan phalanx approached.

One battle tactic the Spartans occasionally used was running away. This tactic had two versions: walking and running. In the first version, the Spartan officers assessed the situation. Were they hopelessly outnumbered? Were they in a poor position, such as fighting uphill or with the sun in their eyes? If the officers decided they didn't have a good chance of winning, they would simply walk away from the battle. They didn't care if the other Greeks thought it was a cowardly move. The Spartans knew they were not weaklings. They were practical. It made sense to wait until the odds were in their favor.

The other tactic involved running away in a fake retreat. If the battle wasn't going well, the commander would yell, "Retreat!" Everyone would spin around and run away from the enemy. Of course, the enemy would charge after them at full speed. The Spartan commander led his troops to a better position, such as on a slope, where they would have the uphill advantage.

Then, the Spartan commander screamed, "Turn!" All the Spartan troops wheeled around, holding their spears before them. Caught off guard, the enemy soldiers couldn't stop in time and ran right into the Spartan spears. The Spartans used this fake-retreat tactic often, and the enemy almost always fell for it.

What About Spartan Women?

Spartan girls and women were free spirits in the Greek world. Women in the rest of Greece wore head coverings and ankle-length gowns. They weren't involved in public life. Spartan women wore short skirts. They ran races, wrestled, and threw javelins. Spartan girls lived at home, but they attended school, where they learned reading, writing, singing, dancing, and self-defense moves.

A Spartan girl competing in a race.[96]

There was no such thing as a normal home life for young Spartan couples. All Spartan men lived in the military barracks until they were thirty. They married around the age of twenty, but they didn't live with their wives until they were thirty. The young men occasionally snuck out of the barracks to spend a little time with their wives. Much of the time, they were away at war.

The birth rate in Sparta was much lower than in the rest of Greece. Since the men weren't around, the women handled the family finances and decision-making. Spartan women could buy and sell property.

The men in the rest of Greece were shocked to learn that Spartan women had opinions. Spartan women aired their views in public and even discussed politics. And their husbands listened to them! The non-Spartan Greeks found it odd that Spartan law required that parents give their girls the same quality of care and food as they gave their boys.

Helots and Hoplites: An Oppressive System

In the Bronze Age, the Dorian people migrated into the Peloponnese Peninsula from Macedonia. The Dorians grew in strength and rebuilt the city of Sparta in the early Archaic era. As their population grew, they needed more land for farming. To get that land, they started a twenty-year war with the neighboring city-state of Messenia. It all began with a quarrel over cows.

An Olympic athlete from Messenia named Polychares leased land from a Spartan named Euaiphnos. Polychares grazed his cattle on the land. One day, Euaiphnos told Polychares that pirates had stolen his cattle. Polychares thought his story seemed fishy, so he asked around. He discovered Euaiphnos had sold his cattle. He confronted Euaiphnos, who apologized. "I'll give you the money I got from the cattle. Send your boy over later today, and I'll give him the money."

Instead of handing over the money, Euaiphnos murdered Polychares's son. The distraught father charged into the Spartan council, demanding justice. But the council refused to discuss the matter. Outraged, Polychares went on a killing spree. He murdered any Spartans that he caught walking alone. The Spartan council messaged Messenia. The councilors demanded that Polychares stand trial. The Messenians retorted, "Of course! We'll send Polychares to you as soon as you send Euaiphnos to us. He needs to stand trial for murdering Polychares's son!"

The negotiations did not go anywhere. Both sides started bringing up offenses from decades earlier. The two Spartan kings used the dispute as an excuse to launch a surprise attack on Messenia. Although tensions were high, the city-state of Messenia wasn't expecting war. The two city-states had coexisted peacefully for over a century. The Spartans attacked the town of Ampheia at night, killing the unarmed people in their beds. A fierce war raged for two decades. Sparta won in 720 BCE. One of the towns the Spartans conquered was Helos. Its people were called helots.

Sparta took the land it had stolen from Messenia and divided it into nine thousand estates, all the same size. Each Spartan citizen got a plot of land to farm. Since the Spartan men were full-time soldiers and often off fighting wars, who could do the farming? The Spartans used the helots to tend the fields. The helots weren't exactly slaves because no Spartan owned a helot. They couldn't buy and sell helots. Instead, the helots were more like serfs. Technically, the helots belonged to the state and were assigned work. The helots did all the labor and got half of the profit; the Spartan landowners got the other half. This freed up the Spartan men to form the most formidable military in the ancient Greek world.

So, Sparta had a system where the Spartan men worked full time as soldiers, and the helots farmed the land and did other menial work. But what about merchants and artisans? Sparta had a third class called the *Perioikoi*. They were free people, but they came from other places and couldn't be citizens. Only Spartans who could trace their ancestors back for centuries could be citizens. Thus, the Perioikoi couldn't serve in the military. But they could run shops, make pottery and weapons, and engage in trade. The Perioikoi grew wealthy, but they couldn't own land.

5ᵗʰ century BCE statue of a Spartan hoplite. [97]

Everything was working out for the Spartans. Every Spartan citizen owned land, but he didn't have to do the demanding farm work. But a new problem arose. The helot men lived at home with their wives and had large families. The Spartan men were off fighting wars or living in Sparta's military barracks. It wasn't long before the helot population outnumbered the Spartans. What was to keep them from rebelling against Sparta and taking over the city-state?

Plutarch was a 1st-century CE historian. He was also a priest at Apollo's temple in Delphi, where the Oracle was. In his book *Parallel Lives*, Plutarch said the Spartans came up with a devious plan to decrease the helot population. They picked Spartan teens who displayed exceptional skills in the agoge to join a force called the **Krypteia**. It was similar to a secret police. Every autumn, the Spartans declared war on the helots. This meant no Spartan could be found guilty of killing a helot. The young men who joined the Krypteia took a dagger and went into the countryside to find and kill helots.

What Was Sparta's Lasting Legacy?

Spartan culture influenced Western ideas about self-discipline, courage, self-sacrifice, and patriotism. Sparta was light-years ahead of the rest of Greece in terms of women's contributions to society. Women weren't hidden at home. They aired their opinions, were physically strong, and enjoyed rights like buying and managing property. Aristotle said that women owned two-fifths of Sparta's land.

Yet, Sparta had a dark side. The Spartans killed weak or sickly newborns. Spartan men lived apart from their wives and barely saw their children. Children belonged to the state, not to the family. Mothers only cared for their male children for six years. Parents had no say in their children's education or anything else about their lives from that point on. The family breakdown made Sparta militarily strong, but Sparta suffered horrific losses sometimes. At times, almost all of the adult males died. Sparta didn't have enough children to rebuild its population. Then, there were the helots. The Spartans essentially enslaved their neighbors and occasionally murdered some of them when the helot population grew larger than the Spartans.

These Spartan ideals of a strong military and state influenced later societies. The classical Greek philosopher Plato liked how the state controlled children's lives and education. Hitler thought Sparta was a model civilization. German children were taught strict discipline, endurance, and the importance of self-sacrifice. Hitler believed Sparta was a prime example of a warrior class.

Round-up Activity: Review Questions

1. How did Sparta's culture and society differ from other ancient Greek city-states?

_____

_____

_____

2. What role did military service play in Spartan society?

_____

_____

_____

3. What was the agoge? How did it shape the upbringing and education of Spartan boys?

_____

_____

_____

4. What challenges did Spartan boys face in their rigorous training and education?

_____

_____

_____

5. What were some positive aspects of Sparta's legacy?

_____

_____

_____

6. How has Sparta's legacy negatively impacted some civilizations?

Chapter 5: The Persian Wars: Marathon and Thermopylae

For 160 years, the Persian Empire, also known as the Achaemenid Empire, and Greece fought each other. For the first six decades, Persia had the upper hand. But three epic battles turned the tide for Greece. This chapter will unlock the remarkable heroism and canny strategies the Greeks used to achieve victory.

What Caused the Persian Wars?

It all began with Cyrus the Great, King of Persia. His empire was located in what is today southern Iran. He united with his kinsmen, the Medes of northern Iran, and they conquered central Asia. Then, they charged through Turkey, taking more territory, until they arrived in Ionia, across the Aegean Sea from Greece. Shockwaves rippled through the Greek world when Ionia bowed to Persia in 547 BCE. These were colonies settled by Greek city-states centuries before. Now, the Persian-Achaemenid Empire had swallowed them up.

In 499 BCE, the Ionians rebelled during the reign of Persian King Darius the Great. Athens and the neighboring city of Eretria sent ships and troops to the Ionians. They sacked and burned Sardis, the Persian capital of Ionia. In 494, the Persians trounced the Greek army, and the revolt fell apart. Yet, Darius was seething. "How dare Athens and Eretria interfere in my war!"

Darius sent his relative Mardonius overland to Greece, but the bloodthirsty Byrgi tribe blocked his way. Meanwhile, a brutal storm sank three hundred of the Persian ships sailing toward Greece. Darius simmered in rage. He wasn't done with Greece yet!

Inconceivable Victory at Marathon

In 490 BCE, Darius sent his ambassadors to the Greek city-states, demanding they submit to his authority. Most Greek city-states agreed to give "earth and water," meaning they recognized Persia as their overlord. But there were some holdouts. Athens and Sparta refused to yield. Darius roared, "Athens, again? They interfered in Ionia. I won't stop until I burn Athens to the ground."

A fleet of triremes.[98]

When Darius's navy with six hundred *triremes* (warships) sailed across the Aegean Sea toward Greece, the people of Eretria panicked. They had destroyed Sardis in the Ionian revolt. Surely, the Persians would punish them. Most fled to Mount Olympus, where they hid out. The Athenians sent four thousand men, but Eretria's city leader sent them back home. "Our citizens aren't planning to fight the Persians. There's no sense in dying for a lost cause."

As it turned out, two Eretrians opened the city gates to the Persians, hoping for a reward. That didn't go well for them. The Persians killed every man left in the city and enslaved the women and children. They sacked and burned Eretria and destroyed its temples. A few days later, the Persians sailed toward Athens, expecting a similar triumph.

Meanwhile, the Athenians sent a long-distance runner named Philippides to run 132 miles (213 kilometers) to Sparta. When the Spartans heard that the Persians had crushed Eretria, they agreed to help, even though Sparta and Athens were usually bitter rivals. Sparta had some weird religious rules about when they could and could not fight.

"Yes, of course, we'll help. The Persians are probably targeting us next since we didn't give them 'earth and water.' If we join forces, we can beat them. But, right now, we're in the middle of the Carnelian festival. We can't go to war until the full moon."

This news was discouraging, as the Persian ships were on the way. The Athenians brightened when the city of Plataea, north of Athens, sent a thousand warriors to help. The Athenians were still outnumbered, but they had a few tricks up their sleeves. They chose a daring strategy. Instead of letting the Persians lay siege to Athens, they marched across the Attica Peninsula to meet their attackers in Marathon. The Persians weren't familiar with Marathon's landscape, but the Greeks knew it well. Marathon was in a swampy valley. **Quagmire**, soft marshy areas that gave way under a person's weight, covered the area. If a person stepped on it, they got sucked in. Any struggle increased the downward force until the doomed person drowned in the bog.

The Persians had just laid anchor at Marathon when the Greeks showed up. The Persians had planned to ride their horses across the peninsula rather than sailing around the bottom of it. They wanted to avoid the lethal storms in the open sea that had wiped out their fleet earlier. When the Persians saw the Greeks coming over the mountains, they smiled.

"Look! The Greeks don't have any horses! They're all on foot! And they only have spears and swords. Our cavalry and archers will wipe them out!"

This was the first time the Persians faced off against the Greeks in a land battle. The Greeks always fought on foot, using their phalanx maneuvers. The Persians were skilled cavalrymen, and their terrifying archers would darken the sky with arrows. But when the Persians came ashore, they realized they couldn't use their horses on the marshy, mountainous terrain.

The Greeks formed their phalanx position on the mountain while the Persians assembled on the small plain below. The Greeks charged downhill, running full speed, catching the Persians by surprise. The Persian archers barely had time to shoot off two volleys of arrows. Most of the arrows hit helmets or shields and bounced off. The Greeks quickly outflanked and encircled the Persians, confusing them.

Panicked, the Persians ran toward their ships, Greek spears flying into their unprotected backs. They had to navigate through the marshland. Many fell into the quagmire. They finally reached the sea, but the Athenians plunged in after them. The Athenians captured seven Persian ships and set others on fire.

The Greeks attack the Persian ships.

The rest of the Persians hoisted their sails and sailed out to sea. The Greeks joyfully assessed the losses. They counted 6,400 dead Persians. Who knew how many more had sunk in the quagmire? The Athenians only lost 192 men, and 11 men from Plateau died.

"Look!" someone shouted, pointing out to sea. "The Persians are sailing south! They're not sailing back to Asia! They're headed around the peninsula to Athens!"

The Greek officers hurriedly called the men to order. "We've got to get back to Athens! If our army isn't there when those ships arrive, the people in the city might surrender to the Persians."

Would they make it in time? Athens was twenty-five miles away. Exhausted after the battle, the Greeks raced back, stumbling over roots and rocks in the dim light of the full moon. They got there before the Persians and collapsed at the temple of Heracles on the cliff overlooking the Saronic Gulf. The Persians saw their campfires as they sailed into the gulf. They dropped their anchor and discussed their next move.

Should they lay siege? They had already lost thousands of men and many ships. The Greeks were pumped up by their victory, and other Greek cities, like Sparta, would likely come to help the Athenians. After floating in the gulf for a while, they weighed anchor and sailed over the horizon to Persia. This was when the Spartans finally showed up, as it was now a full moon. But the Athenians embraced them, and they all hurried back to Marathon to see the dead Persians and hear how the battle went down.

The Greeks had scored an outstanding victory, but they knew the Persians would return. One of Athens's generals, Miltiades, had overseen the battle at Marathon. He realized that Athens had to build up a navy that could take on the Persians. General Themistocles heartily agreed. They ordered the construction of two hundred new triremes. From this point, Athens's nearly unbeatable navy ruled the seas.

Spartan Sacrifice at Thermopylae

Darius the Great died soon after. He never realized his dream of conquering Greece. His son Xerxes now stood before the Persian council. "We cannot let Greece get away with this! They have insulted my father and the Persian Empire. I'll build the largest army the world has ever seen. One million men! All of humanity will be under our yoke. Persia will be the empire upon which the sun never sets!"

The men on the council drew in a collective breath but stayed silent. Xerxes had a hot temper, and they wanted to keep their heads. The Persian Empire stretched from Egypt to Afghanistan, so a million-man army was doable. However, Persia had suffered horrific losses in their previous battles with Greece. Finally, Xerxes's uncle, Artabanus, cleared his throat and reminded him of the grave risk. Xerxes was adamant.

"Artabanus, you're a coward! Stay here with the women. We must strike first! Otherwise, they'll invade us!"

The Greek historian Herodotus said that Xerxes had second thoughts while lying on his bed that night. Artabanus was right! Attacking Greece could spell Persia's doom. He drifted asleep. A ghost appeared in his dream. "Are you changing your mind, Persian? Follow your original plan!"

Xerxes awoke the following day, rubbing his head. What a crazy dream! He called his council and apologized to his uncle. He announced that Persia would *not* invade Greece. But that night, the ghost appeared again. "If you don't invade Greece, you will experience a sudden and violent end."

Xerxes jumped up and ran into Artabanus's room. "I keep seeing a ghost. It's insisting I attack Greece. I don't know whether it's real or just my imagination. Why don't you lie on my bed? See what happens."

Artabanus lay down on his nephew's bed. The ghost appeared and tried to gouge out his eyes. "You! You're the one telling Xerxes not to invade Greece! You now face judgment! Judgment now and in the afterlife!"

Artabanus jumped up and ran screaming to Xerxes. "I've changed my mind! Invade Greece!"

After four years of preparation, Xerxes marched his massive army to the Dardanelles, where Asia meets Europe. Instead of simply ferrying his men over the one-mile-wide strait, he decided to do the unthinkable. He would build a bridge! He had his engineers strap 674 ships together and put a path of planks over them. The engineers finished the job, but a storm struck. The wind and churning waters destroyed the bridge.

The boat bridge over the Dardanelles. [100]

Xerxes erupted in anger. He cut the heads off the engineers and ordered his men to punish the water. They branded the water with hot irons and whipped it three hundred times! Now, he had to get new engineers to rebuild the bridge, which meant spending the winter there and using up precious food stores to feed his large army.

Were there really a million soldiers in Xerxes's army? The Persian Empire was the largest the world had yet seen, and they had the manpower. However, all the planning, organization, and food needed for that many men would have made it impractical, if not impossible.

The bridge was eventually rebuilt. Xerxes's army crossed over and marched toward Greece. Meanwhile, his navy of 1,200 ships sailed across the Aegean Sea. None of the city-states of northern Greece dared resist his massive army. But then, the Persian soldiers reached a high and rugged mountain range that cut through Greece. The Persians had to go through the Thermopylae Pass to get to southern Greece. But six thousand Greek warriors barred his way. Sparta had allied with Athens, Thebes, Arcadia, Corinth, and other southern Greek city-states. Some allied Greek forces stayed behind and shored up defenses in southern Greece. Meanwhile, the Spartans and other Greeks blocked the sixteen-foot-wide pass and quickly rebuilt a crumbling defensive wall.

Xerxes chuckled. He believed as soon as the Greeks saw his gigantic army pouring into the valley, they would run away. But he was dealing with Spartans, the best fighters of ancient Greece. After four days of staring at each other, Xerxes sent an ambassador to Spartan King Leonidas. "This is your last chance. Lay down your weapons and avoid bloodshed."

Leonidas growled, "You will have to take them!"

The Greeks put the phalanx formation into play. They stood shoulder to shoulder, their shields overlapping and spears sticking out. The ones in the back held their shields overhead, forming a bronze ceiling that deflected the thousands of arrows shot by the Persians. If one man was hit, another quickly stepped into his place from behind. The ancient defensive wall protected the men on the front line from a cavalry charge.

The Persians only had wicker shields. These were no match for the Greeks' long spears. For two full days, the Greeks blocked the Persians from entering the pass. Xerxes sent his ten thousand "Immortals," Persia's elite forces, to charge forward with their battleaxes, javelins, and swords. Even these great warriors failed. The seven-foot Greek spears kept them from getting close enough to use their own weapons.

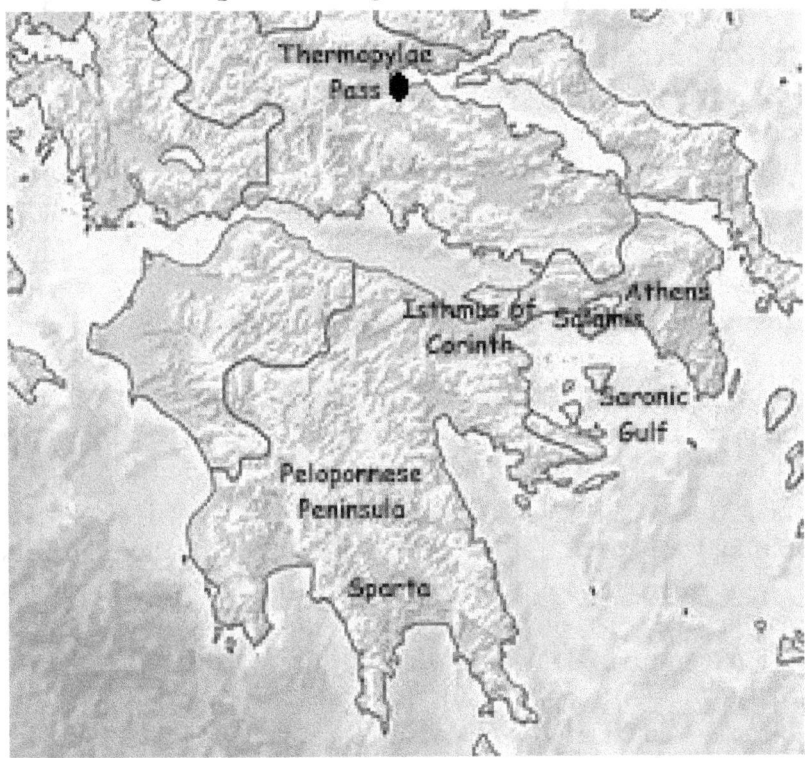

Thermopylae Pass (top of map). [101]

On the third day, a Greek traitor showed the Persians how a few men could get over the mountain on a narrow shepherd's path. Some Immortals scaled the mountain and approached the Greeks from behind. Leonidas ordered a few hundred men to continue holding the line against the Persians. He sent a small unit to attack the Persians who had just crossed the mountain. He ordered the rest of the Greeks to get out of the pass and escape to southern Greece.

There was no way the Greeks could continue to hold the pass with Persians in front and behind them. Why should all six thousand Greeks die when they could live to fight another day? They were desperately needed in southern Greece because Xerxes was headed there next. Leonidas and the small remaining force continued holding off the Persians until more Immortals crossed over the mountain, trapping them in the pass. The Immortals shot volleys of arrows at the Greeks, killing King Leonidas. Soon, every Greek man was dead. The Spartans and their allies sacrificed themselves to save Greece.

Naval Battle at Salamis Turns the Tide

The Persian forces charged south toward Athens, but the city was empty. Most of the citizens evacuated to the island of Salamis. Xerxes looted the city's treasures. He burned its stunning temples and killed anyone he could find. He received the terrible news that two storms had wiped out half his naval fleet. Cursing the gods, he considered his next move.

He couldn't do anything about the Athenians until the rest of his fleet arrived. But he had a score to settle with Sparta. To get there, he needed to cross the Isthmus of Corinth into the Peloponnese Peninsula. However, the Spartans and their Peloponnesian allies were one step ahead of him. While Leonidas and his men held off the Persians at the Thermopylae Pass, the rest of the Greeks had been busy rebuilding an ancient four-mile wall that spanned the Isthmus of Corinth.

When Xerxes laid siege to the newly built wall, the Greeks knew they couldn't hold Xerxes off for very long. They needed to lure the Persians away. The Athenian, Corinthian, and Spartan fleets were moored near Salamis in the Saronic Gulf. The Athenian naval commander Themistocles messaged Xerxes. He convinced Xerxes that the Greek alliance was falling apart and the Spartans were sailing home. Themistocles told Xerxes he was willing to come over to the Persian side. If Xerxes sent his fleet to Salamis the next day, he would give the Athenian navy to the Persians.

Xerxes fell for it. He sent his fleet to the Saronic Gulf. He headed to the gulf and climbed a mountain to watch the battle play out below him. Most of the Greek ships hid behind Georgios Island in the Saronic Gulf. When the Persian navy entered the gulf, they saw fifty Corinthian ships floating in front of them. Suddenly, the Corinthian ships sailed into the strait between Salamis and Athens on the mainland. The Persian ships followed them into the narrow strait. They realized too late it was a trap!

An illustration of the Battle of Salamis. [103]

The rest of the Greek ships came out of hiding and encircled the Persian fleet. The Persians had no way to escape. The Greeks chanted a hymn to Apollo as they shattered the Persian ships with their battering rams. Floating bodies and sinking ships covered the surface of the water. Xerxes watched in horror from the mountaintop as the Greeks destroyed his naval fleet. This was the watershed moment for Greece. The tide had turned in the long war with Persia. Greece would ultimately prevail.

Round-up Activity: Fill in the Blank

The Persian Wars with Greece began when Cyrus the Great conquered _____ in 547 BCE, making these Greek colonies a province of the Persian-Achaemenid Empire. When Ionia revolted in 499 BCE, Athens and _____ sent ships and troops to help. After ending the revolt, the Persian king, Darius the Great, sent his fleet to punish Athens. However, the Athenians chose the battleground in a marshy area where the Persians couldn't use their horses. They soundly defeated the Persians in the _____ ____ _____. Xerxes, the son of Darius, sought revenge and marched into Greece with a huge army. Led by the Spartan king _____, the Greeks held off the Persians at the _____ _____ while the rest of the Greeks evacuated _____ and rebuilt the wall at the _____ ____ _____. The Greeks sacrificed themselves at the pass, but in the end, the Greeks scored an astounding victory in the naval _____ ____ _____.

- Athens
- Battle of Marathon
- Battle of Salamis
- Eretria
- Ionia
- Isthmus of Corinth
- Leonidas
- Thermopylae Pass

Chapter 6: The Golden Age of Athens: Art, Philosophy, and Democracy

From 480 to 423 BCE, Athens shone like never before. It made mind-blowing strides in the arts, philosophy, and democracy. What shaped these glory days that left such an imprint on world history? Athens formed the Delian League, uniting the Greek city-states and pushing pirates and Persians out of Greek waters. This relative peace allowed Athens to focus on culture and trade.

Astounding Architecture

Gleaming temples with graceful pillars leap to mind when one thinks of Athens. Like many Greek cities, Athens was centered around a steep hill called an *Acropolis*, or "high city." The Athenians built elegant government and temple buildings on this "Sacred Rock." But when Xerxes stormed Athens with his huge army, he destroyed the Acropolis.

After the Greeks sank Xerxes's navy and sent him scurrying back to Persia, the Athenians began rebuilding. Once the walls were up to protect the city, they built a breathtaking new complex on the Acropolis. A person climbing the Acropolis entered through the marble Propylaea Gate. A thirty-foot-high statue of Athena stood just behind the gate. Ships on the gulf three miles away could see the shining bronze statue reflecting the sun.

Another temple to Athena on the Acropolis was the Erechtheion, which still stands today. It has an unusual type of pillar called *caryatid* on its "Porch of the Maidens." Sculptures of lovely young women support its roof. Each caryatid pillar is different. They might represent real teenagers from ancient times.

Caryatid pillars in the Temple of the Erechtheion.[108]

Impressive Artistry

Around 530 BCE, the Greeks invented a type of pottery called "*red-figure*" or "red-on-black." Artists first painted the pottery black. Then, they painted people or animals in red or gold over the black paint. The earlier style had black figures painted on a red background. One example of this artwork is a painting of a Greek hoplite and a Persian archer on a shiny black amphora jar. The Greek soldier wears a short skirt and bronze armor. The Persian soldier wears long pants and a long-sleeved shirt.

Red-on-black amphora jar.[104]

Another example of a red (or gold) on black ceramic painting is a vase with a singer and a bunny. A bearded man relaxes on a couch under a basket. He is singing and reaching down to pet his spotted rabbit. Have you ever thought of people having bunnies thousands of years ago? The painting is on a *kylix*, a ceramic drinking cup with a wide bowl and horizontal handles.

Singer and bunny.[105]

Another red-on-black vase has a painting of Dionysus, the god of wine. Two **maenads** are dancing on both sides of Dionysus. What were maenads? They were young priestesses who worshiped Dionysus through dance. The word "maenad" means demented or crazy. As these young women danced, Dionysus's spirit possessed them. Don't be fooled by their seemingly harmless appearance! When these women were "under the influence," they developed superpowers and could kill an animal or person with their bare hands.

Dionysus and dancing maenads.[106]

Classical Greek statues had perfect, lifelike bodies. The artist Phidias built an imposing thirty-eight-foot-high statue of Athena for the Parthenon temple on the Acropolis. It had a wooden frame covered by sheets of gold. The goddess's arms and face were ivory. Her statue was eventually destroyed, but its image on Greek coins helps us know what it looked like. The white marble Parthenon temple still sits on the highest point of the Acropolis in Athens.

A life-sized replica of the Athena Parthenos.[107]

Groundbreaking Philosophy

Famous philosophers lived during the Golden Age of Athens. They discussed almost everything. They thought about what was right and wrong. How can a person really know the difference? They also talked about human nature. Were humans more important than animals? How does reason set humans apart from other creatures? They shared their theories on politics, math, science, and many other topics.

Hippias lived in the Peloponnese, but he visited Athens to argue with Socrates and Plato. He was a **_Sophist_** or an expert in wisdom. Plato loved to poke holes in his reasoning. Hippias discussed a wide range of topics, such as art, astronomy, history, math, music, and philosophy. He attended the Olympic Games. Anybody there could ask him to give a speech about any topic. He could speak about just about anything without preparing.

Hippias pointed out that society constantly changes its ideas about right and wrong. Because of this, he reasoned that we can't depend on society to define morality. Instead, he said a **_natural law_** applies to all places and times. This law never changes. What is right is always right, no matter where or when. Evil is always evil. For example, it's always right to help the weak and helpless.

The most famous philosophers from Athens were Socrates, Plato, and Aristotle. Socrates taught Plato, and Plato taught Aristotle. Aristotle taught Alexander the Great, who conquered much of the known world. Socrates never told his students what to think. Instead, he asked questions. He wanted them to think for themselves. Socrates admitted that he did not know everything. He knew he didn't have all the answers. He called this "simple ignorance." Socrates said this was better than clueless people who claimed to have all the answers. He called this "double ignorance."

Socrates said that an unexamined life is not worth living. What is an unexamined life? Some people live life thinking they already know everything they need to know. They are not interested in learning new things. Other people know that they have only tapped the surface of knowledge. An entire world is out there to explore. In their eyes, a worthy life is spent doing that.

Socrates faced trial on charges of impiety and corrupting Athens's youth. **_Impiety_** means "godlessness." The authorities said that Socrates did not believe in the gods of Athens. Socrates was not an **_atheist_** (someone who does not believe in a higher power). He did believe in his own god. However, he pointed out that the Greek gods were constantly cheating on their spouses, stealing things, and lying. They set a bad example for people to follow. The city leaders said that Socrates believed in "new spiritual things," and he did. His god was perfect, wise, and moral. By introducing this new idea of god and criticizing the Greek gods, Socrates was found guilty of leading young people away from the true religion. He was forced to commit suicide by drinking hemlock poison.

Socrates had to drink hemlock for corrupting Athens's youth. [108]

Plato taught that what we see around us isn't actual reality. He said it's like we're all living in a cave. The sun is outside, but we can't see the sun. All we can see are the shadows the sun casts into the cave. In his *Theory of Forms*, Plato said that philosophy was about understanding that something outside was causing these shadows. There's more to life than the cave. True reality is outside the cave, where there is sunshine, blue skies, and fresh air. If a person could escape from the cave, they could see that a better world is out there.

Plato's student Aristotle talked about the perfect, eternal, **unmoved mover**, who set everything into motion. He said this being brought order into the world. Aristotle came to this conclusion through deduction. What is ***deduction***? Aristotle said that if "premises," or ideas, about something are true, we can "deduce" or come to the correct conclusion.

For example, let's say we have the idea or premise that all kangaroos are mammals. Our second premise is that all mammals are warm-blooded. Our conclusion is that all kangaroos are warm-blooded. But what if we exchange kangaroos for elephants? Both premises would still be true. Elephants are mammals; thus, they are warm-blooded. But can we exchange elephants for jellyfish? No, because they aren't mammals. Both premises have to be true for a correct conclusion. Aristotle used this understanding of deduction to move on to ***induction***, which uses known facts to assume universal or well-known truths.

Developments in Democracy

All these philosophical discussions led to innovative ideas about democracy. That brings us to Pericles, who brought Athens to new political heights. In fact, the Golden Age of Athens is sometimes called the "Age of Pericles." He transformed Athens's government system into "the rule of the many instead of the few." His vision was to write a constitution that other Greek city-states could follow. Under Pericles's "radical democracy," everyone had equal justice by law. It didn't matter whether they were poor or lower class. They had the same rights. Well, the men did, at least. Women had few rights and had to depend on someone to represent them in court.

Pericles said the middle and lower classes should serve in government positions. He even paid for jury service so working-class citizens could take time off from their jobs to participate in the court system. Previously, only the wealthy served as city administrators because everyone else had to work. Now, city officials got paid so that anyone could do the job.

Pericles.[109]

The Delian League Ejects the Persians and Pirates

After most of southern Greece's city-states allied to squash Xerxes and his Persian invasion, they realized that cooperation was the key to keeping the Persians away forever. The Athenian colonies in Ionia revolted again. This time, they were successful. The allied Greek navy conquered part of Thrace on Greece's northeastern border. In 478 BCE, they captured Byzantium on the Bosporus Strait between Europe and Asia. Centuries later, Roman Emperor Constantine rebuilt Byzantium. He renamed it Constantinople, and it served as the capital of the Eastern Roman Empire.

With these victories, the Greeks controlled the Aegean Sea. At this point, Sparta was ready to withdraw from allied warfare. Sparta always had an independent streak. Plus, they were concerned about Ionia, which was just next to Persia's territory. They didn't think protecting Ionia was possible. They suggested moving all the Ionian Greeks to mainland Greece. This idea infuriated the Ionians, who had lived there for hundreds of years. The Athenians said, "They're our colonies. We can protect them ourselves!"

In 478 BCE, the Athenians took over the Delian League. This was the Greek alliance of Ionia and other islands and coastal cities in the Aegean Sea. The league's first naval commander was Cimon. He had fought in Marathon and Salamis against the Persians. The 330 cities that belonged to the alliance provided warships or money in the war against the Persian-Achaemenid Empire.

Meanwhile, the Persians assembled another enormous army and navy to attack Greece again. But Cimon struck first in a land and sea battle at Pamphylia in today's western Turkey. He sunk two hundred Persian ships and chased off their army. The Persians stayed out of the Aegean Sea for the next fifteen years. Cimon also drove the Dolopian pirates out of the Aegean, ensuring peaceful trade that enriched the Greeks.

After a successful battle in the north Aegean, Cimon and his Greek allies captured many prisoners. They also gained gold jewelry and priceless purple robes. Cimon asked the allies if they wanted the loot or the prisoners. "Choose whatever you want, and I'll take the other."

"Ha! These prisoners are all upper class. They've never worked a day in their lives. They'll be no good as slaves. We'll take the gold and the robes. You can have them."

So, Cimon took the prisoners. It wasn't long before their affluent families and friends paid Cimon money to free them. He put some money in the Delian League's treasury. He used some to support his navy and used the rest to host meals for the poor in his home.

Egypt had been an unwilling part of the Persian Empire. It revolted in 460 BCE. Pericles sailed 250 Greek ships to aid Egypt against the Persians. The Greeks suffered a devastating loss of twenty thousand men and most of their fleet. This disaster prompted Pericles to move the Delian League's treasury to Athens for "safekeeping." The payments from the city-states went to Athens. Pericles spent it on his building projects on the Acropolis. Athens was now an empire. Yes, the city-states grumbled. Some even tried to pull out of the Delian League, but they were severely punished by Pericles.

Pericles captured the island of Cyprus in the northeastern Mediterranean, but the Persians took it back. In 451 BCE, Cimon sailed with two hundred ships to reclaim Cyprus. He died in the battle, but his officers kept his death a secret until they won the battle. Greece and Persia signed the Callias Treaty, which brought thirty years of peace. The Persians promised to leave Ionia alone and to stay out of the Aegean Sea. The Greeks returned Cyprus to the Persians and promised not to interfere in North Africa or Turkey.

Round-up Activity: You're a Greek Artist!

Below is a blank amphora vase. Use your creativity and imagination to design a picture on the vase. Review the scenes in the book so far for inspiration. Greek vase decorations included battles, everyday life, and Greek deities. You might want to color the picture in gold or red and the background in black.

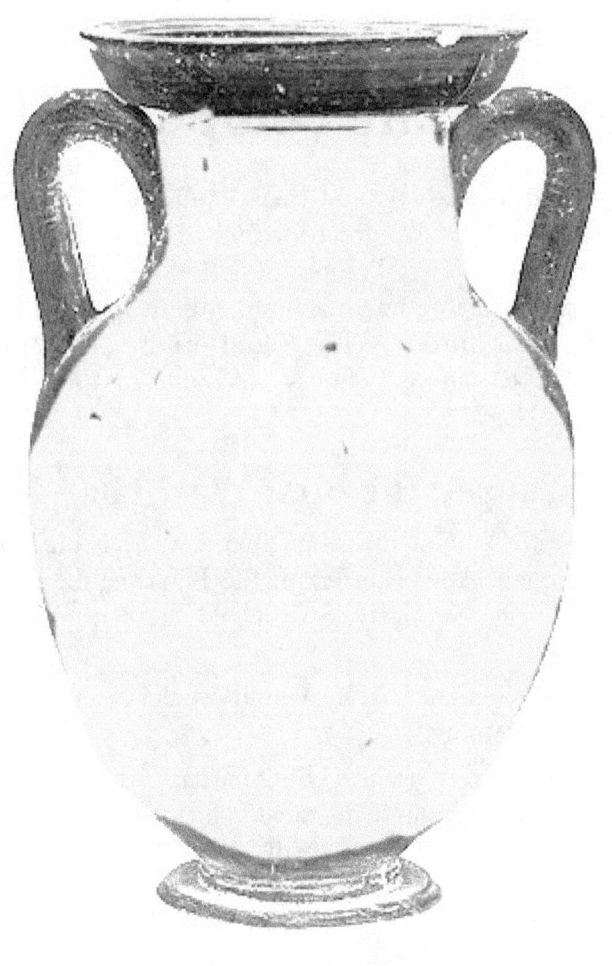

Chapter 7: The Peloponnesian War

For twenty-six years, Athens and Sparta were at each other's throats. It wasn't the first time the two great forces had clashed. An earlier conflict, sometimes called the First Peloponnesian War, raged for fifteen years. Sparta was an unbeatable war machine. Athens had the Delian League's unparalleled naval force. Who would win? The Athenian general Thucydides wrote an eyewitness account in his *History of the Peloponnesian War*.

What Caused the First War? (460–445 BCE)

It all started with a helot uprising. Sparta was stirring up trouble even before that, though. After chasing off the Persians, the Athenians started rebuilding their city. Strangely, Sparta told them not to rebuild the city walls.

"Those crazy Spartans! Why would we leave Athens unprotected? They're up to something!"

The Athenians were right. The Spartans were planning to invade Athens. But two disasters distracted the Spartans. An earthquake occurred, killing thousands. Shortly after, the helots revolted. The Spartans sent word to all their allies, asking for help. Athens was still an ally then. After all, they had fought side by side against Persia. But when Athens sent four hundred men, the Spartans sent them back home.

The Athenians were offended. "Really? They took everyone else's help but not ours? Do they think we'd fight on the helots' side?"

The Spartans finally got the helots under control. But what would keep them from rebelling again? It was time for them to leave! The Spartans kicked them off the Peloponnese Peninsula, which dramatically changed Sparta's structure. Now, not all its men could serve full-time in the army. Somebody needed to stay home and do the farming. The Athenians inserted themselves into the situation by resettling the helots at Naupaktos (today's Nafpaktos) on a narrow strait where the Ionian Sea flows into the Gulf of Corinth. That meant the helots controlled the region's sea trade and ships.

Key cities in the Peloponnesian War.[110]

What Happened in the First War?

The Athenians knew they would soon come to blows with Sparta. They had the Delian League, but they needed to cement other partnerships. They allied with Argos and Megara, which were located between Sparta and Athens. These cities were strategic for controlling the Saronic Gulf and the Isthmus of Corinth. But Megara and Corinth were at war. If Athens allied with Megara, it would get sucked into the war. This conflict began the First Peloponnesian War in 460 BCE.

Athens fought on two fronts at the same time. It helped Libya and Egypt in their attempt to leave the Persian Empire. After sending two hundred ships to North Africa, Athens was short of men and ships to fight Corinth. Athens lost the land wars but scored a victory when its navy captured seventy Peloponnesian warships. When Corinth attacked Megara, most of the Athenian soldiers were at sea. The elderly men and young boys of Athens formed a small army and marched to aid Megara. They won the battle!

Sparta initially stayed out of the fray. It only got involved to help the city of Doris fight Phocis. Both towns were near the helots' new location at Naupaktos, and Sparta wanted friends in the area. The Spartans beat Phocis, but the Athenian navy blocked their way back to the Peloponnese. The enraged Spartans marched toward Athens. The Athenians tried to stop them at Boeotia, but they lost the battle. Sparta also took a brutal hit. The Spartans decided not to attack Athens and headed home.

Athens's navy came into play at this point. It sailed around the Peloponnese Peninsula and attacked its coastal towns. Sparta had never built a navy, so it could not fight the Athenians at sea. To the Spartans' relief, the Persians scored a stunning victory in Egypt, destroying Athens's fleet there. Athens quickly agreed to the Thirty Years' Peace with Sparta and its Peloponnesian allies. However, the peace would only last half that time.

What Started the Second War? (431–404 BCE)

The Corinthians sparked the breakdown in the Thirty Years' Peace. They had a falling out with their colony of Corcyra in northern Greece. When the Corinthians began to build a naval fleet with its Peloponnesian allies, Corcyra begged Athens for help. Athens sent a small fleet to Corcyra. The commander had strict instructions, though. "You're only there to protect Corcyra. Do not attack the Corinthian fleet! If you do, you will break the Thirty Years' Peace."

The Athenian commander couldn't resist launching an attack. He assumed it would be an easy win. It wasn't. Athens had to send more ships to save the day. Meanwhile, other city-states in northern Greece had become increasingly dissatisfied with the Delian League. They were sending a lot of money to Athens and not seeing any benefits. What's worse, the Athenians were bossing them around, telling them how to run their cities.

Corinth thought the time was ripe to get the upper hand over Athens. The Corinthians visited the Spartans to see if they could stir things up. The Athenians heard about it and crashed the party. The old men of the Spartan assembly scowled as the Corinthian and Athenian delegates traded jabs. Then, the Corinthians challenged the Spartans. "You're too passive! If you don't act soon, you'll be surrounded by Athenians!"

The Athenians jumped in, saying, "You'll lose if you break the Thirty Years' Peace. You don't even have a navy! And we have the best navy in the world!"

The Spartans replied, "The way we see it, you Athenians have already broken the treaty. War is on the table!"

General Thucydides of Athens tried calming the hotheads down, "My brothers! Think! War is unpredictable. Count the cost before committing to war. The longer a war lasts, the more things can go wrong. Everyone does war the wrong way around. They leap into action without thinking. It is only after suffering that they begin to think."

Thucydides. [111]

The Second War Begins

By this point, Megara had fallen out with Athens and allied with Sparta. Athens set up a blockade, keeping ships from delivering grain to Megara. Megara asked Sparta for help. The Spartans and Athenians ended up fighting outside Megara's walls. Athens had never won a land battle against Sparta's fierce army. It didn't win this one either. The Athenians left, but Sparta took the war to Athens.

The Siege of Athens

The Spartans surrounded Athens and stole all the produce from the farms around Athens. But General Pericles brought the rural people inside the city, warning everyone not to fight the Spartans. That would be suicidal. He ordered grain from Ionia and Egypt to feed the people. Meanwhile, the Athenian navy blocked any ships from reaching the Peloponnese. Sparta and its allies could not get grain or supplies.

A Horrifying Plague Strikes Athens

The Athenians were receiving plenty of grain shipments. They had enough food. However, the ships brought something else: the plague! Rats on the ships probably carried it. Thucydides got the plague. He was one of the few who recovered. It caused diarrhea, vomiting, and lung infection. People went blind. Their fingers and toes turned black and fell off. The plague killed one-third of the Athenians, including Pericles.

No one knew much about how disease spread in those days. Thucydides noticed that if the vultures ate the dead people, the birds died. He also observed that if someone got the plague and recovered, they didn't get it again. An upside to the plague was that once the Spartans heard about it, they raced away from Athens as fast as their legs could carry them. The people in the Peloponnese peninsula didn't get the plague. The Athenian blockade had kept ships from reaching the peninsula.

The Peace of Nicias

The plague eventually ended, and Athens slowly recovered its strength. The Athenians built forts around the Peloponnese, and its navy resumed attacking the coastal towns. One day, the Spartans attacked an Athenian fort, Pylos. The Athenians beat the Spartans this time! That had never happened before in a land battle. The Athenians were hopeful they could win the war.

That hope turned to worry when the Spartans marched to Thrace. They conquered Athens's colony of Amphipolis, which had silver mines. The angry Athenians exiled General Thucydides for not getting to Thrace in time. General Cleon of Athens and General Brasidas of Sparta died in the Battle of Amphipolis. Athens and Sparta were tired of fighting and agreed to stop the war.

Athens and Sparta formed the fifty-year Peace of Nicias. They exchanged prisoners of war and returned most of the territories they had taken from each other. The peace treaty only lasted six years. The rest of the Peloponnesian cities wanted nothing to do with it. They formed a separate alliance and attacked Sparta. Sparta defeated the rebels and forced them to join the Peloponnesian League.

The Sicilian Expedition

General Alcibiades was Athens's young and handsome new star. He was a con man. When Sparta's ambassadors came to Athens to hash out the details of the Peace of Nicias, he snatched power. He targeted Syracuse in Sicily. Sicily is the island at the toe of Italy's boot. Syracuse was one of the world's richest cities. It was allied with Sparta at that time.

Indigenous people lived in Sicily long before the Greeks set up colonies there. Segesta was a small indigenous city under attack by the city-state of Selinus, located on Sicily's western coast. Selinus had close ties to Syracuse and Sparta. Segesta begged Athens to help. Athens was happy to help. Maybe they could conquer Syracuse in the process. The Sicilian Expedition set sail in 415 BCE with 284 ships and 6,300 soldiers. They were led by generals Alcibiades, Lamachus, and Nicias.

Ship route from Athens to Syracuse.[118]

As the fleet approached Sicily, the three generals discussed their strategy. Nicias wanted a moderate approach. "We'll stop Selinus's attack on Segesta, sail around Sicily so everyone can see the size of our fleet, and then head home."

Alcibiades thought Nicias's plan didn't go far enough. "We should ally with the Ionian-Greek cities on Sicily. Together, we can take Syracuse!"

Lamachus had an even bolder plan. "Syracuse isn't expecting us. We should sail to Syracuse first and capture the city before they know what's happening!"

After arguing a bit, the generals agreed to do Alcibiades's plan. That didn't go well. The Ionian Greeks didn't want to attack Syracuse. Then, a ship arrived from Athens. Its captain grabbed Alcibiades. "You're coming with us to Athens. You need to stand trial!"

Back in Athens, someone had damaged a number of statues of the god Hermes. Alcibiades was blamed. He boarded the ship but escaped when it got to Italy. Angry at Athens, he turned traitor and offered his services to the Spartans. They welcomed his insider knowledge of Athens.

The Weird Battle of the Walls

When Alcibiades told the Spartans about the Athenian plan to take Syracuse, Sparta sailed its brand new navy to Sicily. Meanwhile, the Athenians had begun a siege of Syracuse. But they had lost the element of surprise. Syracuse quickly built a new wall to protect the city. Then, the Athenians started building a wall to block Syracuse from its harbor. Realizing their plan, the Syracusans began building a counter-wall going directly from the city to the harbor. Both sides raided the other's wall to keep it from going up.

During one raid, the Syracusans killed General Lamachus, leaving only Nicias in control. Nicias had trouble deciding what to do. He wasted a lot of time. He didn't finish the wall blocking the harbor before Sparta's ships arrived. When Sparta's fleet landed with 2,700 men, Nicias decided to launch a sea battle. That didn't go well.

Just when Nicias decided to sail back to Athens, a lunar eclipse happened. Nicias was very superstitious. He visited a soothsayer (someone who predicts the future by consulting supernatural beings or using intuition and logic). The soothsayer told Nicias the eclipse meant he should wait twenty-seven days before doing anything. The delay was fatal. The Syracusan and Spartan fleets trapped the Athenian ships in the harbor and sank them. They surrounded the Athenians' land army, killing thousands of men. They imprisoned the rest. Most of the men starved to death.

The Third Wave

After Athens's devastating loss in Sicily, Sparta launched a fierce assault on Decelea, which was just north of Athens. This cut off supplies from northern Greece. Sparta also retook Athens's silver mines in Thrace. Syracuse sent a fleet to Greece, and the Persians built more ships for Sparta. They wanted Greece to tear itself apart. The Persians also retook Ionia. To make matters worse, Athens experienced a political revolt and rejected democracy. Athens's navy refused to acknowledge the new leadership.

Alcibiades. [118]

Alcibiades switched sides again when King Agis of Sparta discovered he was having an affair with his wife. Athens's navy made him its new admiral. Alcibiades was a good commander. He led the Athenian navy to an incredible victory in 410 BCE. He crushed the fleets of Sparta and Syracuse. He also took back Ionia. The Athenians were so happy that they embraced democracy again.

But then, Alcibiades lost a battle to the Spartans in Ephesus on Turkey's western shore. Athens voted him out as general. Athens executed six other generals. Although they had sunk seventy Spartan ships, a sudden storm kept them from rescuing their own men.

Without Alcibiades and these other experienced generals, the Athenian navy was crippled. Sparta dominated the Aegean Sea and the Dardanelles. The Spartans cut off grain shipments from the Black Sea to Athens. When Athens sailed out to confront the Spartan navy, they suffered a loss at the Battle of Aegospotami. They lost 168 ships and 4,000 sailors.

Outcomes

Without a navy, the war was over for Athens. The city and its allies surrendered in 404 BCE. They had to take down the city walls and give their remaining warships to Sparta. They no longer had city-states sending tribute. Sparta replaced Athens with its own empire. It placed its own governors and military posts in cities throughout Greece. Sparta ejected democracy. It enforced its *oligarchy* system (rule by elders) throughout Greece.

Round-up Activity: True or False?

Can you tell which statements are true and which are false? Check your answers in the back of the book.

1. Homer gave an eyewitness account of the Peloponnesian War. ( )
2. The Athenians resettled the helots at Naupaktos. ( )
3. Athens also fought in North Africa during the first war. ( )
4. Thucydides thought going to war was a great idea. ( )
5. The plague didn't kill many people in Athens. ( )
6. The fifty-year Peace of Nicias only lasted six years. ( )
7. The war moved to Sicily when Athens agreed to help Segesta. ( )
8. General Nicias made quick and sound decisions that won the war in Sicily. ( )
9. Alcibiades switched sides to Sparta and then back to Athens again. ( )
10. Athens won the final Battle of Aegospotami against Sparta. ( )

Chapter 8: Alexander the Great

Who could have guessed that little-known Macedonia would conquer all of Greece? Who would have thought that a united Macedonian-Greek army would wipe out the Persian Empire? Alexander and his father, Philip, were men with big dreams. They had the courage and skill to chase those dreams. And those dreams came true. Alexander ruled an empire covering three continents.

King Philip's Conquests

Macedonia was a large but poor nation north of Greece. Philip II's father was the king. Philip was the youngest of his father's three sons. When Philip's father died, his oldest brother, Alexander II, became king (not to be confused with Alexander the Great). Thebes rose to power over Greece and its neighbors. General Pelopidas forced King Alexander to ally with Thebes. Alexander had to send his youngest brother Philip as a hostage to Thebes. This was to make sure Alexander stayed loyal to Thebes.

Ptolemy, Philip's mother's lover, murdered Alexander so he could take control of the throne. Although the middle brother, Perdiccas, was officially king, he was too young to rule. Ptolemy ruled as his regent (adult representative ruler) until Perdiccas grew up and killed him. In the meantime, Philip II lived in Thebes as a hostage. He was well treated and schooled in Theban military arts.

Perdiccas died in battle, so Philip II became king. Philip wanted to be the ruler of the world's greatest empire. He invented a new weapon, the *sarissa*, a spear three times longer than a man. With his unbeatable army and deadly sarissas, he set out to achieve his dream. Philip captured today's Albania, Bulgaria, Serbia, and Kosovo. He invaded Thrace, grabbed Athens's silver mines, and took control of central Greece.

Alexander and Aristotle

Alexander III (Alexander the Great) was the son of Philip's fourth wife, Olympias. Philip hired Aristotle to teach Alexander when he was thirteen. The famous philosopher taught Alexander ethics, politics, and logical thinking. Alexander found these skills helpful when making quick judgments. They also helped him when he had to set up a government in his new empire.

Aristotle gave Alexander many of the Greek classics to read. Alexander's favorite book was the *Iliad*, the story of the Trojan War. He read it a lot. It was practical information that Alexander could apply to warfare. Alexander couldn't get enough of the stories of Achilles, who became his role model. When he led his army to northwestern Turkey, he stopped at the ruins of ancient Troy to honor Achilles's grave.

The Art of War

Aristotle taught Alexander how to think, but his father taught him how to fight. Alexander learned to ride a horse and fight when he was a child. When Alexander was sixteen, Philip put him in charge of Macedonia when he went to war. Alexander had to fend off rebel tribes in his father's absence. Both of them often went to war together. Sometimes, Philip sent his teenage son to lead an army on his own.

When Alexander was eighteen, he and Philip fought the Battle of Chaeronea against Thebes, Corinth, and Athens. Philip was on the right side of the Macedonian army facing Athens. Alexander commanded the left against Thebes. Other Macedonian officers fought the Corinthians in the middle. The Greek military stretched for three miles. Alexander destroyed the Thebans. Philip and his other generals beat Athens and Corinth.

Macedonia's victory convinced the Greeks to join the Macedonians. In 337 BCE, Greece's city-states united with Macedonia in the League of Corinth. They swore not to fight each other so they could fight Persia together. Philip would be their commander in chief. Philip's first move was to send General Parmenion across the Aegean Sea with ten thousand soldiers. His orders were to free the Greek city-states in Ionia from Persian rule.

Philip II of Macedonia. [114]

Persian Poison

Meanwhile, the Persian Empire was in chaos. The Persian kings had many wives and concubines. Concubines were sexual partners of the king and other men of high status. They were usually foreign women and not official wives. Concubines generally held a servant status, but some achieved a fairly high standing through palace intrigues.

Because of their many wives and concubines, Persian kings often had one hundred children or more. One king, Artaxerxes III, killed eighty of his half-brothers in one day shortly after he came to the throne. He didn't want any of them to lead a revolt against him. Several years later, his chief officer Bagoas poisoned him and any other royal males who survived the earlier purge.

With all the royal males dead, Bagoas introduced a young man to the court. "This is Darius III. He's the great-grandson of Darius the Great!"

Darius III had served as governor of Armenia. He was also the royal postmaster. Nothing had prepared him to lead an empire. Bagoas wanted Darius to be a figurehead so Bagoas could run things. Darius didn't want Bagoas to be in control. So, Bagoas decided to poison him too. But then, Darius handed Bagoas his cup of wine. "Drink a toast to me!"

Bagoas took the cup, trembling. He knew it had poison in it, but what could he do? With Bagoas dead, Darius could focus on defending his empire against the Macedonian-Greek threat.

Unexpected Murder

In Macedonia, King Philip threw a wedding for his daughter. As he entered the banquet hall, his bodyguard and jealous former lover shoved a dagger between his ribs. Philip collapsed to the floor in a pool of blood. The Macedonian nobility looked in horror at their dead king. Philip only had three sons. Arrhidaeus was *cognitively* (mentally) challenged. Caranus was still a baby. Macedonia's generals surrounded Alexander and crowned him as their new king.

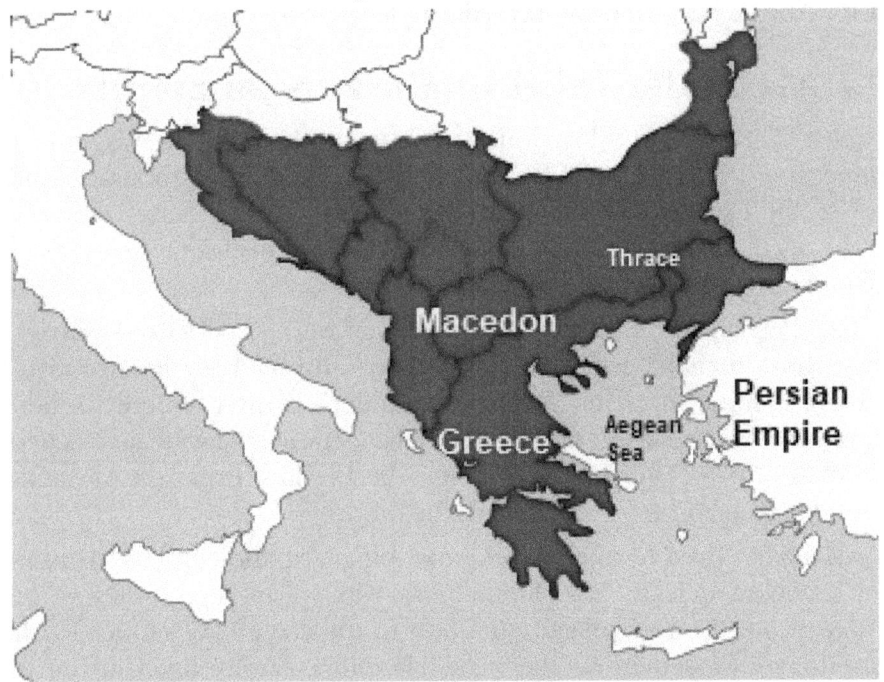

Philip ruled most of the Balkan Peninsula at the time of his murder. [115]

Reconquering Greece

After hearing of Philip's death, Athens and Thebes dropped out of the League of Corinth. Thessaly, Thrace, and Corinth followed their lead. Other cities considered their options. The Macedonians' planned Persian Empire takeover was in trouble.

Alexander marched to northern Greece. The Theban army was waiting for him at the Mount Olympus pass. Alexander took them by surprise. He took a different way around the mountain at night. When he showed up at the Thebans' rear the following morning, he caught them off guard. They immediately surrendered.

Alexander marched into southern Greece, where Athens and Corinth met him apologetically. The Greeks there assured him they would rejoin the league. Alexander turned north. His next target was Thrace. It took a year to make Thrace submit.

Meanwhile, Athens and Thebes had backed out again. Alexander was exasperated and tired of this game. He had spared them the first time. He knew he needed to set an example of what happens to rebels. He hammered Thebes, enslaved its people, and gave its farmland to nearby towns. Athens begged for mercy. Alexander gave it.

Alexander Takes on the Persian Empire

Greece, Thrace, and Macedonia were together again. It was time to pounce on Persia! In 334 BCE, Alexander and forty thousand men crossed the Dardanelles into Asia. When word reached King Darius III, he shrugged and stayed in his palace. "What can this twenty-two-year-old do? My generals will chase him off."

The Persian generals in western Turkey were experienced warriors. They chose their battlefield at the Granicus River. They lined up on a cliff overlooking the river, forcing Alexander's army to come to them. The swift, churning river was sixty feet (eighteen meters) wide and as deep as a man's thigh. The sun was setting. The Persians expected Alexander to set up camp and cross the river in the morning.

Alexander loved to catch his enemies off guard, though. His men took their positions quickly. His elite infantry, with spears three times as long as a man, set up their phalanx position in the center. Alexander led his Macedonian horsemen on the right. His other cavalry lined up on the left. They were guided by an experienced general named Parmenion.

Alexander led the charge as the sky turned black with Persian arrows. His cavalry galloped across the river and climbed the steep bluff. This distracted the Persians and allowed the Greek infantry to wade across the river.

As Alexander's horse reached the top of the steep bank, Alexander thrust his spear into Mithridates, King Darius's son-in-law. But the battleax of a Persian governor, Spithridates, came crashing down on Alexander's helmet, breaking it in half. Miraculously, Alexander was not seriously hurt. His best friend, Black Cleitus, speared Spithridates.

By this point, the rest of Alexander's army was crossing the river. They clawed their way up the bluff. When they reached the top and moved into formation with twenty-foot-spears, the Persians' knees buckled under them. They had never faced off against a Greek phalanx. They had never seen such long spears. The panicked Persians raced off the battlefield.

Alexander, sculpted in the 3rd century BCE by Menas. [116]

After this victory, the Ionian cities under Persian control surrendered. Alexander attacked the ports of Miletus and Halicarnassus, paralyzing the Perian navy. As he passed through Phrygia, someone pointed out the Gordian Knot. "They say King Midas tied this. Anyone who can untie it will be the ruler of all Asia!"

Alexander inspected the knot. It actually consisted of multiple knots all tangled together. Alexander frowned. Then, he grinned. "Ruler of all Asia, you say?"

He pulled his sword and sliced the knot in two. "Done!"

Darius Runs Away

"Idiots!" King Darius growled. "They ran off the battlefield! I'll have to lead the next battle myself."

Alexander's army marched south along the Mediterranean coast, near Turkey's border with Syria. Without warning, Darius and his army surprised them from behind. They trapped the Greeks between the mountains and sea at the Pinarus River. But Alexander's men knew the drill. They fell into formation like clockwork. They used the same tried-and-true positions as in the previous battle.

The Persians used Greek mercenaries to fight for them. Darius's Greek forces were in the center. Darius's cavalry was by the sea. His Persian foot soldiers stretched along the river into the foothills.

Some Persian foot soldiers crossed the river. They wanted to draw out the Macedonian cavalry. Meanwhile, the Persian cavalry charged over the river, crashing into General Parmenion's cavalry on the left side.

Alexander led a cavalry charge on the right wing. His men broke up the Persian infantry. However, his foot soldiers in the center were getting stuck in the swift river. They couldn't move with their heavy shields and long sarissas. They did not dare to go deeper. When Alexander glanced over and saw his infantry pulling back from the river, he charged directly toward King Darius's chariot. When Darius saw Alexander racing toward him, he wheeled his chariot around and raced off the battlefield. When his men saw their king run away, they looked at each other, wondering what to do. One glance at the Greek horses charging their way settled the matter. They ran off at full speed with the Greeks in hot pursuit.

King Darius III from a mosaic in Pompeii. [117]

Darius was so panicked that he left his mother, pregnant wife, and two daughters behind. The Persians had a habit of taking their women along when they went to war. Alexander took the women and girls with him. He treated them kindly. When the queen died in childbirth, he honored her with a royal funeral. After conquering the empire, Alexander married Stateira II, one of Darius's daughters.

Alexander's army marched south. All the Phoenician cities on Lebanon's coast surrendered. Ancient Tyre was the only holdout. The city was on an offshore island and surrounded by high walls. For seven long months, Alexander tried to break into the city. He built a causeway to the island, but ships from Tyre constantly attacked the workers. Finally, the Ionian Greeks, the other Phoenicians, and the people of the island of Cyprus offered their ships. Alexander attacked Tyre with a fleet of 220 ships and took the city. He crucified two thousand men and enslaved the rest.

Egypt had spent centuries trying to get rid of the Persians. The Egyptians cheered as Alexander marched in. They crowned him their new pharaoh and turned over the royal treasury. Alexander built the city of Alexandria on the Mediterranean coast. Alexandria became the capital of Egypt. It was a key naval base and a bustling center of *Hellenistic* (Greek) artists, scientists, philosophers, and religious leaders.

May I Have My Women Back?

While Alexander was in Egypt, Darius wrote him, asking him to return his mother and daughters. "I'll give you half my empire, a fortune in gold, and one of my daughters in marriage."

Alexander chuckled. "I have both daughters, and I don't plan to stop until I have the whole empire."

The two kings faced off at the Battle of Gaugamela in northern Iraq. This time, Darius had war elephants and scythed chariots. The chariots had three-foot blades sticking out from the wheel hubs. They could cut a man's leg off. However, the Macedonian phalanx was highly flexible. The infantry simply moved over to let the chariots pass.

King Darius was in the center of his army. Alexander led his cavalry around the side. They outflanked the Persians and drew them out from the center. Darius panicked and raced off, followed by his men. He tried to regroup, but one of his governors murdered him, ending the Persian-Achaemenid Empire.

Battle of Gaugamela. [118]

Cultural Interchange

Alexander marched south and entered Babylon. He respected the Middle Eastern culture and began dressing like the locals. His Greek and Macedonian men thought this was a bit odd. They felt he'd gone too far when he started requiring them to bow down and kiss the ground. Babylon became Alexander's headquarters, and he made plans to restore it to its former glory.

Alexander appointed leaders to oversee all the provinces and cities he conquered. He kept most of the same rulers in place. All they had to do was pledge their loyalty to him. He founded dozens of cities named Alexandria. They became hubs for a new cultural fusion of Greek and Middle Eastern ways.

On to the Indian Subcontinent!

Alexander headed to the eastern border of the Persian Empire at the Jaxartes River in today's Tajikistan. He conquered the nomadic tribes of Central Asia. On the way, he captured Roxana, a beautiful princess of the Sogdian people, and married her. When Alexander reached the Jaxartes River, he kept going. He crossed the Hindu Kush mountains into Pakistan. But his soldiers had been away from home for ten years. They were worn out. They wanted to be with their families. So, they refused to take another step east.

Sudden Death and Split Empire

Alexander had no choice but to return to Babylon. He threw a wedding. Eighty Persian princesses married his officers. He married two princesses on the same day: Darius III's daughter and Artaxerxes III's daughter. Soon after hearing the thrilling news that his first wife, Roxana, was pregnant, he became ill. He died at the age of thirty-two. He had never lost a battle.

Alexander's unexpected death plunged the new empire into confusion. He had no chosen heirs. Was Roxana's unborn child a boy or a girl? Who should rule now? How could one person rule three continents? Finally, his generals decided to divide the empire among themselves. Roxana's child (if it was a boy) and Alexander's cognitively challenged brother Arrhidaeus would be joint kings. General Perdiccas would be regent. The generals each took a section of the empire to govern. However, their plans fell apart within months.

Alexander followed in his father's footsteps. He successfully united Greece. Alexander even conquered the world's superpower of his day. He ranks as one of history's most successful military commanders. His military tactics are still studied today. By the age of thirty-two, he had created the largest empire the world had yet seen. Alexander's conquests spread the Greek-Hellenistic culture across his new empire, starting the Hellenistic Age, an era of astonishing scientific and artistic advances.

Round-up Activity: Quiz

1. In what ways did Alexander's upbringing and education influence his leadership style and approach to warfare?

2. What were some of the key military tactics that Alexander the Great used in his conquests? How did these tactics contribute to his success?

3. What events destabilized Persia shortly before Alexander's invasion?

4. How did Alexander view Eastern cultures? What cultural changes did he encourage, and how did he do that?

5. What was Alexander's lasting legacy?

Chapter 9: The Hellenistic Age

"This is Alexander's ring!" General Perdiccas held the ring high. "He gave it to me on his deathbed. I shall rule as the regent for Arrhidaeus and Roxana's son."

The council of generals erupted in anger. "How do we know Roxana will have a son? Arrhidaeus isn't even fit to rule."

"He's Alexander's only living brother. Yes, he's not bright, but we can guide him," Perdiccas insisted. "If Roxana has a girl, Arrhidaeus will be our king. If she has a boy, we'll have two kings."

"And you'll have all the power," the generals complained.

"We will *all* have power," Perdiccas stated. "Each of you will rule a chunk of the empire."

The Partition of Babylon

What did the new leadership plan—the Partition of Babylon—look like? Perdiccas was to command the army and be the regent for Roxana's baby (if a son) and Arrhidaeus. The other generals, called the ***Diadochi*** (successors), each took a section of the empire. Antipater, Ptolemy, and Antigonus were the primary players. General Antipater continued to rule Greece and Macedonia. Alexander had appointed him as regent when he was away conquering the Persian Empire. Egypt went to General Ptolemy. One-eyed Antigonus got southwestern Turkey.

With that settled, Perdiccas walked through the palace to Roxana's room. "Time to tie up some loose ends."

Roxana nodded. "I have everything ready."

They swept into the room of Alexander's two Persian wives, Stateira and Parysatis II. Perdiccas nodded to the princesses. "The generals have made their decision. They will govern the provinces. I will be regent for Arrhidaeus and Roxana's child if it's a son."

Princess Parysatis frowned. "What happens to us?"

Roxana smiled reassuringly. "You can return to Persia or stay here in Babylon. Now, let's drink a toast to our departed husband and the future of his empire."

Perdiccas opened a new bottle and poured out four cups. He handed one to each woman and took a long drink from his cup. "May Alexander's legacy live on."

The three women drank from their cups. Then, Perdiccas and Roxana spoke a few more assuring words and left. As they walked down the corridor, Perdiccas turned to Roxana. "How?"

Roxana laughed. "The poison was in the cups, not the bottle. They'll be dead within hours."

Wars of the Diadochi

Roxana had a baby boy two months later. She named him Alexander IV. Arrhidaeus married his niece, Eurydice, in a match arranged by Perdiccas. Meanwhile, General Ptolemy stole Alexander's body when it was on its way to Macedonia for burial. He said, "Alexander wanted us to bury him in Egypt! I'm honoring his request." To this day, no one knows where Alexander's tomb is located.

In 322 BCE, Athenians rebelled against Antipater's rule over Greece in the Lamian War. They chased him out of southern Greece. Antipater would have lost the war if General Craterus of Macedonia hadn't come to the rescue. Together, they crushed the Athenian army in Thessaly. After this devastating loss, Antipater ended democracy in Athens. He forced the Athenians to submit to a council of elders.

Seleucus I.[119]

Perdiccas didn't last long as regent. His officers rebelled and killed him. The generals worked out a new arrangement. Antipater became regent for Arrhidaeus and two-year-old Alexander IV. He brought them to Macedon. Seleucus, one of the officers involved in the plot against Perdiccas, became the ruler of Babylon. He eventually formed the Seleucid Empire, which covered the Middle East at its height.

Antipater died in 319 BCE. He appointed General Polyperchon as his replacement in his will. But Antipater's son, Cassander, refused to accept it. He allied with Ptolemy and Antigonus. They attacked Polyperchon. Polyperchon couldn't fend off three armies. He took Roxana and little Alexander to Epirus in northwest Greece, where he hoped they would be safe.

Alexander the Great's mother, Olympias, got involved in 317 BCE. Arrhidaeus was the son of her rival, one of Philip's other wives. She wanted her grandson, Alexander IV, to sit on the throne. She attacked

Macedonia with General Polyperchon. The soldiers refused to fight Alexander the Great's mother. Olympias ordered Arrhidaeus's execution. Eurydice committed suicide.

Olympias, Alexander the Great's mother.¹³⁰

The tables turned against Olympias when Ptolemy, Antigonus, and Cassander successfully attacked Macedon. Olympias was stoned to death. Polyperchon escaped to southern Greece. Cassander now ruled Macedonia and northern Greece. He locked Roxana and the boy-king Alexander in a tower for years. Eventually, he poisoned them. By that point, no one cared. The generals had become so powerful they were kings in their own right. Antigonus ruled Turkey, Lebanon, and Syria. Ptolemy was still the pharaoh of Egypt. Seleucus controlled much of the Middle East.

Showdown at Ipsus

In 302 BCE, southern Greece (except Sparta) united under Demetrius, the son of Antigonus. His enemy Cassander drummed up support in northern Greece. He also had the support of General Lysimachus in Thrace. Cassander invited Seleucus to join them in the war against Antigonus and Demetrius. Seleucus was wrapping up a war in north India. He lost, but he hashed out an agreeable settlement. King Chandragupta Maurya gave him five hundred war elephants. Seleucus gave Chandragupta his daughter to marry.

Seleucus marched to Turkey from India with his elephants. With Lysimachus marching in from Thrace, Antigonus desperately needed Demetrius to come help him. Demetrius blocked the Dardanelles when Cassander tried to send troops. Cassander then put his men on ships, but only one-third of the vessels made it. Demetrius captured some, and a storm sank the others. In the Battle of Ipsus, Antigonus and Demetrius had seventy thousand troops, ten thousand cavalry, and seventy-five elephants. The allies had sixty-four thousand foot soldiers, fifteen thousand cavalry, and Seleucus's five hundred elephants.

Seleucus launched a charge of two hundred elephants. Demetrius's seventy-five elephants were outnumbered. The main problem was that Demetrius's cavalry wasn't up to the challenge. The horses galloped off the field. However, Antigonus's foot soldiers began pushing the allied forces back.

Demetrius got his calvary under control, and the horses raced back on the field. It was time for Seleucus to bring out the rest of the elephants! The massive beasts frightened Demetrius's horses right back off the field. Seleucus brought his horses around on the other side, shattering Antigonus's phalanx. King Antigonus died in a hail of javelins. Demetrius ran off to Greece.

Hellenistic Culture Transforms Asia, Africa, and Europe

As the Greeks established cities in North Africa and Asia, they spread their philosophical, artistic, and scientific knowledge. The Greeks picked up aspects from the cultures of North Africa, the Middle East, and India. As Rome interacted with Greece, it imitated Greek sculptures, literature, and other cultural elements, spreading the Hellenistic culture throughout Europe.

Antioch in Syria and Alexandria in Egypt were two dynamic centers of Hellenism. Alexandria was the intellectual center. It had a mind-blowing library of a half million scrolls on history, literature, religion, and science. It had observatories for studying astronomy and laboratories for developing science. Mathematicians like Euclid and Eratosthenes taught there.

Ptolemy II, Egypt's second Macedonian pharaoh. [191]

Alexander the Great and his successors spoke and wrote Koine Greek. It became the common language around the Mediterranean and in the Middle East. Ptolemy II, Egypt's second Macedonian pharaoh, had the Jewish Tanakh (Old Testament) translated into Koine Greek. This Septuagint translation was used in Jewish synagogues in Jesus's day. The Apostles wrote the New Testament in Koine Greek.

What Happened to the Greek City-states?

Sparta's population was dwindling fast. Over two-thirds of its men died in battle. The fighting men had trouble maintaining their farms once the helots left. A few wealthy families held much of the land. Everyone else suffered under crushing debt. They had no way to feed their families. In 245 BCE, Agis IV became one of Sparta's kings. He had ideas for radical reform. He planned to forgive all debts and redivide all the farmland so every family had an equal plot again.

The wealthy landowners did not want to give up their land. They had the other king, Leonidas, on their side. When the council voted, Agis lost by one vote. But then Agis pulled out his trump card. "May I remind the council that Leonidas is more Persian than Spartan? He grew up in Persia and married a Persian woman, which is against our law. He lives a life of luxury rather than our simple Spartan ways."

It worked. The council kicked Leonidas out. Agis decided to hold off on land redistribution. That policy seemed too radical. However, he did cancel everyone's debts. But when he headed out to war, Leonidas snuck back into town and took his throne back. When Agis returned, Leonidas strangled him.

Cleomenes was Leonidas's son. One day, he returned from a hunting trip when his father announced he had arranged a marriage for him.

"To whom?"

"To Agiatis, the widow of Agis."

Cleomenes knew his father wanted the wealthy woman's estate. How on earth would this crazy marriage work? His father had killed her husband! Against all odds, the unlikely couple got along. Agiatis enthusiastically supported her first husband's reform plans. She convinced Cleomenes to follow through on them.

When Cleomenes became king, he introduced Agis's land redistribution plan. He started with his own land, which he handed it over to be divided up. His friends and family followed his lead. All the large landowners were eventually shamed into giving up their land. Sparta only had two thousand male citizens left, and the land was divided among them and the Perioikoi non-citizens.

Cleomenes's reforms were a good start, but Sparta's population was dropping at an alarming rate. The young men continued living in the barracks, so their wives didn't have many children. And then, in 222 BCE, it happened. Sparta suffered a horrifying loss against Macedonia in the Battle of Sellasia. Only two hundred of Sparta's men survived. Sparta was on the brink of extinction.

The Macedonian kingdom threatened to swallow up all of Greece's city-states. If they wanted to survive, they had two choices. The Greek cities could place themselves under another powerful Hellenistic kingdom, like Egypt or the Seleucid Empire. Option two was joining a Greek league and uniting with other Greek city-states. Athens took option one and allied with Egypt. It didn't work. Athens fell to Macedonia in 261 BCE in the Chremonidean War.

The Aetolian League and the Achaean League were the two most powerful Greek leagues. The Aetolian League in central Greece successfully fought Macedonia. In 279 BCE, it protected Apollo's temple at Delphi from a Celtic invasion. Initially, the Aetolian League allied with the Roman Republic, but later, it fought with the Seleucid Empire against Rome.

The Achaean League was in the Peloponnese Peninsula, but Sparta never joined it. The league scored a thrilling victory by removing the Macedonians from the Peloponnese in 243 BCE. But then the league made the mistake of asking Macedonia for help fighting King Cleomenes of Sparta. They almost wiped the Spartans off the face of the earth, but the Macedonians were lording over them again. In the Second Macedonian War, the Achaean League joined forces with its former enemies, the Aetolian League. Success! They got rid of Macedonia's control.

King Pyrrhus of Epirus. [122]

Rome Emerges as a Superpower

Initially, the Roman Republic controlled only central Italy. In 280 BCE, it began to attack the wealthy Greek colonies in southern Italy. The Greeks asked King Pyrrhus of Epirus to help. Epirus was a poor city-state in northern Greece, but Pyrrhus had visions of grandeur. He dreamed of being another Alexander the Great. He rounded up ships and soldiers from his royal relatives in Egypt, Macedonia, and the Seleucid Empire. Then, he sailed to Italy.

Pyrrhus technically won his first battle against Rome. Still, he suffered such devastating losses that it was a **Pyrrhic victory**, which means it was not worth the win. His subsequent two battles were even worse. He went home, where he was killed by an old lady who threw a roof tile at him and knocked him off his horse.

Rome conquered the Greek city-states of Sicily in the First Punic War (264–241). While fighting Carthage and the Sicilian Greeks, Rome got involved in the Macedonian Wars. The Romans joined forces with the Aetolian League against Philip V of Macedonia. Sparta also jumped into the fray and allied with Rome and the Aetolian League. That didn't go well. The Peloponnese Greeks lost to Philip in 209 BCE.

However, in 198 BCE, Rome kicked Philip out of Greece. On Philip's way back to Macedonia, the Romans launched a surprise attack on his rear guard, killing two thousand of his men. Philip fought the Romans again in Thessaly the following year. An early morning fog covered the valley where the battle occurred. The Romans used war elephants for the first time in the Battle of Cynoscephalae. The Macedonians could hear them stomping and trumpeting. Then, the elephants suddenly appeared in the swirling mist. Philip lost eight thousand men that day. He had to give up his navy and army.

The Achaean League initially allied with Rome, but that relationship soured when Rome said the league couldn't expand its territory. The Achaean League revolted against Rome in 146 BCE. It lost most of its men in the Battle of Scarpheia near central Greece's eastern coast. Most of the survivors committed suicide. A few escaped to Corinth, but the Romans followed.

In less than a day, Rome defeated the Greeks at Corinth. Most of its citizens snuck out of the city, but the Romans killed any men who were left and enslaved the women and children. The Romans stripped Corinth of its precious statues and artwork. They burned the ancient city to the ground. The rest of the Greek cities surrendered to Rome.

The Last Embers of the Hellenistic Kingdoms

What happened to the Hellenistic kingdoms? King Perseus of Macedon started the Third Macedonian War in 171 BCE. He made outlandish promises to get the Greek city-states to ally with him. When he conquered Thessaly, Rome sent troops to counter him. The Macedonians pounded the Romans into the dirt. They killed two thousand Romans and only lost four hundred of their own.

Perseus let the victory go to his head and let down his guard. Without warning, Rome's consul, Crassus, stormed in with his war elephants. Eight thousand Macedonians fell in one day. Perseus abandoned his army at Pydna, but the Romans tracked him down and dragged him to Rome. He spent the rest of his life in prison. After 168 BCE, Rome controlled Macedon. Macedon was divided into four provinces.

The Seleucid Empire was a dynamic hub of Hellenistic culture. At its height, it stretched from Syria to Afghanistan. However, the empire slowly declined after Seleucus's death. Persia's Parthian Empire eventually swallowed up the eastern part of the Seleucid Empire. The western part of the empire suffered civil wars and invasions until it fell under Roman control. General Pompey of Rome reorganized it into Roman provinces in 63 BCE.

Before the Seleucid Empire collapsed, its king triggered the Maccabean Revolt in Judea. In 167 BCE, Antiochus IV Epiphanes tried to force the Jews to mix the Greek religion with Judaism. When Jerusalem rebelled, he killed forty thousand Jews, including children and babies. He sacrificed a pig to Zeus in Jerusalem's temple. The enraged Jews fought against the Seleucid Greeks and kicked them out of Judea.

Egypt was a Macedonian kingdom for three centuries. Its pharaohs all came from Ptolemy. The Egyptian pharaohs married their sisters, and the Macedonian pharaohs did the same. Quarrels and power plays within the royal family weakened Egypt. Cleopatra was a co-pharaoh with her thirteen-year-old brother, Ptolemy XIII. She was also his wife. When Ptolemy got mad at Cleopatra and kicked her out, she started a steamy romance with a Roman named Julius Caesar. Caesar went to war against Egypt. Ptolemy XIII ended up drowning in the Nile.

Cleopatra, the Macedonian pharaoh of Egypt.[128]

Another of Cleopatra's brothers came to the throne. He was only twelve. It is believed he also married Cleopatra. However, she ran off with Caesar. She lived in his villa in Italy until the senators assassinated him in 44 BCE. Cleopatra then started a romance with a Roman consul, Mark Antony. Octavian was Antony's co-consul, and his sister, Octavia, was Antony's wife. He was furious when Antony abandoned his sister for Cleopatra. Octavian declared war against Egypt. Antony and Cleopatra lost the war. Both of them committed suicide, and Egypt became a Roman province.

Round-up Activity: Timeline

( ) Agis IV begins reforming Sparta.
( ) Antigonus dies in the Battle of Ipsus.
( ) Athens falls to Macedonia in the Chremonidean War.
( ) Maccabean Revolt begins. The Jews kick the Greeks out of Judea.
( ) Olympias orders Arrhidaeus's execution.
( ) Partition of Babylon.
( ) Peloponnese Greeks lose to Philip V of Macedonia.
( ) Rome attacks Greek colonies in southern Italy.
( ) Rome burns Corinth to the ground and steals priceless art.
( ) Roxana has a baby boy, Alexander IV.

Chapter 10: Greek Science and Technology

The ancient Greeks changed the world. They gave rise to awe-inspiring breakthroughs in science and technology. As the Greek culture spread to Egypt and the Middle East, it created an exciting exchange of ideas. People became even more interested in science, math, and medicine. This intellectual growth took the world by storm.

Pythagoras

Pythagoras was a math genius who lived in the 6th century BCE. He grew up on the island of Samos. As a young adult, Pythagoras lived as a hermit in a cave. He did not eat meat. Pythagoras later moved to southern Italy and set up a school. His students were also vegetarians and lived a simple life. It was similar to a commune. Everyone shared everything.

Most people back then thought the world was flat. Pythagoras challenged this idea. He taught that it was a sphere, like a ball. He might have been the first to introduce this groundbreaking idea. Pythagoras was the first in the Greek world to develop the ***Pythagorean theorem***, although the Babylonians used it centuries earlier.

What is the Pythagorean theorem? It starts with a triangle with a right angle (a ninety-degree angle). Opposite the right angle is the longest side of the triangle: the hypotenuse. If you square each of the two shorter sides, it equals the hypotenuse squared.

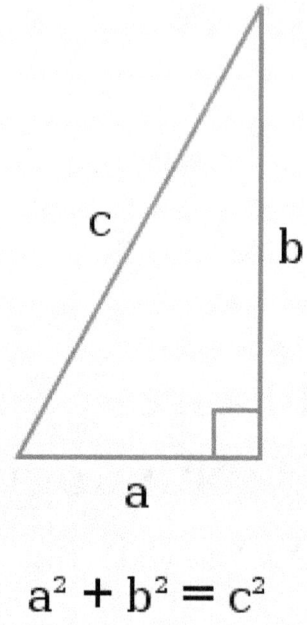

In this right triangle, "c" is the hypotenuse or longest side.[134]

Hippocrates, the Father of Modern Medicine

Our medical legacy owes an outstanding debt to Hippocrates. He lived in the 5th century BCE and learned medicine from his father and grandfather. Plato said he was an "Asclepiad," or a healing priest. In his day and age, people thought sickness was a curse from the gods. Hippocrates taught a revolutionary new idea. He said that diseases had natural causes. He suggested that what a person ate, how they lived, and their environment affected their health.

Hippocrates was the first to use *clinical diagnosis*. This included things that are a normal part of doctor visits today, like checking a person's pulse and temperature. He observed a person's range of motion and asked about their urine and bowel movements. He used all this information when making a diagnosis. He thought the body could heal itself and that the doctor's job was to help this process. For some health problems, he recommended fasting for a short time. He also used a mixture of honey and vinegar for some illnesses.

Hippocrates, Father of Modern Medicine.[135]

New doctors still quote the Hippocratic Oath, although the words have changed over the centuries. The original oath included some of the following promises:

1. I will soothe the pain of anyone who needs my art, and if I don't know how, I will seek the counsel of my teachers.
2. I will never harm my suffering friend because life is sacred.
3. I pray that the attention I give to those who put themselves in my hands is rewarded with happiness.
4. I swear to care for anyone who suffers, prince or slave.

Leucippus and Democritus Develop Atomic Theory

Leucippus and his student Democritus lived in the 5th century BCE. These brilliant ancient scientists developed the early principles of atoms and nuclear physics. What did they have to say about atoms?

1. The universe is made of "Being" (the physical world or matter) and "Void" (empty space).
2. Atoms are countless super-tiny particles that can't be changed or divided.
3. These atoms constantly move and form everything in the physical world.
4. Groups of atoms can change into various arrangements, making distinct types of matter.

Democritus was also interested in genetics. He wrote a letter to Hippocrates, saying that a man and woman both make "seeds." These seeds contain information about every part of the body. They come together to form a new body.

Architectural Wonders

Polycrates was the tyrant of Samos when Pythagoras lived there. Remember, tyrants were not necessarily evil. They often improved the lives of people. For instance, Polycrates built a **_mole_**. This was like a causeway sticking out into the sea. A mole kept waves and strong currents from destroying the harbor.

What really made Polycrates famous was the Tunnel of Eupalinos. The tunnel was named after its engineer. It was a half-mile (one-kilometer) aqueduct that went straight through a mountain! Two teams carved the tunnel. They began on opposite sides of the mountain and met in the middle. The Greek historian Herodotus said this was one of the most extraordinary feats in the Greek world.

Ictinus was an architect who pulled off another engineering triumph in the 5th century BCE. He built the lovely Parthenon temple in Athens. It had elegant Doric columns. It was a breathtaking showcase of balance and had intricate details. Ictinus put **_entasis_** into play. He put slight bulges in the columns to create an optical illusion of perfectly straight pillars.

The Parthenon. [196]

Giant amphitheaters were also popular in ancient Greece. Even before the Dark Ages, the Greeks built semi-circular outdoor theaters for dramatic performances. How did people hear the actors in the days before microphones? Well, the architects used incredible acoustic engineering technology. Modern scientists tested it on the ancient theater ruins at Epidaurus, near Athens. Even today, if one drops a coin, it can be heard throughout the theater.

By the 3rd century, these arenas had become huge. The one in Ephesus could seat twenty-four thousand people! Greek architects built theaters where there was a beautiful view, such as on a mountain or overlooking the sea. If people got bored with the show, they could enjoy the view!

Theaetetus of Athens

Theaetetus was a 4th-century BCE mathematician. He was a student of Socrates. He made giant leaps in the field of geometry. Theaetetus figured out that there could only be five *Platonic solids*. A Platonic solid has "faces" that are *polygons*, flat shapes with straight edges. Only three polygons can make a Platonic solid: squares, triangles, and pentagons (a shape with five sides). In a Platonic solid, all the faces have to be identical. The same number of polygons meet at each corner of the shape.

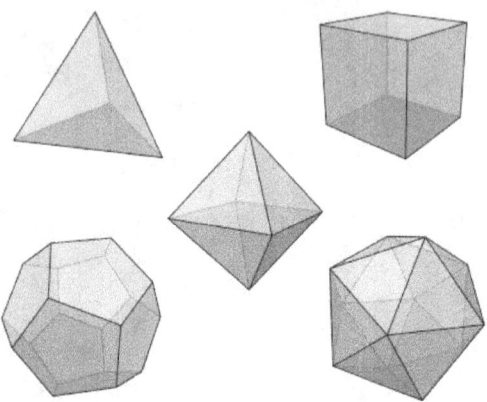

The five Platonic solids are the tetrahedron (or pyramid), cube, octahedron (eight faces), dodecahedron (twelve faces), and icosahedron (twenty faces).[197]

Theaetetus explored *irrational lengths*. What are those? The Greeks believed that numbers measured the length of something. Irrational numbers are numbers that aren't rational. They have no repeating pattern and cannot be fractions. Irrational numbers aren't usual numbers like one, four, seven, or nine. They are numbers like pi (π), which starts with 3.14159.

Euclid of Alexandria

Euclid was a 4th-century BCE mathematician who wrote the *Elements*, a collection of thirteen textbooks on math and geometry. His book was a collection of earlier mathematicians' work. Euclid developed their work further. For instance, he tweaked Theaetetus's theorems so they were more accurate. Euclid provided solid proof of the theories of earlier mathematicians. He ran a school in Alexandria, Egypt, in the early 300s when it was a new city.

Aristarchus of Samos

Aristarchus was a 3rd-century BCE astronomer. He was the first to say that the earth rotates on its axis once a day. Aristarchus said the sun was at the center of the universe. He believed the earth revolved around the sun once a year, along with the other planets. He also thought the stars were suns that were far, far away. Most people thought Aristarchus was a bit crazy thinking these kinds of things. They believed the earth was the center of the universe. It took eighteen centuries before Nicolaus Copernicus's model of the universe with the sun at its center caught on.

Archimedes of Syracuse

Archimedes was a 3rd-century BCE mathematician, scientist, and inventor. He founded *theoretical mechanics* (how things move under the action of force). Archimedes developed the *law of the lever*. Think about a see-saw. If the person on one end weighs twice as much as the person on the other, the smaller person would be stuck in the air. But what if the heavier person moves toward the center (*fulcrum*) of the see-saw? Then, they would both be balanced. We can use this principle to move heavy objects with a long stick and a big rock. Archimedes supposedly said, "Give me a place to stand, and I shall move the earth!"

Law of the lever. [128]

Archimedes built on the lever concept and made the first *compound pulley*. A compound pulley consists of a fixed pulley that doesn't move and a moveable second pulley attached to the load. The combination of pulleys gives greater lifting ability because the weight is distributed. It also allows more flexibility when changing directions. He demonstrated this tool's power by moving a ship all by himself!

Archimedes also discovered that if you place a solid in a fluid, it is lighter than the fluid it displaces. For instance, let's say you're a bigger person. You go swimming, and you notice that you can easily float despite your weight. In fact, you find it easier to float than your thin friend. Why? The buoyant force pushes you up. The water is denser than your body is, especially if you have a lot of body fat. That's why ships can float. Rocks can't float, though; they're denser than water.

Archimedes didn't stop with levers, compound pulleys, and floating heavy objects. He worked out a formula for the volume of a ***sphere*** (a ball shape). He also discovered the ratio of the distance around a circle (its ***circumference***) compared to its ***diameter*** (a line going through the circle's middle). He called this the "ratio of circumference to diameter pi" (π) and calculated it to be 3.14159.

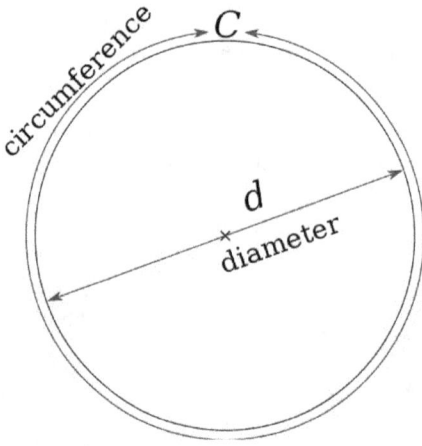

Diameter and circumference of a circle. [189]

Eratosthenes of Alexandria

The bustling city of Alexandria on Egypt's Mediterranean coast had a priceless library of books on science, math, history, religion, and literature. In the 2nd century BCE, its head librarian was Eratosthenes. By his time, Greeks had gradually accepted that the earth was not flat but a sphere. "How big is the earth?" Eratosthenes wondered. And this is where things get wild—he figured it out!

As a librarian, Eratosthenes tended to read a lot. One day, he read something interesting about the nearby city of Syene (Aswan, Egypt). On the summer solstice (June 21st), the sun lit up the bottom of a well at noon. This meant the sun was directly overhead. "I wonder if the same thing happens in Alexandria?" he mused.

So, Eratosthenes went outside on the summer solstice at noon and plunged a stick into the ground. It cast a slight shadow that had an angle of about seven degrees. Syene was fifty miles (eighty kilometers) from Alexandria. "If the sun casts a shadow here at noon but not in Syene, it's because the earth is curved," he decided. "Seven degrees is about 1/50th the circumference of a complete circle."

Using his knowledge of geometry, Eratosthenes worked out some figures. He decided that the distance around the earth was about twenty-eight thousand miles (forty-five thousand kilometers). He was really close! Calculations today place the earth's circumference at 24,901 miles.

What a mind-blowing legacy the ancient Greeks left us! These sharp-witted people discovered things that we take for granted. The knowledge they accumulated and built on is almost overwhelming to think about. We owe so much to them in the fields of philosophy, medicine, mathematics, science, and astronomy. The accomplishments of the ancient Greeks stretch through time to touch our lives today.

Round-up Activity: One-pager

In this activity, you will create your own Greek history page focusing on science and technology in ancient Greece. It can be a normal-sized page, like the size of copy paper, or you can make a poster. Use pictures to illustrate important people or their contributions. Draw your own or print photos off the internet. Describe key players and how they advanced science, math, or technology. You may want to include a timeline. You can choose to cover one unit of time, such as the Classical period or the Hellenistic Age. Or you could focus on a specific field, such as geometry, medicine, or architecture. Get creative with your favorite colors (or colors that symbolize Greece). Don't forget to make an eye-catching border.

Use your imagination and have fun!

Answer Key for Round-up Activities

Chapter 1: Timeline Game

(2) A catastrophic volcanic eruption wipes out all life on the island of Thera.

(7) A horrible plague kills one-third of Athens's population.

(10) Battle of Corinth: Rome conquered the Greek Achaean League.

(5) Cleisthenes brings democratic reform to Athens.

(4) First Olympic Games.

(3) The Greek Dark Ages.

(1) Minoans develop Greece's first writing system, Linear A.

(8) The Greek League of Corinth forms to invade the Persian Empire under Alexander.

(6) The Greeks unite to crush the Persian fleet in the naval Battle of Mycale.

(9) When Alexander the Great dies, his generals fight for control in the Wars of the Diadochi.

Chapter 2: Who's Who?

1. Aphrodite
2. Apollo
3. Ares
4. Artemis
5. Athena
6. Demeter
7. Dionysus
8. Hephaistos
9. Hera
10. Hermes
11. Poseidon
12. Zeus

A. King of the gods and of rain
B. Queen of the gods and vengeful wife of Zeus
C. Goddess of love and mother of Aeneas
D. The disabled god of crafts and volcanoes
E. God of the sun, music, archery, and healing
F. God of war and one of Aphrodite's lovers
G. Goddess of nature, wild animals, and hunting
H. Goddess of wisdom who split open Zeus's head
I. Goddess of farmers and the earth's fertility
J. The messenger god with winged sandals
K. God of the seas and father of the Cyclopes
L. God of wine, insanity, theater, and festivals

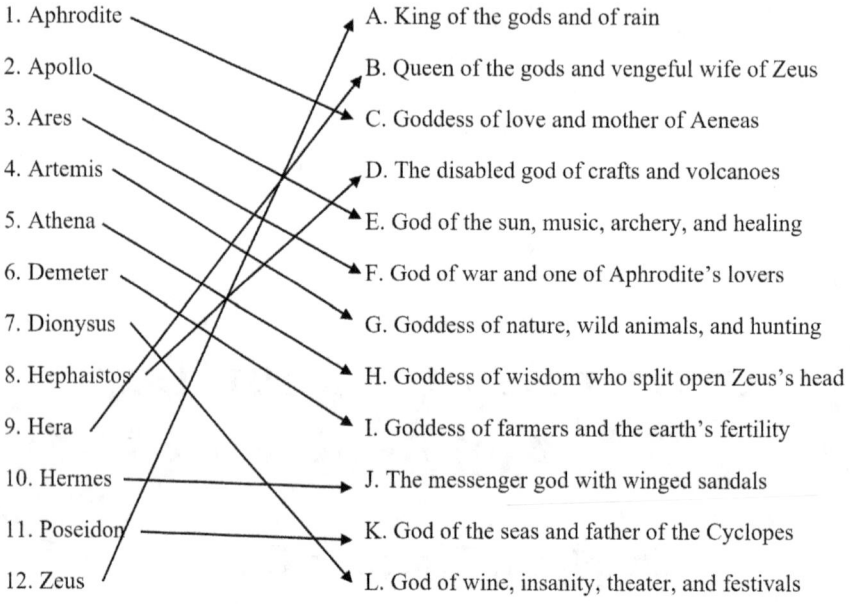

Chapter 3: Word Search

E	S	P	A	L	L	O	C	E	G	A	E	Z	N	O	R	B
T	I		I	N	F	R	A	S	T	R	U	C	T	U	R	E
A	E		C	A			N	Y	M	A	G	Y	L	O	P	
T	R		E	I				A								
S	A		A	N				R								
Y	N		R	O		Y		C								
T	E		G	C		R		H								
I	C		A	A	W		T	N	A	R	Y	T				
C	R		N	R	O											
	E		G	D												
	M		A													
			M													

1. The sudden fall of multiple civilizations in the eastern Mediterranean around 1200 BCE (Bronze Age collapse)
2. Marriage to more than one person (polygamy)
3. One large independent city ruling over towns and villages in the surrounding area (city-state)
4. "Great Greece" region of southern Italy (Magna Graecia)
5. An absolute ruler who came to power outside the usual channels (tyrant)
6. Something that is inhumane or unusually cruel (draconian)
7. Money or property a bride brings into a marriage (dowry)
8. Disorder because of governmental breakdown (anarchy)
9. Public works like roads, bridges, and sewers (infrastructure)
10. Soldiers who are paid to fight for another city-state or country (mercenaries)

Chapter 4: Review Questions

1. How did Sparta's culture and society differ from other ancient Greek city-states?
    - It had a different political system with two kings.
    - Boys were educated away from home from age seven.
    - Women had more rights.
    - The helot system provided labor. Spartan men did not work their own farms.
2. What role did military service play in Spartan society?
    - All Spartan men under age sixty were full-time soldiers.
    - Boys trained for military life from the age of seven.
    - Young married men lived in barracks rather than with their wives.
3. What was the agoge? How did it shape the upbringing and education of Spartan boys?
    - The agoge was the military training and educational system for boys from age seven to thirty.
    - It taught the boys discipline, endurance, simplicity, patriotism, and military skills.
4. What challenges did Spartan boys face in their rigorous training and education?
    - They endured harsh treatment, like sleeping outside and hazing.
    - They often did not have enough food.
5. What were some positive aspects of Sparta's legacy?
    - The culture promoted self-discipline, self-sacrifice, and courage.
    - Women had an elevated status (compared to other Greek women) in Spartan society.
6. How has Sparta's legacy negatively impacted some civilizations?
    - It influenced the state control of families
    - The goal of military conquest was more important than a healthy family life.
    - They practiced infanticide and ethnic cleansing (killing the helots).

Chapter 5: Fill in the Blank

The Persian Wars with Greece began when Cyrus the Great conquered _Ionia__ in 547 BCE, making these Greek colonies a province of the Persian-Achaemenid Empire. When Ionia revolted in 499 BCE, Athens and _Eretria_ sent ships and troops to help. After ending the revolt, the Persian king, Darius the Great, sent his fleet to punish Athens. However, the Athenians chose the battleground in a marshy area where the Persians couldn't use their horses. They soundly defeated the Persians in the _Battle of Marathon_, where the marshy terrain kept the Persians from using their horses. Xerxes, the son of Darius, sought revenge and marched into Greece with a huge army. Led by the Spartan king _Leonidas_, the Greeks held off the Persians at the __Thermopylae Pass_ while the rest of the Greeks evacuated _Athens_ and rebuilt the wall at the _Isthmus of Corinth_. The Greeks sacrificed themselves at the pass, but in the end, the Greeks scored an astounding victory in the naval _Battle of Salamis_.

Chapter 7: True or False?

1. Homer gave an eyewitness account of the Peloponnesian War. (It was Thucydides) **(F)**
2. The Athenians resettled the helots at Naupaktos. **(T)**
3. Athens also fought in North Africa during the first war. **(T)**
4. Thucydides thought going to war was a great idea. (He warned them to count the cost) **(F)**
5. The plague didn't kill many people in Athens. (It killed one-third of the population) **(F)**
6. The fifty-year Peace of Nicias only lasted six years. **(T)**
7. The war moved to Sicily when Athens agreed to help Segesta. **(T)**
8. General Nicias made quick and sound decisions that won the war in Sicily. (He constantly delayed and made mostly poor decisions) **(F)**
9. Alcibiades switched sides to Sparta and then back to Athens again. **(T)**
10. Athens won the final Battle of Aegospotami against Sparta. (Sparta crushed them, ending the war) **(F)**

Chapter 8: Quiz

1. In what ways did Alexander's upbringing and education influence his leadership style and approach to conquest?
   - Aristotle taught him ethics, politics, and logic, which shaped his leadership skills. He learned military strategies from reading the *Iliad*. He also learned Classical Greek culture, enabling him to communicate effectively with his Greek forces.
   - His father, Philip II, taught him military arts and provided him with opportunities to put them into practice.
2. What were some of the key military tactics that Alexander the Great used in his conquests? How did these tactics contribute to his success?
   - He used the element of surprise.
   - He used a blend of skills and tools: a new phalanx position, the sarissas, cavalry, and ingenious siege technology.
   - He tended to use the same line-up for his battles. His soldiers always knew what to do.
   - He made effective decisions on the spur of the moment.
3. What events destabilized Persia shortly before Alexander's invasion?
   - Most of the Persian royal males were poisoned.
   - Darius III was abruptly brought to the throne with little preparation to rule an empire.
4. How did Alexander view Eastern cultures? What cultural changes did he encourage, and how did he do that?
   - He admired Eastern culture, adopted some customs, and planned to restore Babylon.
   - Eastern and Western cultures were fused. For instance, Greek officers married Persian princesses.
   - He built over two dozen cities named Alexandria that promoted Hellenistic culture.

5. What was Alexander's lasting legacy?
    - He developed military strategies that are still studied today.
    - He developed a cultural fusion of Eastern and Western cultures.
    - He spread the Greek Hellenistic culture to Asia and North Africa.

Chapter 9: Timeline

(7) Agis IV begins reforming Sparta. (245)

(4) Antigonus dies in the Battle of Ipsus. (302)

(6) Athens falls to Macedonia in the Chremonidean War. (261)

(9) Maccabean Revolt begins. The Jews kick the Greeks out of Judea. (167)

(3) Olympias orders Arrhidaeus's execution. (317)

(1) Partition of Babylon. (323)

(8) Peloponnese Greeks lose to Philip V of Macedonia. (209)

(5) Rome attacks Greek colonies in southern Italy. (280)

(10) Rome burns Corinth to the ground and steals priceless art. (146)

(2) Roxana has a baby boy, Alexander IV. (323)

Part 3: Ancient Rome for Teens

An Enthralling Guide to the Roman Republic and Empire

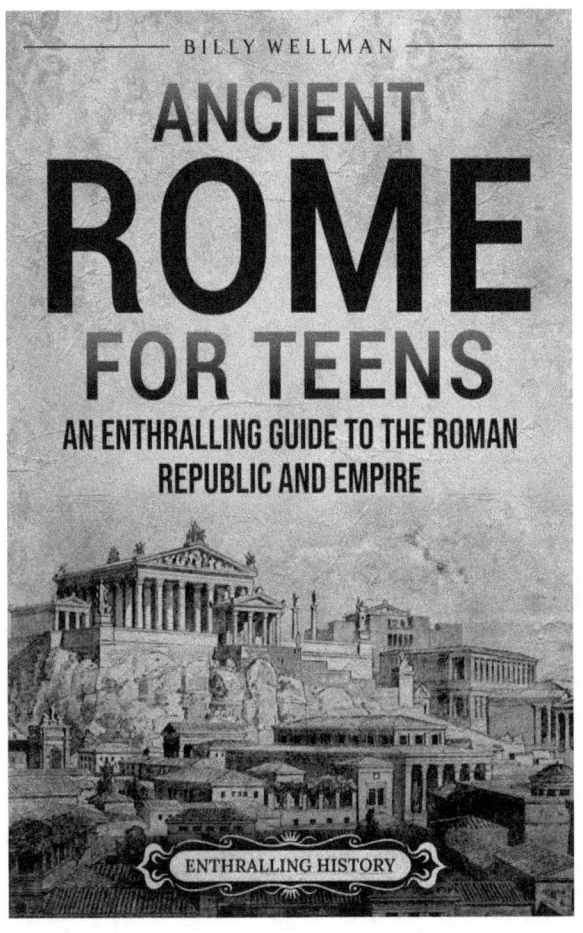

Introduction

Rhea Silvia gasped in pain. She had hidden her pregnancy, but now, she was in labor. What would her uncle Amulius do? He had stolen the throne from her father and forced her to become a Vestal Virgin. If anyone found out, she would be buried alive. Maybe she could give birth in secret and hide the baby somewhere. Suddenly, she heard screams from the temple and someone running down the corridor. Her door flung open. It was Dora, another priestess, wide-eyed in terror.

"Rhea! The eternal flame has gone out. We are all doomed! The goddess Vesta is angry! Someone has broken their vow of virginity!"

Dora's face paled as she realized Rhea was giving birth. "It was you!"

What happened to Rhea and her newborn twins? We'll unwrap that in the first chapter, along with the story of Aeneas, who fled the flames of Troy to build a new city. Ancient Rome rarely had any dull moments. This book explores the political drama and inspirational stories of the fascinating men and women who built Rome, developed a republic, and conquered an empire.

How did its sensational stories unfold? Why was the Roman military such an unstoppable force? Why did Rome's slaves revolt, and how did that go? What social problems led to several civil wars? What happened when the lower classes couldn't take it anymore? This journey through ancient Rome's history will examine all this and more.

What made Rome extraordinary? Rome morphed from a modest city-state into an incredible empire stretching from the Middle East to North Africa to Britain. Its politics, philosophy, architecture, language, and religion left a lasting legacy that continues to influence our world today. Above all else, Rome is a story of people. Good people, brilliant people, psychotic people, power-hungry people, hopelessly poor people—they were all part of Rome's astounding ancient history. This book will bring their despair, craftiness, and triumphs to life.

Why study history? It gives us insight into our present and future. Some of Rome's stories are uplifting, but others are lessons in what *not* to do! Knowing Rome's history and culture helps us understand why things are the way they are today. How many countries worldwide have a government based on the Roman Republic? Analyzing Rome's leaders helps us realize how good politicians can lift their country into peace and prosperity while inept leaders can plunge it into desperation.

Let's travel back in time to explore what happened to the twins and how everything played out after that.

Chapter 1: Romulus and Remus

What happened to the twin babies, Romulus and Remus? First, we need to explore another myth that sets the stage. When diving into ancient myths, we have to remember they aren't pure fiction. Most myths have an inner core of real history. The challenge is separating truth from fiction. Over the centuries, ancient stories were retold over and over. Some parts got left out, and others were added in.

Adventures of Aeneas

The story of Aeneas begins in ancient Troy. Recent evidence points to Troy being an actual city on Turkey's northwestern coast. Greek history books say the Trojan War happened around 1200 BCE. Aeneas was the son of Prince Anchises of Troy and, according to myth, the goddess Aphrodite. His mother hovered over Aeneas, saving his life several times as he fought in the Trojan War. The Greek warrior Achilles killed Aeneas's cousin, the crown prince Hector. One night, Aeneas had a nightmare of his cousin's ghost.

"Aeneas! Get up! The Greeks have gotten into the city! Get your family out! You have a long journey at sea, and then you will build a new city."

Aeneas jumped up. The city was going up in smoke. Aeneas carried his old father on his back. His little son Ascanius and his wife Creusa ran with him as they dashed toward the city gates. Just as they ran out of the gates, Aeneas realized Creusa wasn't there. He ran back into the city, but her ghost met him. The Greeks had killed her. "Leave Troy! Save our son! Sail to Italy!"

Aeneas escapes Troy with his family. Painting by Pompeo Batoni.[180]

As black smoke rose from Troy, Aeneas found his father and son and guided other refugees to Mount Ida. They built twenty ships and sailed down the Aegean Sea. On their journey, they met another survivor, Prince Helenus, who told Aeneas, "When you find a white pig with thirty piglets, stop. Build your new city there."

Aeneas and his group sailed to Sicily, where they narrowly escaped the Cyclopes, one-eyed monsters. But when they tried to sail to Italy, they hit a fierce storm that knocked them off course. After many days, they landed on a peaceful beach. They were in North Africa, where some Phoenicians had recently arrived from Lebanon. Their queen was Dido, and they were building the city of Carthage. Aeneas and Queen Dido were instantly attracted to each other. Aeneas forgot all about the prophecies of establishing a city in Italy.

Finally, the god Mercury visited Aeneas. "Don't forget your destiny given to you by the gods. You are to rule in Italy!"

Dido was beside herself when she heard Aeneas was leaving. "I can't live without you. If you leave, I swear I'll kill myself!"

But Aeneas and his followers weighed anchor at dawn and sailed up the west coast of Italy. They followed the Tiber River inland, where King Latinus ruled the land. Latinus had just dreamed that his daughter would marry a foreigner and that the Latins would rule the world. Meanwhile, Aeneas and his men were about to sacrifice a white pig to celebrate their arrival in Italy. However, she got away and ran into the forest. Aeneas ran after her and found the sow the next morning. She had given birth to thirty piglets! The prophecy was fulfilled. Aeneas would build his city on this spot.

The Latins and Trojans allied, and Aeneas married Princess Lavinia, the daughter of King Latinus. Aeneas named his new city Lavinium after his lovely wife. Five years later, when Lavinia was pregnant with their first child, Aeneas mysteriously disappeared during a battle against the Rutuli people. No one ever found his body. Ascanius, Aeneas's son from his first wife, became the next king.

King Latinus introduces Aeneas to Lavinia. Painting by Giovanni Battista Tiepolo. [181]

Alba Longa: City on a Lake

Lavinia was worried. She was supposed to give birth soon, but her husband had disappeared without a trace. Would her unborn child be safe from her stepson Ascanius? If it were a boy, would Ascanius consider him a threat and try to kill him? Lavinia decided to go into hiding with the help of Tyrrhenus, the chief herdsman. He hid her in a house in the mountains, where she gave birth to a son she named Silvius. The boy grew up in the forests.

Meanwhile, King Ascanius was unhappy with Lavinium. "This city is nothing but a smelly swamp! Its vapors are making my people sick, and these mosquitoes are unbearable! There's hardly any farmland. So much for a prophecy about a pig!"

Ascanius built a new capital he named Alba Longa at the bottom of Mount Alba, overlooking a large lake. The mountain and lake gave the capital natural protection from enemies. Alba Longa was about twelve miles from where Rome would later be built. After thirty-eight years, Ascanius died. Who would be the next king?

At this point, Tyrrhenus brought Lavinia and Silvius down the mountain to Alba Longa. Of course, Ascanius's son, Iulus, challenged Silvius, but the city's people talked it over. Silvius was the grandson of King Latinus and the son of King Aeneas. Both Latin and Trojan blood flowed in his veins. Iulus was only Trojan, and the Latins wanted representation. The people took a vote, and Silvius won. Prince Iulus became a priest. Centuries later, his descendant, Julius Caesar, became Rome's dictator for life. For the next several centuries, Silvius's descendants ruled Alba Longa. The twelfth king was Numitor.

Romulus and Remus

Numitor was king of Alba Longa, but his younger brother, Amulius, wanted the throne for himself. One reason for this, aside from a desire for power, was a disturbing prophecy. A seer had told him that a descendant of his brother would kill him. He needed to ensure there were no descendants. Numitor had only one son, Aegestus. Amulius took his nephew on a hunting trip, and the boy died in an unfortunate accident. Amulius had only one other child of Numitor's to worry about: his daughter, Rhea Silvia.

Amulius staged a palace takeover. He kicked Numitor out, and he forced Rhea Silvia to become a **Vestal Virgin**. The temple of the goddess **Vesta**, the chief goddess of the Trojans and Latins, had six priestesses. They swore to remain virgins for thirty years. If they broke their vow, they would be buried alive. If Rhea was a virgin, she would have no children, and Amulius could enjoy being king without fear of being killed by his brother's descendants.

Except Rhea did get pregnant.

"How did this happen?" Amulius shouted when he arrived at the temple. "You should be buried alive!"

Rhea told her story. "I went out to draw water from the well. Suddenly, I saw a wolf! I ran to a cave to hide, and just then, a solar eclipse darkened the sun. At that moment, the wolf turned into the god Mars! He forced himself on me but promised that my children would be heroes."

Amulius paced back and forth. There had been a solar eclipse nine months earlier. Maybe these babies really were half-divine. But they were descendants of Numitor! One of them might fulfill the prophecy and kill him. He ordered Rhea to be locked in a tower and then turned to his guard. "Take these babies out to the river and drown them!"

The guard picked up the basket holding the twins and walked out. He arrived at the river and sat down to think. What if their father really was Mars? If he killed the god's children, Mars might kill him. Instead of drowning them, he placed their basket in the Tiber River.

"Let Mars decide. If they are his children, he will save them. If not, they will drown."

The basket floated down the river with the babies inside until a sudden wave pushed it up on a small beach. A female wolf was passing through the area. She had recently given birth, but her pups had not survived. Hearing the babies' cries, she looked up, her ears twitching and her nose sniffing the air. The sound was coming from the river! She tentatively walked toward the basket and looked down at the babies, who were screaming in hunger. Gently, she picked up the twins and laid them on the grass. Then, she lay next to them and nursed them from her painfully swollen teats.

Statue of the twins with the wolf at the Maison de la Louve in Brussels.[182]

A little while later, a shepherd walked to the river to draw water. His name was Faustulus, and his wife's baby had just died. He saw the wolf with the infants. How bizarre! The wolf snarled but then slunk into the forest. Faustulus placed the babies in the basket and carried them home. His wife's tears turned to joy when she saw the twins. She held them close to her as Faustulus told her how he had found them. "The gods have replaced our baby with two sons!"

Faustulus had no idea where the boys came from. He knew Numitor was living in exile nearby, but he had no clue his foster sons were grandsons of the former king. The boys grew up in the humble shepherd's home, thinking they were his children. They became shepherds like Faustulus, but their lives took a sudden turn when they fought with Numitor's shepherds.

Remus killed one of the shepherds, and Numitor seized him. Romulus escaped and ran home to get Faustulus. The shepherd knelt before Numitor, pleading for Remus's life. He told him the boys must have come from the gods, explaining how he found them with the she-wolf.

"How long ago was that?" Numitor asked.

"Eighteen years, sire."

"Eighteen years! That's when my daughter had twin boys. We never found out what happened to the babies. These must be them! These are my grandsons!"

Numitor wrapped the two young men in his arms, sobbing. Finally, they all sat down, and he told them how Amulius had stolen his throne. "He ordered you two to be killed as well."

"We'll get revenge." Romulus and Remus swore. "We'll kill him and put you back on the throne of Alba Longa!" And that's what they did, fulfilling the prophecy that a descendant of Numitor would kill Amulius.

Once Numitor was king again, the twins looked at each other.

"Now what?" Romulus asked.

"We could stay here in Alba Longa with our grandfather. But let's build our own city!"

"Yes! We'll build it where Faustulus found us. By the river, where the seven hills are."

Cities of Lavinium, Alba Longa, and Rome.[188]

Founding of Rome

Full of enthusiasm, the young men hurried back to the seven hills, planning to build their new city on one of the hills. But which hill? And which one of them should be king? Romulus and Remus loved each other very much, but they had always been hotheads. Their quarrel became so intense that Romulus killed Remus. He wept when he realized what he'd done. But then he dried his tears.

It was time to start building his new city, which he named Rome after himself. Romulus only had a small band of followers. He chose the Palatine Hill and built a wall around it. However, he needed more workers. Romulus sent invitations out to the surrounding region. Everyone who joined him would be a citizen. Yes, even if they were not from the nobility. And yes, even formerly enslaved people could be citizens.

The area where he built Rome already had towns and villages. Before the Trojan War, a Greek named Evander of Arcadia had established the city of Pallantium in the region, importing Greek customs and deities. Most of Rome's first citizens came from Alba Longa or Pallantium. Other people living near the seven hills were the Etruscans and the Sabines. The fledgling city of Rome was a cultural blend of Greek, Trojan, Latin, and other nearby cultures.

A new city needed a government. What would that look like? Romulus called a council of his followers to hash things out. It would be a monarchy, and Romulus would be king. Yet, it would be an unusual monarchy with elected kings. Rome would have a senate, an idea borrowed from the Greeks. Each family clan (*gen*) had a leader called *pater* (plural: *patres*), meaning father. The senators were patres, so each family group had representation. Most of these founding families were from unremarkable backgrounds, but they eventually became Rome's aristocratic *patrician* class. Senators could only come from these families.

One job of the Senate was to elect a new king when a king died. They also served as advisors to the king. The king made the laws, but the senators could suggest what they would be. Since the senators represented all of Rome's people, in theory, the laws benefited everyone. Of course, that became problematic down the road when new people who weren't part of the founding families moved into Rome.

Romulus's biggest problem was that there were a lot of men but not enough women. Romulus started with his fellow shepherds and a band of young men willing to fight for a living. Once he founded Rome, he collected former slaves, traveling workers, and other men looking to make their fortune. However, they were almost all single men. He needed about three thousand young women as wives for his men, but where could he get them? The towns and cities in the area refused to arrange marriages with his rag-tag group of men.

Without wives, the city would have no children and no future. Romulus came up with a plan. He invited the Sabines, a neighboring people, to a religious festival. The Romans gave the Sabine men strong wine, but the Romans *diluted* (made less strong) their own wine. The Sabines got drunk while the Romans pretended to be intoxicated. When the Sabines fell asleep, the Romans kidnapped their young women.

The Romans kidnap the Sabine women. Painting by Nicolas Poussin.[184]

The next day, the Sabines realized what had happened. "Give us our women back!"

"They're ours now," Romulus replied.

Two of the Sabine cities attacked Rome but lost the battle. Then, the Sabines went to all their cities, rallying support until they amassed an enormous army. Yet, months had passed, and many of the young Sabine women had become pregnant. The women ran between the two armies.

"Fathers! Brothers! Why are you doing this?" the women screamed, facing the Sabines. They whirled and faced the Romans. "Husbands! Stop fighting!" The women turned again, pleading with the Sabine men, "Your grandchildren are in our bellies! If you kill our husbands, you kill their fathers! Think of your grandchildren. If you can't, then kill us since you're fighting because of us."

The hardened soldiers on both sides sheathed their swords and threw down their spears. The Sabines and Romans formed a united kingdom, with Sabine King Tatius serving as a co-ruler with Romulus. That worked for about five years. An unknown assassin killed Tatius, and Romulus became king of both the Sabines and Romans.

Romulus was a military genius, but he did not get along with his senators. One day, they got so furious with him that they tore him into pieces. At that moment, a violent wind blew through Rome, and a solar eclipse darkened the sky. The senators hid the body parts and said the wind had blown Romulus away. The citizens scoured the region, looking for him. The senators realized they couldn't elect a new king. Everyone thought Romulus might still be alive. Of course, they couldn't admit they murdered him.

Finally, they hit upon a solution. An elderly, highly respected senator, Proculus Julius, told the people, "I just had a vision of Romulus rising into heaven. He's now the god Quirinus. He said his work here is done, but he will watch over you from above."

The people breathed a sigh of relief and stopped looking for Romulus. Now, they could choose a new king!

Truth or Fiction?

Remember that myths contain elements of actual history, but there is still a lot of fiction woven in. Although Romulus supposedly founded Rome around 753 BCE, the oldest written history of Rome came four centuries later. Did Romulus and Remus even exist? Roman historians said Romulus was buried under the Roman Forum. In 2019 CE, an ancient tomb was discovered under the Forum's northwest corner. An altar in the tomb declared it holy ground. No human remains were in the tomb, but remember, no one (except the senators) knew where Romulus's body was. The "tomb" might have simply been a place to honor him.

A bronze sculpture of a wolf found in Rome dates to the 5th century BCE, and coins from the 3rd century BCE show the wolf suckling Romulus and Remus. Assigning Mars as the twin's father was an attempt to link the Romans' heritage with the god of war. The she-wolf and Remus's murder by his brother aren't in all of the ancient accounts. However, the connection to Aeneas and Troy is. This link seemed important in legitimizing Roman rule. The wicked King Amulius also features strongly, suggesting that this part of the story likely happened.

Roundup Activity

Can you solve the crossword puzzle below? The answers are in the back of the book if you get stuck.

Who or what am I?

Across

3. I was queen of Carthage and lover of Aeneas
6. I was a shepherd who raised the twins
7. A great war happened here
8. I'm a goddess and mother of Aeneas
10. I was a Vestal Virgin who had twins
12. I was Rome's first king

Down

1. The Romans stole our women
2. I was Lavinia's son and king of Alba Longa
4. I'm a god and the father of Romulus and Remus
5. I was Rhea Silvia's father
8. I stole my brother Numitor's throne
9. I was killed by my brother Romulus
11. I escaped from Troy and founded Lavinium

Chapter 2: What Was the Roman Republic?

Beginning with Romulus, kings ruled Rome for over two hundred years. Intrigue and evil marked the reigns of the last few kings, starting with Tarquinius Priscus's murder. This king wasn't supposed to be the king. He was half-Greek and not from Rome, but he was rich and happy to help others out. He became close friends with the previous king, Marcius, who appointed him second in command under him.

When Marcius died, his sons were too young to rule, so the senators elected Tarquinius as king. He ended up being one of Rome's best kings. He was an impressive military commander. He expanded Rome's territory in central Italy. He erected the *Circus Maximus* stadium for chariot races, games, and gladiator contests. He also built the *Cloaca Maxima*, a sewer system, one of the world's first.

Murder Rocks the Palace

Servius Tullius, probably Tarquinius's illegitimate son, grew up in the palace. When Tarquinius named Tullius his heir, this enraged the patricians and Marcius's sons. They hired assassins who murdered Tarquinius. Unwilling to lose power, Queen Tanaquil plotted with Tullius. She knew someone outside the family would become king since her sons weren't old enough. Her sons would never get the chance to rule. So, she stepped out on the balcony overlooking the people gathered below.

"My fellow Romans, before my husband died, he appointed Tullius as regent. When our sons are older, the Senate can elect one of them as king."

Servius Tullius. Painting by Frans Huys.[185]

Queen Tanaquil's plotting backfired. When the boys grew up, Tullius kept the crown. The *plebians* (plebs), or working-class people, adored him. Only people who owned land could vote, so he gave land to the plebs in exchange for their votes. Then, he started talking about freeing the slaves and giving them citizenship. The patricians gasped, "What will we do without slaves to work our farms? The plebians are already swinging the vote!"

Meanwhile, Queen Tanaquil's son Tarquin was plotting to overthrow Tullius. He joined forces with his brother's wife, Tullia, who was Tullius's daughter. Each poisoned their spouse, and then they married each other. The senators were already angry with Tullius. Tarquin fanned the flames in a fiery speech in the Senate.

When King Tullius heard, he rushed to the Senate, but Tarquin shoved him down the steps. No one came to help him, and the bruised and dejected king began limping home. He never made it. Tarquin's co-conspirators murdered him in the street. Meanwhile, the Senate elected Tarquin as king, and a gleeful Tullia congratulated her new husband.

The senators immediately regretted electing Tarquin as king. He surrounded himself with bodyguards and began suppressing the Senate's power. He purged anyone he thought might not support him. Some senators were executed or banished on false charges. Secret assassins murdered other senators. Tarquin even killed his sister's husband. Her son, Brutus, pretended to be mentally disabled and survived.

The Overthrow of the Monarchy

King Tarquin's son, Sextus Tarquinius, was just as brutal as his father. He wanted Lucretia, his cousin's beautiful wife. But she loved her husband, Collatinus, and ignored Sextus. Sextus didn't take rejection well and forced himself on Lucretia. The following morning, Lucretia sent a message to her husband and father, who were away fighting, telling them to come home immediately and bring witnesses. One witness was Brutus, the nephew of King Tarquin, who had pretended to be mentally disabled.

When they arrived, Lucretia tearfully told them what happened. They tried to comfort her. "It wasn't your fault. He was stronger than you."

Lucretia sobbed. "Promise me you will get revenge!"

Then, to everyone's horror, she stabbed herself. Her father and husband collapsed to the floor, wailing. Brutus stood, picked up the knife, and held it in the air. "I will overthrow the evil Tarquin family! Who is with me?"

Brutus vows revenge for Lucretia. Painting by François-Joseph Navez.[186]

The other men raised their daggers. "By fire, sword, and whatever else it takes, we will erase Rome of its kings forever!"

This spearheaded a revolution that toppled Rome's monarchy. They carried Lucretia's body into the Forum and told the senators what Sextus Tarquinius had done.

"Act like men and Romans!" Brutus screamed to the gathering crowd. "Take up your weapons against the enemy of us all!"

The royal family fled the city. Rome's military pledged its support to the revolution. Tarquin rallied help from some neighboring tribes but failed to retake Rome. The Romans formed a new form of government called a republic.

How Did the Romans Structure Their Republic?

The Romans replaced their king with two elected *consuls* who served for a one-year term. The idea was that two heads of state would balance each other out. Each could veto the decision of the other. The two consuls were the commanders in chief of the army. In the early Roman Republic, the consuls appointed the senators. They built the Senate back up to one hundred men after King Tarquin's purge. If there was a crisis, the Senate could recommend a temporary *dictator*. He could only serve as long as the crisis lasted or for six months, whichever came first. The dictator could make quick decisions without passing through the usual channels.

Was the Roman Republic a democracy? Not in the sense that every citizen got to vote. They did have elections for leadership, but only the men in the assemblies could vote. The senators were an advisory council to the consuls and voted on bills. They were appointed by the consuls (and later by the censors). The Roman Senate was a rowdy place, with the senators booing, hissing, heckling, and making personal attacks during debates.

The Roman Senate in a fresco by Cesare Maccari.[187]

The *Centuriate Assembly* elected the consuls, censors, and praetors. A *century* was a unit of one hundred soldiers, and each century got a vote. Rome later added a non-military *Assembly of Tribes*. Each tribe represented a geographic area. This assembly elected some magistrates, made laws, and judged the most serious crimes. In 494 BCE, Rome added the *Plebian Assembly*, which represented the working class. They could propose new laws and veto laws the upper class tried to pass.

The *censors* took the *census* (the count of how many citizens there were) and maintained morality. They could *censor* or try to stop threats to public safety or obscene behaviors or speech. The *praetors* were elected as judges, army generals, and governors of the provinces. If both consuls were away at war, the praetor urbanus ran things in Rome. *Tribunes* had various jobs. One led the Plebian Assembly once that started. Two military tribunes led each Roman *legion*, which consisted of about five thousand soldiers. Other tribunes collected taxes and took care of the treasury. The consuls, censors, praetors, tribunes, and military commanders were all *magistrates* elected to a one-year term.

A Pyrrhic Victory

The Roman Republic took control of central Italy in its first few centuries of existence. The Greeks had ruled southernmost Italy for hundreds of years. In 280 BCE, Rome broke an agreement with Tarentum, a Greek city in the heel of Italy's boot. Rome was supposed to stay out of the Gulf of Taranto in southernmost Italy. Yet, it boldly sailed a fleet of ships into the gulf. A storm blew ten of the ships toward Tarentum. The enraged Tarentines sunk five ships and captured others.

Rome declared war, and the Tarentines called for help from an old friend, King Pyrrhus of Epirus. Epirus was a poor country in northern Greece, but Pyrrhus was a relative of Alexander the Great and had visions of building his own empire. He borrowed money, soldiers, horses, and war elephants from his royal relatives in Macedonia, Egypt, and the Middle East. Pyrrhus technically won the first two battles, but he suffered such heavy losses that they were called ***Pyrrhic victories***. This means the victory was not worth the cost of lives and resources. After losing the third battle, Pyrrhus slunk back to Epirus. Rome grabbed southern Italy.

What Were the Punic Wars? (264-146 BCE)

Carthage, located in North Africa, had a sea empire. It controlled trade around the southern Mediterranean Sea. Rome wanted that empire and fought three legendary wars against Carthage to get it. "Punic" comes from the Latin word for the Phoenicians of Lebanon, who built Carthage. At this point, Rome had never fought a war outside Italy. It didn't even have a navy. The war began on the island of Sicily, just six miles from the toe of Italy's boot. Most of Sicily's cities were colonies of Greece or Carthage.

Rome got involved with Sicily when the Mamertine pirates asked for help. They had been raiding Sicily's ships and coastal towns for decades. Finally, Carthage sent troops to their holdout in Messana on Sicily's east coast. The Romans weren't excited about working with pirates, but they did want a foothold in Sicily. They crossed the Strait of Messina in 264 BCE, took the Carthaginians by surprise, and sent them packing. By 262 BCE, Rome had about twenty thousand troops in Italy.

Rome knew it needed a navy if it was going to beat Carthage. So, in a matter of months, the Romans built 120 warships and trained their men to sail them. The Romans were masters of one-on-one combat, so they made long gangplanks on their ships to hook and board enemy ships. They also used catapults to fire flaming missiles at the Carthaginian ships.

Everyone was shocked when Rome's brand-new navy beat Carthage in its first two battles. The Romans built a hundred more warships and trained fourteen thousand marines. Incredibly, Rome won the Battle of Cape Ecnomus, one of the largest naval battles in history. Together, Rome and Carthage had 300,000 marines and 680 ships.

A Roman trireme warship.[188]

However, the tide turned against the Romans when they attacked North Africa. Greece's invincible Spartans came to help Carthage. Carthage killed twelve thousand Roman soldiers, leaving only two thousand alive. Another Roman fleet arrived to rescue the men, but a cyclone at sea caused history's deadliest shipwreck. It sank 320 ships and drowned 100,000 Roman sailors. Carthage thought Rome would give up after this catastrophe, but that wasn't something Rome did.

The Romans regrouped and charged back into the fray, beating Carthage in two more battles. But then, another killer storm sank 150 ships. And then, there was a problem with chickens. Consul Pulcher was leading Rome's navy on a sneak attack on Carthage. He had some sacred chickens he would consult for the future. However, his chickens refused to eat, an omen that meant the battle wouldn't go well. Pulcher refused to accept what the chickens told him and tossed them all overboard.

The chickens were right. Pulcher lost the battle. It was such a disaster that Rome called him back, charging him with impiety for drowning the sacred chickens. After building a new fleet of ships, Rome got the upper hand in 241 BCE, and Carthage surrendered. Rome won Sicily, its first territory outside of Italy, and Sardinia, a large island north of Sicily.

Carthage had colonies on the coast of Iberia (Spain). After the war, it expanded its power to cover almost all of Spain. The wealth coming from this province helped Carthage recover from the losses of its war with Rome. Carthage's commander in chief was Hannibal. In 219 BCE, he attacked the city of Saguntum in Spain, a trade partner with Rome. He killed all the adults in the city. Rome declared war, and the Second Punic War began.

When Roman General Scipio Africanus arrived in Spain, Hannibal was gone. Where was he? Hannibal was marching north with ninety thousand men, twelve thousand cavalry, and thirty-seven elephants. He passed through Spain, over the Pyrenees Mountains, and through Gaul (France) to the Alps, which separated France from Italy. With his massive army, Hannibal scaled the thirteen-thousand-foot Isère Alps on narrow, icy paths and through deep snow.

His goal was a surprise attack on Italy from the north, but it was costly. He lost over half his army and horses in the treacherous climb. However, his plan worked. The Romans assumed he was still in Spain somewhere. Then, he suddenly appeared in northern Italy! Hannibal blazed through Italy, destroying its farmlands and beating Rome's much bigger army. In the Battle of Cannae, he killed 50,000 Roman soldiers, only losing 5,700.

Meanwhile, Scipio Africanus attacked the Carthaginian forces left in Spain and scored an astounding victory. He captured their treasury and supplies. He then sailed to Carthage with 440 ships. Hearing that Scipio was attacking Carthage, Hannibal hurried home. He sent his eighty war elephants in a charge against the Romans, but Scipio was familiar with elephants. His men stepped aside, letting the elephants stampede by, and then rounded them up with spears and sent the mighty creatures charging toward the Carthaginians. Once again, Rome won the war. Carthage had to give up its navy. It agreed not to fight anyone without permission from Rome.

Rome scored a victory by herding the elephants back at the Carthaginians.[189]

Rome and Carthage had peace for fifty years. Carthage paid tribute money to Rome and did not fight anyone. However, Carthage's neighbor Numidia kept crossing the border and raiding Carthaginian land. When Carthage appealed to Rome, asking for permission to defend itself, Rome said no. Numidia was an ally of Rome. Carthage fought Numidia anyway the next time it invaded. It was a huge mistake. The Numidians were more skilled than the Carthaginians expected, and the Carthaginians hadn't fought anyone in fifty years.

Despite its bitter loss to Numidia in a war of self-defense, Rome punished Carthage for breaking the treaty. Rome made Carthage send three hundred children as hostages. Then, Rome demanded they get rid of their army and hand over their weapons. The Carthaginians obeyed. Rome sent them over the edge by ordering them to move away from the coast and into the desert. They would lose their shipping trade if they couldn't stay by the sea. In the desert, they would be vulnerable to attacks from the Berber tribes, and they would be helpless without their army and armor.

Carthage refused to obey this time, so Rome laid siege for three years. High, thick walls surrounded Carthage, and the Romans couldn't breach them. Malaria put the Romans out of action for weeks. Finally, Rome appointed the handsome and capable Scipio Aemilianus as consul. He was the adopted grandson of General Scipio Africanus. They sent him to crush Carthage, and he did. Scipio had his men build a tower beside the wall and throw a gangplank over. Once the Romans got inside, they flattened and burned Carthage. Anyone who didn't escape was killed. Rome now controlled Carthage's former sea empire.

Conquest of Greece

While fighting Carthage, Rome also fought for control of Greece and Macedonia. King Philip V of Macedonia attacked cities on the Adriatic Sea that were trade allies with Rome. Rome responded by invading Philip's allies in Greece. (Greece wasn't one country but multiple city-states that often fought each other). Philip won this war and gained territory in Greece.

After beating Carthage, Rome headed to Greece and took Philip's territory in 197 BCE. When Philip's son Perseus became Macedonia's king, he tried to unite the Greek city-states against Rome. Rome crushed his efforts and captured Macedonia. Then, the Romans invaded Greece. Rome sacked and burned Corinth in 146 BCE. With that move, it controlled all of Greece.

What Was the Triumvirate?

Julius Caesar and Pompey were brilliant generals who had been fighting nonstop. They gained a lot of territory for Rome. However, the Roman soldiers had little to show for it. Pompey wanted each soldier to get a plot of farmland in the territory they conquered so they could support their families. But the senators opposed him, wanting the land for themselves. Caesar suggested a solution to overcoming the Senate: a triumvirate with three men holding power.

Pompey was popular because of his conquests in Turkey, Syria, and Judea. Caesar planned for Pompey to use his connections to get him elected as consul. As consul, Caesar would pass Pompey's land bill. The third person in the Triumvirate was Crassus, Rome's wealthiest man. His money would help elect Caesar and bribe senators to vote for the land bill. And so, the "Gang of Three" formed. It succeeded in getting Caesar elected as consul and passing the land bill. However, it also led to the fall of the Roman Republic.

Roundup Activity

Circle the correct answer in these multiple-choice questions.

1. Who built the Circus Maximus stadium and the Cloaca Maxima sewer system?
   a. Brutus
   b. Hannibal
   c. Pyrrhus
   d. Tarquinius Priscus
2. Who spearheaded the overthrow of the monarchy?
   a. Brutus
   b. Pompey
   c. Pulcher
   d. Scipio Africanus
3. Who elected the consuls, censors, and praetors?
   a. All the male citizens
   b. Centuriate Assembly
   c. Senate
   d. Tribunes
4. What was one of the largest naval battles in history?
   a. Battle of Cannae
   b. Battle of Cape Ecnomus
   c. Battle of Pydna
   d. Trojan War
5. Who threw his sacred chickens overboard?
   a. Pompey
   b. Pulcher
   c. Scipio Africanus
   d. Julius Caesar

Chapter 3: From Republic to Empire

Julius Caesar set off a chain of events leading to Rome's next chapter. The Roman Republic morphed into an empire. The emperor held far more power than the consuls. Some emperors lifted Rome to new heights of power. Others were unhinged. Early in the empire's history, a baby born in Judaea transformed Rome's religion and changed the course of world events.

Caesar's Civil War

Julius Caesar won the election as consul in 59 BCE and set to work passing Pompey's land bill. When the other consul, Bibulus, threatened to veto the bill, Caesar's followers flung poop at him. Bibulus was so embarrassed that he stayed home for the rest of the year. Caesar easily swung the votes, especially since Crassus padded the senators' pockets.

After Caesar's one-year term as consul, he became the governor of Cisalpine Gaul (northern Italy) and Transalpine Gaul (southern France). The Triumvirate began to fall apart when Caesar's daughter Julia died. She had married Pompey to seal the alliance with Caesar. Pompey adored his wife and was heartbroken when she died in childbirth.

Meanwhile, Rome's politics were a big mess. Politicians openly bribed others to get their bills passed. The Romans were weary of the republic. "Maybe we should return to a monarchy," they whispered. "Wouldn't Pompey make an excellent king?"

Pompey[140]

Pompey was Caesar's greatest competitor in his quest to rule Rome. In 49 BCE, after eight years in Gaul, Caesar began his journey back to Rome. The Senate told Caesar to send his soldiers home before entering Rome. Marching toward Rome with an army was considered an act of war. Caesar ignored the Senate and crossed the Rubicon River with his legion. Today, *"crossing the Rubicon"* means reaching a point of no return or committing to a revolution.

Caesar did not harm anyone in Rome. He spoke politely to the senators who hadn't fled Rome. He did raid the state treasury. He needed the money for his next move: a march to Spain to confront Pompey. His army crossed over the Alps, through France, and down to Spain, catching Pompey by surprise.

Pompey fled to Greece, with Caesar in hot pursuit. After losing a battle in Greece, Pompey sailed to Egypt. That country was experiencing its own drama. Ptolemy XIII was Egypt's thirteen-year-old pharaoh. His wife was his older sister and co-pharaoh, Cleopatra. The two were at each other's throats. While escaping Rome's civil war, Pompey landed in the middle of Egypt's civil war.

Unluckily for Pompey, Ptolemy XIII killed him. He hoped to win Caesar's favor. When Caesar arrived soon after, Ptolemy handed him Pompey's head as a gift. However, Caesar was not pleased. He wept and demanded a proper burial for his former friend.

Cleopatra had a more successful strategy for winning Caesar's support. She became his lover, and they joined forces against her brother-husband. Ptolemy lost the war. He drowned while crossing the Nile.

Caesar was the last man standing in the Triumvirate. Cleopatra married another one of her brothers, Ptolemy XIV. She gave birth to Caesar's only son, Caesarion, in 47 BCE.

Caesar served as consul and eventually dictator in Rome from 49 to 44 BCE. His reforms helped unemployed people and relieved the plebians' debt. He established the *Julian calendar*, which was remarkably close to what we use today.

In 44 BCE, Caesar became the dictator for life. He rejected a crown, but the senators knew Rome was headed for a monarchy again. They had to stop Caesar from gaining more power. On the Ides of March (March 15th), 44 BCE, they attacked Caesar in the Senate, stabbing him twenty-three times. Rome's citizens loved Caesar. His funeral turned into a riot, and the senators fled Italy.

The senators murdered Caesar on the Ides of March.[141]

The Second Triumvirate

Caesar named his teenage nephew Octavian as his heir. However, Rome's new consul, Mark Antony, blocked Octavian from receiving Caesar's titles. Rome was in chaos. Some of Caesar's assassins promised freedom to Rome's enslaved people if they fought for them. But people from Italy's provinces loved Caesar for his land acts. They formed an army to punish his killers.

When Antony finished his year as consul, the Senate appointed him as governor of Macedonia. However, Antony wanted to be close to the action in Rome. He demanded northern Italy instead and took his army to claim it. The senators sent Octavian after him, but Antony went to Gaul. He joined forces with his friend, Lepidus, the governor of Hispania and parts of Gaul.

Octavian came back to Rome to discover that the senators were plotting his murder. They had made Brutus commander in chief of the army. He was one of the senators who killed Caesar. However, part of the army was made up of Caesar's legions from Gaul. These men were fiercely loyal to Caesar. They came over to Octavian's side, and Octavian declared himself Rome's new consul.

The enemy of your enemy is your friend (sometimes). Octavian needed help to confront the senators. So, he joined with Antony and Lepidus in the Second Triumvirate in 43 BCE. They crushed their enemies, but the Triumvirate quickly crumbled. First, Octavian and Lepidus quarreled. Then, Antony fell in love with Cleopatra. They secretly plotted to make Cleopatra's son, Caesarion, Caesar's heir. They planned to rule Rome through him. Octavian declared war against Antony and Cleopatra. The lovers lost and committed suicide. The Roman Republic was already transforming into the Roman Empire, but no one realized it just yet.

Octavian (Caesar Augustus) was Rome's first emperor.[149]

How Were the Republic and Empire Different?

What changes came into play as Rome transitioned into an empire? When Octavian returned from Egypt, he planned to become an emperor. Yet, he was smart enough to do so stealthily and slowly. He pretended to be humble. He acted like he was in favor of the Senate and the republic. The change was so gradual that people hardly noticed anything was different.

Octavian became a consul in 31 BCE and worked to make Rome stable again. He restored the Senate's power, but it handed a lot of authority back to him. The senators asked him to continue as consul past the one-year term. The provinces were in chaos after the civil war. When the Senate asked Octavian to take control of the provinces, he agreed, smiling to himself. Controlling the provinces meant controlling the military.

In 27 BCE, the Senate gave Octavian the title *Augustus*. It means "exalted" or "magnificent." Since Caesar was his family name, his new name was Caesar Augustus. Later on, Caesar became a title for the emperors. The Senate also gave him the title *Princeps Senatus, Princeps Civitatis*, which means "first in the Senate, first among the citizens." This had been the title for the Senate's leader, but now, it basically meant "emperor."

Augustus would not wear the gold crown and purple toga that Julius Caesar wore. They stood for royalty. Augustus desired supreme power, but he didn't want anyone to know he wanted it. Four years later, the Senate gave Augustus full power over Rome's military and all the governors of the provinces. With this power, Augustus doubled the empire's territory, taking more of Africa, the Middle East, and Europe.

Augustus set up Rome's police and fire departments and a postal service. He restructured Rome's economy and organized a census and tax system. He built roads stretching from Rome to the farthest points of the empire. Even though Rome transitioned into an empire, its citizens welcomed the change. They enjoyed the peace and prosperity it brought, at least in the empire's early days.

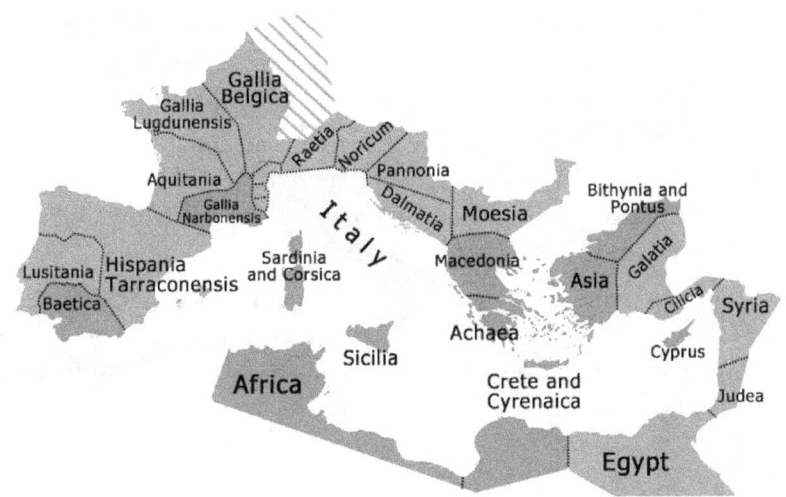

Rome's territory at the end of Augustus's life in 14 CE.[148]

A substantial change was religion. Rome had always been *polytheistic*, which means the people worshiped many gods and goddesses. That began to change in the empire's earliest days. Jesus Christ was born in the Roman province of Judaea during Augustus's reign. Jesus's teachings and miracles upended Judaea. Some Jews hoped for a Messiah to rescue them from Rome's oppression. When the Romans crucified Jesus, they thought that was the end. However, it was only the beginning.

The first generation of Jesus's followers spread his message throughout the Roman Empire. Some of the emperors tried to stamp it out. Yet, the attempts to suppress and persecute Christians only fueled the flames. Eventually, Christians were part of all layers of Roman society, even the Senate. By 300 BCE, 10 percent of the Roman Empire's population was Christian.

A Two-Century Rollercoaster Ride

Caesar Augustus had no sons, so he adopted his daughter Julia's two sons from her first marriage. He planned for one of them to become the next emperor. His backup was his stepson, Tiberius. Augustus forced Tiberius to divorce his beloved first wife to marry Julia. Julia's sons died young, so Tiberius took the throne in 14 CE when Augustus died. Tiberius suffered severe bouts of depression and spent most of his time away from Rome.

Tiberius's nephew, Germanicus, co-ruled with him until he was poisoned. Drusus was Tiberius's son from his first wife, and he also died of poisoning. Tiberius couldn't bear it. He abandoned Rome forever. He left his praetorian prefect, Sejanus, in charge, not realizing he was the poisoner.

When Germanicus's two older sons also died suddenly, Tiberius paced back and forth in his palace on the island of Capri. "Rome is unsafe for my family! Is Sejanus the killer? I trusted him! Now, I only have Germanicus's youngest son as my heir. I need to keep Caligula safe! I'll bring him here to live with me in Capri."

Eventually, the Romans became so fed up with Sejanus's schemes that he was arrested and executed. When Caligula became emperor in 37 CE, he did well for the first seven months. He gave bonuses to soldiers and started the elections again. He improved the economy and began elaborate building projects.

But then, Caligula got sick with a fever, probably from meningitis or encephalitis. After that, he had seizures. As a result, his personality changed. He became cruel. He often killed people for no reason. Caligula made his horse a priest and kept it in an ivory stable. After four years of this madness, the **Praetorian Guard**, an elite unit that served as the emperor's bodyguard, killed Caligula.

Emperor Claudius.[144]

Caligula's uncle Claudius was the only male adult left in the family. He had some odd ticks. He would suddenly laugh when nothing was funny. If he was stressed, he would blurt out weird things. Yet, Claudius was a good emperor. He built roads, aqueducts, and ports. His armies took more territory in Europe. Claudius's third wife was Caligula's sister, Agrippina. She talked him into adopting her son Nero and then fed Claudius poison mushrooms.

In 54 CE, Nero became the next emperor. He was unable to trust his mother, so he exiled her and later had her murdered. As he got older, Nero became increasingly unstable. By age thirty, he was behaving very irrationally. The western European provinces led a revolution, hoping to make Galba, governor of Spain, the new emperor. Then, the Roman army turned against Nero. He decided his only option was suicide, so he asked his servants to dig his grave. But he was too afraid to kill himself.

He turned to the few friends who were with him. "Someone else go first!"

When none of his friends volunteered, he handed his knife to his secretary. "You do it! Kill me now!"

Rome's Year of Four Emperors followed Nero's assisted suicide in 68 CE. On the night Nero died, the senators announced that Galba was the new emperor. Galba marched to Rome from Spain, crushing any cities that refused to accept him as their emperor. He only lasted seven months in Rome. The people grew tired of his cruelty. The Praetorian Guard killed Galba and made Otho emperor.

However, in Germany, the Roman legions had already made Governor Vitellius their new emperor. He marched over the Alps, and the Roman forces in northern Italy switched to his side. As Otho approached Rome, he killed himself. Vitellius spent all of Rome's money on banquets. He would eat until he couldn't eat anymore. Then, he would make himself vomit so he could eat more. He fed his rivals to the lions or forced them to fight as gladiators.

Meanwhile, the Jews in Judaea had rebelled against Roman rule. The Romans, led by General Titus Flavius Vespasian, fought them. When the Roman soldiers in Judaea heard about the chaos in Rome, they cried, "Rome needs a real leader! Vespasian should be the new emperor!" Vespasian left his son Titus to squash the Jewish revolt and headed to Rome. Vespasian's forces killed Vitellius, and Vespasian ruled for ten years, beginning the Flavian dynasty.

The Colosseum, built in the reigns of Vespasian and Titus.[145]

In 70 CE, Vespasian's son Titus burned Jerusalem. He destroyed the temple and killed over a half million Jews who had gathered in the city to celebrate Passover. He enslaved another sixty thousand and sent them to Rome to build the Colosseum. Meanwhile, Vespasian raised taxes to repair the damage done by the civil war. People even had to pay a tax to use the public bathrooms. They mockingly named the toilets *vespasiano* after their emperor.

When Vespasian died in 79 CE, Titus became the emperor. He was the first emperor whose biological father was also an emperor. He finished building the Colosseum, the world's largest amphitheater. Romans came to the Colosseum to see chariot races, gladiator fights, and animal hunts.

Three disasters struck Italy during Titus's two-year reign. Rome burned for three days, and an outbreak of disease killed thousands. Mount Vesuvius also erupted in southern Italy, shooting pumice and ash ten miles up. Hot ash and poisonous gases killed anyone who didn't escape. The ash covering the bodies hardened into a shell. In the 1800s, archaeologist Giuseppe Fiorelli poured plaster into the shells. It formed statue-like casts of the victims.

Cast of a victim from the Mount Vesuvius eruption.[146]

Titus's younger brother, Domitian, was the Flavian dynasty's last emperor. He was a bit weird, like many of Rome's early emperors. He liked catching flies and sticking a needle in them. He stripped the Senate of its power and imposed crushing taxes. Domitian also persecuted Jews and Christians. He was desperately afraid of being assassinated. His fears came true when a palace servant stabbed him to death.

The Senate installed the elderly Nerva as the new emperor, which began the Antonine dynasty. He was the first of the **Five Good Emperors**, who restored Rome to order and prosperity. He reformed the economy, reduced taxes, and gave land to people experiencing poverty. After less than two years, he died of a stroke. His adopted son Trajan became emperor. Trajan was an insightful ruler who formed a welfare program for orphans and poor children. During his reign, the Roman Empire contained about 25 percent of the world's population. His adopted son Hadrian became emperor when he died of heatstroke in 117 CE.

Hadrian's twenty years as emperor elevated the empire to new heights. He spent much of his time in western Europe, Africa, and the Middle East. He built roads and cities.

When he died in 138 CE, his adopted son, Antoninus Pius, became emperor. His reign was more peaceful than that of any other emperor. Pius was so good with finances that he filled Rome's treasury with money to spare. He was the first emperor to initiate diplomatic relations with China. His death in 161 CE left his adopted sons, Marcus Aurelius and Lucius Verus, as co-emperors.

Marcus Aurelius was scholarly, while Lucius Verus was into hunting and sports. The Parthians of Persia invaded Armenia, so Verus headed east to chase them away. When his men drained a section of the Orontes River to build a shipping channel, they discovered an eighteen-foot coffin with a giant's bones. Verus successfully evicted the Parthians and returned to Rome as a hero.

Meanwhile, Marcus Aurelius freed enslaved people and oversaw the care of Rome's orphans. In 165 CE, the Antonine Plague struck. It was likely either a measles or smallpox outbreak. It killed five million in the empire, including Lucius Verus. Marcus died in 180 CE, ending the Pax Romana.

What Was the Pax Romana? (27 BCE–180 CE)

The *Pax Romana* is Latin for "Roman Peace." Everything wasn't perfect during this time. Rome certainly had its ups and downs. Yet, the Roman Empire stretched from Britain to North Africa to western Asia. This area enjoyed a peace never seen before. It lasted two centuries, from Octavian to Marcus Aurelius. The Roman legions enforced law and order throughout the provinces. They kept the empire's roads mostly safe from bandits and the seas free of pirates.

This entire area had one central government and two main languages (Latin and Koine Greek). The Pax Romana led to astounding growth in trade, engineering, and culture. Christianity spread like wildfire. The Roman Empire reached its greatest size during this era. Its population grew to about seventy million.

Roundup Activity

Define the word or phrase listed below. Remember, the answers are at the end of the book if you need some help.

1. Transalpine Gaul
2. "Crossing the Rubicon"
3. Julian Calendar
4. Ides of March
5. The Second Triumvirate
6. Princeps Senatus, Princeps Civitatis
7. Polytheistic
8. Colosseum
9. Antonine Plague
10. Pax Romana

Chapter 4: The Roman Army

The Roman military repeatedly shocked the ancient world by winning battles against all odds. Rome's army and navy were the key ingredients in building an empire that stretched over three continents.

What led to such unbelievable success? The Romans were so stubborn that they refused to give up. Even if they lost the first time, they would charge back into battle. When they combined this determined nature with their organizational skills, lethal weapons, and stunning technology, they were an unstoppable force.

How Was the Roman Army Set Up?

A *century* was the smallest unit. It consisted of one hundred soldiers. Later, it had eighty soldiers, with eight men sleeping in each tent. An officer called a *centurion* was the leader of each century. How did someone become a centurion? First, he had to be an outstanding soldier to receive this promotion. He had to be strict with the men under him and lead by example.

Six centuries made up a *cohort*, which consisted of about 480 to 600 men. A *legion* was ten cohorts or about four thousand to six thousand men. The first cohort in a legion was the most experienced and skilled warriors. The tenth cohort was the new recruits.

How many legions did Rome have? In the early Roman Republic, Rome only had about twelve thousand soldiers in two legions. When it grew to four legions, Rome was able to conquer southern Italy. When Rome transitioned into an empire, it had around twenty-eight legions serving in Europe, North Africa, and western Asia. A *Legatus Legionis* was the commander of a legion. Military tribunes served under him. They organized command, handled logistics, and led the armies into battle.

This mural of a Roman soldier was in a house in Pompeii. It was covered by nineteen feet of ash from the Mount Vesuvius eruption in 79 CE.[147]

How Were Soldiers Recruited?

In the early Roman Republic, soldiers were usually drafted. However, they had to be landowners. Most soldiers came from Rome. The neighboring Etruscan, Latin, and Sabine tribes also sent one thousand soldiers each year to serve in the army. Since most soldiers were farmers, Rome usually only waged war in the summer after the farmers planted their crops and before the fall harvest. Rome did not have a full-time army at that time.

General Marius became one of Rome's consuls in 107 BCE. Rome was fighting a long war in Numidia (Algeria) in Africa. Marius wanted to win the war quickly, but he had a problem. Rome didn't have enough soldiers. Why? Well, Rome didn't have enough landowners. So, Marius decided to reform the military. His first change was to allow men who didn't own land to join the army.

Another dramatic change was recruiting soldiers as volunteers, although Rome still used draftees. "If they volunteer, they're more willing to fight!" Marius told the Senate. Marius also rewarded faithful service in the military by giving land grants. Getting land wasn't guaranteed, but it was an incentive. Poor people now had a way to work their way up into the middle class and own land. This change in recruitment got mixed reviews from the wealthier Romans.

"What is he thinking? Fighting is a noble art meant only for the upper classes. It has always been this way. Now, anybody can volunteer."

"Yes, but is that so bad? Now, we have enough soldiers to defeat Numidia."

"Nonsense! He just wants to build favor with the middle class. They're the ones who got him elected."

"Maybe, but these men without property don't have farms back home to worry about. They don't have to come back to plant their farms. Marius is forming a full-time army that can fight all year. Rome can have the power to rule the world!"

"Ha! Your head is in the clouds. Have you heard that our government must pay for the soldiers' armor and weapons? We'll be bankrupted!"

"We can pay for that with the loot from conquests. And some of our soldiers were going into debt. They were getting drafted and had to spend money they didn't have for swords, spears, and armor. Then, they had to leave their farms to fight and sometimes didn't get back in time for harvest. They had no way to feed their families or pay off their debts. Did you know some came home from war only to be sent to debtors' prison?"

Gaius Marius[148]

A century later, Caesar Augustus formed the ***Praetorian Guard***, which protected the emperor and sniffed out any plots against him. However, the Praetorian Guard sometimes joined the plots against emperors they hated. Augustus only used full-time, well-trained men instead of having a mixture of part-time and full-time soldiers. Soldiers didn't only come from Italy. By Nero's reign, half the Roman soldiers came from provinces in Europe, North Africa, and western Asia.

What Was the Training Like?

Roman soldiers needed to run long distances while carrying their gear. Soldiers were required to be exceptionally strong and able to endure hardships. Training drills taught them to fight in an organized way. Josephus was a Jewish commander and historian who fought against the Romans. He reported how the rigid discipline of the Roman soldiers helped them defeat much larger armies.

After being recruited, Roman soldiers went through four months of training. First, they learned how to march and run in formation. They had to speed-march with their heavy gear for 20 Roman miles (18.4 of today's miles or 29.6 kilometers) in 5 hours. They also had to learn to swim since they would need to cross rivers. Next, they trained in using their weapons and practiced mock battles against each other. Another important lesson was instantly obeying commands from their officers.

How Were They Punished for Stepping Out of Line?

If a soldier didn't immediately follow an order, he faced harsh punishment. If he ran away from battle, he got the death sentence because this put his fellow soldiers in danger. He would be beaten or stoned to death. Sometimes, soldiers were executed for things like stealing from the camp, giving false evidence, or committing the same crime three times. Other punishments included having money deducted from their pay or getting whipped in front of everyone.

How Were They Rewarded?

Roman generals made a point of rewarding soldiers who were brave or skilled. After a battle, the general would give a speech praising the soldiers who did especially well. He gave special awards for certain things. If a soldier wounded the enemy, he got a new spear. A gold crown went to the first person to climb over the wall of a city. Special decorations on their uniforms rewarded other feats.

The soldiers cheered on those who got these rewards. When they went home, their families celebrated their achievements. They proudly hung up their rewards so everyone could see them when they entered the house. Their hometowns threw parades, where the soldiers wore crowns or other decorations. The attention given to rewards encouraged the soldiers to be better fighters.

Weapons and Armor

Roman soldiers carried three weapons: a sword, a dagger, and a spear. The dagger, or *pugio*, came in handy if the enemy knocked a soldier's sword out of his hand. Roman officials carried them around Rome for self-defense. One never knew when his fellow senators might try to kill him! In the 2ⁿᵈ century BCE, soldiers started using the iron Spanish sword. Its blade was twenty-five inches (sixty-three centimeters), which was ideal for one-on-one combat on a crowded battlefield.

The ***pilum*** was a spear that weighed up to five pounds (two kilograms). It was six-and-a-half feet long (two meters). Its handle (shaft) was wood, and the rest was iron. Soldiers usually threw their spears. The iron was somewhat soft, and the spearhead often bent on impact. This might have been on purpose so the enemy couldn't pick up a spear and use it against them.

Soldiers of the Roman Republic carried a round shield called a ***scutum***. During the Roman Empire, they used a long, rectangular red and yellow shield. The shields had a ***boss*** in the center, a cone-shaped protrusion that could be used as a weapon when smashing the shield into the enemy. Soldiers in the Roman Republic wore Montefortino helmets that looked like an iron baseball cap worn backward. In the Roman Empire, helmets were more elaborate. They often had a cheek guard and a section protecting the nose.

Statue of a soldier's armor around 130 BCE.[149]

Roman soldiers in the empire often wore armor made of overlapping metal strips that covered their shoulders, upper arms, chest, and back. Sometimes, the part covering the chest was a solid piece of metal. Another type of armor was chain mail, which was made from small circles of iron linked together. It was flexible, so it gave the soldiers better movement. A third type of armor was scale armor. Small metal scales were sewn on fabric so they overlapped.

Tactical Formations

In the early days, the Roman soldiers copied the Greek phalanx position when lining up for battle. They stood shoulder to shoulder with their shields slightly overlapping. This formed a wall that protected the front line from arrows and spears. The soldiers behind the front line pushed the soldiers in front of them with their shields. The hundreds of men moved in unison in a tightly packed group with their spears sticking out in front. After Alexander the Great conquered western Asia, the Romans copied his formation with their own twist. The *manipular formation* had smaller units of 120 men each. Each *maniple* acted on its own, with a junior commander giving orders.

Siege Technology

The Roman army used engineers. They had many strategies to break into cities with high, thick walls. They built towers on wheels that they pushed close to the walls. Soldiers at the top of the tower could shoot arrows into the city. They could even get into the city using a gangplank. Catapults flung huge rocks into the walls, breaking them down. They also filled a pot with oil, set it on fire, and used the catapult to fling it over the wall. Titus used this method against Jerusalem.

Roman soldiers climbed over the walls using portable ladders. Engineers dug tunnels under the city walls that destabilized them, sending the walls crashing down. When Roman General Vespasian attacked Jotapata in Galilee, General Josephus was in the city. It was on a steep hill that kept the Romans from getting close with their siege engines. He wrote that the Romans cut down trees and used dirt and rocks to build a bank.

Once they built the bank, the Romans could put their catapults and battering rams into action. A battering ram was a huge beam with an iron head at one end. It hung by ropes from a tower on wheels. The soldiers would pull the beam back and then let go, letting it smash into the wall. Eventually, the wall would crumble. Although the Jews poured pots of burning oil on their attackers, the Romans ultimately broke into the city.

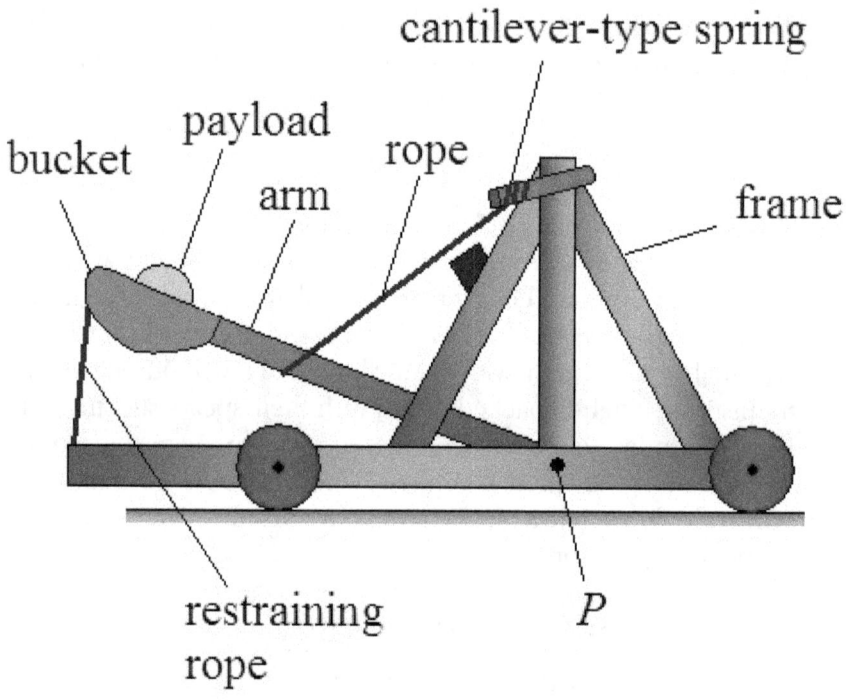

Catapults flung rocks or fiery pots of oil at a city under siege.[150]

Why Did They Set up Base Camps?

As the Roman army marched across vast territories, they set up *marching camps* where they would rest. They protected their camp by digging a ditch around it and erecting a rampart or defensive wall. Logs with pointed ends protected the wall. These camps had supplies and served as a base of operations. If the soldiers went out to fight and lost the battle, they could run back to the camp, which provided a safe place to regroup.

What Was a Triumph?

Victories deserve a celebration. The Romans celebrated their war victories with a *triumph*. It involved a breathtaking parade led by the commander, who wore a purple robe and a laurel-leaf crown. As flags waved and music played, the generals and their soldiers displayed their loot like elephants, chariots, jewels, and gold. The crowd went wild at the sight of captured kings and queens wearing golden shackles. The ceremonies lasted the entire day with speeches, rewards for the soldiers, and feasting.

Roundup Activity

Ten keywords/phrases are hidden in the puzzle. Read the definitions below to figure out the keyword and then find it in the puzzle. The answer key is at the back of the book.

D	R	A	U	G	N	A	I	R	O	T	E	A	R	P
M	L	K	J	I	H	G	F	E	D	L	C	B	A	U
T	M	A	R	I	U	S	S	R	Q	U	P	O	N	G
T	O	W	T	E	N	O	Z	Y	X	P	W	V	U	I
A	E	V	I	F	R	U	O	F	E	A	E	R	H	O
O	N	M	L	K	J	I	H	G	F	T	E	D	C	B
I	Z	Y	N	X	W	V	U	T	S	A	R	Q	P	L
I	G	E	O	B	T	R	O	H	O	C	E	H	T	I
H	W	E	I	H	T	S	A	W	G	N	I	N	N	A
P	H	T	G	D	N	A	D	R	O	P	I	L	U	M
M	A	W	E	D	R	O	D	G	O	I	O	W	E	N
U	G	H	L	T	D	S	L	O	G	O	I	W	S	I
I	T	D	V	E	L	O	S	E	V	N	A	D	O	A
R	D	R	Y	T	X	S	U	S	E	O	W	E	H	H
T	G	S	O	U	J	A	W	Y	R	U	T	N	E	C

1. A Roman army unit with eighty to one hundred soldiers
2. Six centuries with 480 to 600 men
3. Ten cohorts or about four thousand to six thousand men
4. An elite unit that protected the emperor
5. A Roman dagger
6. A Roman spear
7. A siege engine used to fling rocks or fiery pots of oil at the enemy
8. A parade and ceremony celebrating a Roman war victory
9. A Roman consul who reformed Rome's army
10. Small circles of iron linked together to form armor

Chapter 5: Patricians, Plebians, and Slaves

Patricians, plebians, and enslaved people were the three main groups of ancient Roman society. The patricians believed they had the right to rule over everyone else. The plebians were the folks in the middle. They were working-class people who initially had no influence on government, but that changed as time passed. The slaves had little power and no say at all in what happened in the government.

What Was the Life of a Patrician Like?

The patricians were at the top of society. They were rich landowners from noble families. When Rome was a kingdom and an early republic, the patricians controlled politics, religion, and the military. They were the senators, the high priests, and the military officers. Most patricians had large plantations farmed by enslaved people. The plebians and freed slaves (freedmen) who worked in the towns and workshops connected to the plantations were called *clients*.

A patrician father, or *patron*, took care of his "clients," who were part of the extended "family." If they had to go to court, he represented them. He arranged marriages, helped them with business deals, gave loans, and provided food and protection. At dawn, the patron met with any clients who needed help. After finishing business, his clients escorted him to the Forum. Arriving at the Forum with a large group of clients was a status symbol for patrons.

Where did the patricians live? Most patrician families owned two homes. One was a townhouse in the city called a ***domus***. The other was an elegant villa in the suburbs or on a plantation. The patrician men usually stayed in the domus during the week and relaxed in their villas on the weekends. Women and children spent more time in the villas, but they came into the city for dinner parties and festivals.

Elaborate murals and statues decorated the entrance to the domus. It led to the ***atrium***, where an opening in the roof let in the light and rain. A pool under the opening caught the rainwater, with pipes leading to an underground ***cistern***, a container that holds water. Rooms surrounding the atrium included the patron's office, where his clients would meet him in the early morning. He also handled business deals there.

The villa had lots of room for children to play. There were beautiful gardens. A domus and a villa both had a large dining room with tile mosaics on the floor and bright murals. The patricians loved throwing dinner parties. Guests reclined on couches and ate from small tables.

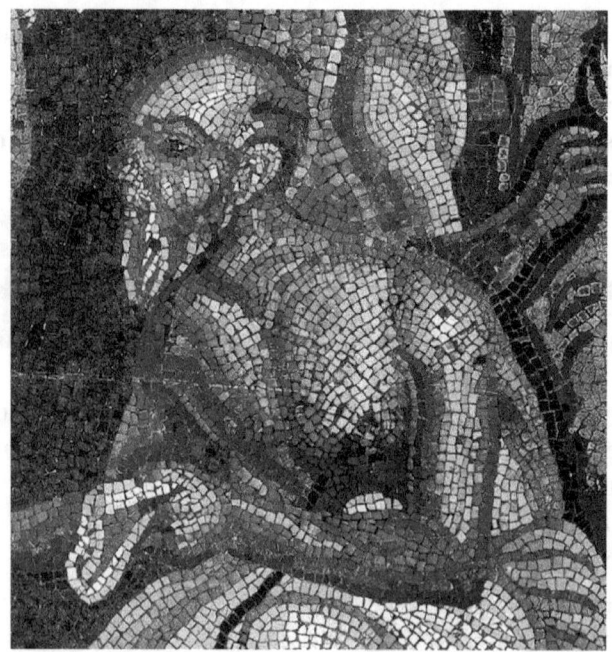

A tile mosaic of Livius Andronicus, Rome's first schoolmaster.[161]

What about school? In Rome's early days, fathers taught their children. In 272 BCE, a patrician named Livius bought a Greek prisoner of war named Andronicus. He was highly educated, so Livius had him tutor his children. Later, Livius Andronicus (he took his owner's surname, like most slaves) won his freedom. He opened a private school. It became fashionable for patricians to buy Greek slaves to teach their children or send them to a school taught by a Greek freedman.

Most patrician boys and girls were educated. Upper-class boys and girls could learn at home or attend a *ludus* or primary school. These schools were informal. They met in a house, a public building, or a quiet spot outside. The tutors taught reading, writing, and math. Students learned to read both Latin and Greek, focusing on the Greek historical poetry written by Homer and Hesiod.

The *grammaticus* was a type of middle school for boys aged eleven to fourteen. Girls usually didn't attend because they got married in their early teens. In the grammaticus, the boys learned public speaking, history, geography, literature, and mythology. Some teens finished school at fifteen, but a few boys continued to study *rhetoric* (giving a speech) by a teacher called a *rhetor*. When a patrician boy turned sixteen, he graduated from school. After a special ceremony, he could wear the white toga, which meant he was a full citizen. Togas were mainly worn for special events to show off one's social status.

What Was the Life of a Plebian Like?

The plebians were everyone who wasn't a patrician or an enslaved person. Some had small farms. The rest lived in towns or cities. They were shopkeepers, craftsmen, construction workers, and bakers. The ones who owned land could serve in the army. After Marius's reforms, more plebs volunteered or got drafted into the army. Some plebians became military officers.

Plebian parents taught their children basic reading, writing, and math. Most plebian children worked with their parents in the shops or on the farms, so they had little time for school. As some plebian families grew wealthy, they hired tutors or sent their children to school. Girls married between the ages of twelve to fourteen. In one type of marriage, the husband "bought" the right to control his wife from her father. Other times, the couple simply moved in together. If they lived together for a year, the husband "owned" his wife. However, if she stayed away from the home for three nights in a year, he could not have control over her.

The plebs in towns and cities lived in apartment buildings called *insulae*. Up to fifty people lived in a three- to five-story building. There were shops on the first floor. At one time, the insulae were higher than five stories. However, Rome's earthquakes toppled the tall buildings every few years. Fire was also an issue. Caesar Augustus passed laws requiring apartment buildings to be no higher than five stories. They also needed thicker, stronger walls. Nero ordered the builders to use less wood and more brick and stone. There had to be a gap between each building.

An insula built in the 3rd century BCE.[163]

Initially, Rome's plebians had almost no political influence. Tension between the patricians and plebs erupted occasionally, beginning in the early republic. When the patricians became abusive, the plebs found a clever way to turn the tables. They went on strike. They closed their shops and headed to the countryside for a vacation. This brought Rome to a standstill. No shops were open. There was no one to clean the streets, bake bread, or deliver things. The plebian soldiers even refused to fight.

After several days, the patricians were ready to discuss the issues upsetting the plebs. What was their top complaint? The senators passed new laws but didn't announce them to the public. They waited until someone broke the law and then arrested them. The plebs were unhappy about paying fines or going to jail for a law they knew nothing about. Over the centuries, the plebians gained more political control. In 494 BCE, they got their own Plebian Assembly. Beginning in 312 BCE, they could be senators. Many plebians grew wealthy and powerful.

Who Were the Gracchus Brothers?

In the late Roman Republic, the rich were growing richer, and the poor were growing poorer. Tiberius and Gaius Gracchus were plebian tribunes trying to bring social reform. Rome was getting a lot of new land. The Romans had conquered cities and provinces in Europe, North Africa, and western Asia. When he became a tribune in 133 BCE, Tiberius wanted this land divided into small farms for war veterans and the poor so they would have a way to support themselves. However, the wealthy senators wanted the land for themselves. They falsely accused Tiberius and stirred up a mob. The Romans beat him to death with wooden chairs.

A decade later, Gaius became a tribune. He supported his brother's land redistribution. He also wanted the government to pay for the soldiers' weapons and armor. Poor men drafted into service often went into debt buying their equipment. The Senate declared Gaius an enemy of the state and stirred up a mob again. Gaius committed suicide before they could kill him. About two decades later, Consul Marius had the government start paying for the plebs' armor and weapons. However, something still needed to be done about land for the veterans and poor plebs.

Marcus Livius Drusus became a tribune in 91 BCE. He continued to push for the reforms the Gracchus brothers fought and died for. He tried to get more land for the plebs. Another issue was citizenship for people living in Italy who were from other tribes. Many Italian cities provided soldiers and support for Rome's wars, and they wanted the right to vote and the protection of Roman law. An assassin snuck into Drusus's house and killed him, cutting short his untiring advocacy. Finally, in 59 BCE, Julius Caesar and Pompey passed the land redistribution bill.

What Was the Life of a Slave Like?

In ancient Rome, enslaved people made up about 20 percent of Rome's population, but they had no rights. Most slaves were prisoners of war. Before being captured, they came from all walks of life. Some enslaved people were plebians who sold themselves or their children into slavery to pay a debt or because they didn't have enough food. If a slave woman had a baby, the child was automatically enslaved, even if the father was a free man.

Pirates sailed the seas, capturing ship crews and passengers and selling them as slaves. Cilician pirates even captured Julius Caesar when he was a young man. However, they didn't sell him since he was from a noble family. Instead, his family paid a ransom to get him back. In the months it took to negotiate his freedom, Caesar warned the pirates he would crucify them. They laughed, but he wasn't joking. After they freed him, he formed a militia. He sailed back to their island hideout and captured and crucified them.

When Rome fought Carthage in the Second Punic War, Hannibal captured thousands of Roman soldiers. He offered Rome the chance to pay a ransom for them, but the Senate refused. Hannibal sold his prisoners of war to the Greeks. They worked as enslaved people in Greece for twenty years until Rome's General Flamininus rescued 1,200 of them when invading Greece.

In this 2nd-century mosaic, an enslaved person on the left holds water and towels, and the two large slaves pour wine.[158]

Enslaved people's work depended on their education and past occupations. Child and female slaves often worked as servants in the homes of wealthy patricians. The patrician plantations had hundreds of slaves doing the farmwork. Enslaved people carried out Rome's massive construction projects. Those with advanced skills or education worked as craftspeople, dancers, teachers, scribes, doctors, painters, engineers, or architects. Some slaves with a military background were trained to be gladiators.

Roman law gave no protection to enslaved people. Some masters were kind, but others beat their slaves. They even raped, tortured, and killed them. The government did nothing during the Roman Republic. As Rome transitioned into an empire, enslaved people received more rights.

Emperor Nero allowed them to complain to the courts about harsh treatment. Emperor Pius said that a master who killed his slave could be found guilty of murder.

Some masters let their slaves buy their freedom. Some set them free without payment and helped them establish a new life. The Greeks found it amazing that formerly enslaved people could become citizens. The Romans remembered that Romulus had welcomed former slaves into his new city and given them citizenship. A Roman slave could not marry, but he could enter into a relationship with a woman and have children. If they later both got their freedom, they could legally marry.

A slave owner could set an enslaved woman free and then marry her. She had no choice in the matter, and she could not divorce him even though divorce was usually permitted in Rome. Technically, slave owners could split up a slave family, but they usually respected and supported the relationship. They even put instructions in their wills to keep slave families together.

What Happened When Italy's Slaves Revolted?

Spartacus was a soldier in Thrace (today's Bulgaria) who the Romans captured and sold to a gladiator school. The school trained men and women. Yes, Rome had women gladiators. They had to learn a particular type of combat performed in the Circus Maximus or the Forum (before the Colosseum was built). The gladiators followed a choreography when fighting, which sometimes required them to accept a death blow from their opponent depending on their master's wish. Not all the competitions ended in death, but few gladiators lived past the age of twenty-five.

Mosaic of Roman gladiators.[154]

In 73 BCE, Spartacus and seventy-eight of his fellow gladiators plotted an escape. "We'll certainly die if we stay here," they agreed. "Why not take our chances on the outside?"

"Where would we go?" someone asked.

"We could go north and cross the mountains into freedom!" Spartacus answered.

So, the gladiators stole knives and cleavers from the kitchen and escaped. They hiked to Mount Vesuvius (152 years before it exploded and buried Pompeii). On the way, other enslaved people joined them. They raided villages, towns, and fields for food and more weapons. Rome sent Commander Clodius to capture the escapees.

"Ha! They're up on the mountain, and my army is down here. They're trapped! We'll sit here and let them starve!"

One side of Mount Vesuvius was a sheer cliff face. The Romans didn't worry about protecting that side. However, the slaves wove rope ladders from vines and scaled down the cliff to freedom. The Roman troops were still stationed at the bottom of the mountain when they got word the escapees were roaming through Italy. The Senate was enraged. "They've grown to ten thousand fighting men now!"

The Senate ordered both consuls to take their legions and kill the slaves. Meanwhile, the slave army split into two groups. One stayed in southern Italy, thinking they could continue living as desperados. That plan didn't end well. A Roman legion surrounded and killed most of that group. The escapees led by Spartacus took the long trek north to the Alps. They wanted to cross over. However, on the way, they got trapped between two Roman armies. Spartacus had a trick up his sleeve, though.

Spartacus and many of his men were from Thrace and were excellent horse riders. While roaming around Italy, they collected hundreds of horses and formed a cavalry. At this time, the Roman army wasn't using horses in battle very much. The slave army took the Romans entirely by surprise by charging *at* them with their horses and stealing their supplies! They then raced toward northern Italy.

They got to the base of the Alps, but the men lost heart at the sight of the towering peaks. "Look at all the snow and ice up there. Our horses can't climb that! We need to wait until summer."

"Well, what do we do now? We can't stay here and let the Romans trap us!"

"Let's head back south and cross over to the island of Sicily. Their slaves rebelled fifty years ago. They lost, but I bet we can start a new rebellion. With our joint forces, we could take over Sicily!"

So, they trekked back south to the toe of Italy's boot. They had to figure out how to cross the strait, so they found some pirates who agreed to sail them to Sicily. However, the pirates took their money and disappeared over the horizon, leaving them behind. Roman Commander Crassus thought he had them trapped at the Messina Strait. He dug a long canal to keep them penned in. He didn't expect them to build a dam over the canal and escape.

By this time, the slave army had divided into several smaller groups to elude the Roman forces more efficiently. Spartacus's group even won one battle against Crassus when the Romans had the uphill advantage. But then, they got cocky and thought they could beat the Romans no matter what. Spartacus tried to warn them, but they wouldn't listen and insisted on another battle. So, Spartacus killed his horse.

"If I die, I won't need the horse. If we win, I'll steal one from the Romans."

As it turned out, he didn't need the horse. Spartacus and many of the slaves died in the battle. The Romans captured six thousand escapees and crucified them. Rome rewarded Crassus for defeating the slaves by making him consul in 70 BCE.

Roundup Activity

Pretend you're the same age as you are now, but you live in ancient Rome. Decide whether you're a patrician, a plebian, or an enslaved person. Write a diary entry describing your day.

Chapter 6: Leisure, Entertainment, and Economy

What did ancient Romans enjoy doing during their free time? A favorite activity was to head to the Forum or the Circus Maximus. They could see jugglers, dancers, gladiators, and chariot races. After the Colosseum opened in 80 CE, people flocked there. They watched mock sea battles, dramas, and, of course, gladiator contests and chariot racing. Sadly, a lot of the Roman entertainment was cruel to people and animals.

Gladiators

Most gladiators were prisoners of war or criminals. However, in the early Roman Empire, men actually volunteered to fight. They were eager to show off their fighting experience to the roar of the crowds. Of course, there was also the fame and prize money that went to the winners. Even patricians joined in a few mock battles to prove their skills. In the 2nd century CE, Emperor Commodus jumped into the arena dressed as the god Mercury.

When did Rome start having gladiator contests? In early Rome, families held gladiator fights at the funerals of noblemen to honor their skills. They believed the blood that flowed from the fighters purified the dead person's soul. These funeral gladiator shows were still going on in Julius Caesar's day. He organized contests with hundreds of gladiators to honor the memory of his father and daughter.

Most gladiator fights were between two men of comparable size and had similar abilities. A referee in a white tunic supervised each fight. About one in five contests ended in the death of a fighter. Usually, if one wounded the other, the referee ended the contest.

Gladiator contests had several variations. A typical fight was between two men with a sword or shield. Others fought on horseback or from chariots. The *retiarius* gladiators fought with a fish net and *trident* (a three-pronged spear). They would try to capture their opponent with the net.

A 3rd-century CE mosaic of retiarius gladiators and a referee.[155]

Before a gladiator contest, promoters plastered billboards everywhere. They advertised who would be fighting, the kind of music, and what kind of food and sweets would be for sale. The owner of the gladiator school threw a banquet for the gladiators the night before. The contest began with a parade into the arena and musical performances. Executions of condemned prisoners were next, and then, the gladiators began their contests. The winners got a palm branch and a prize, like a crown or money. Some even won their freedom.

Animal Hunts

Another bloodthirsty event that drew crowds was wild animal hunts. It came to Rome from Greece in 189 BCE after Rome defeated Greece's Aetolian League. This type of entertainment went back to at least the days of Alexander the Great, who held contests with lions against men and dogs. In Rome, animal hunts first involved gladiators fighting big cats, like panthers and lions.

What kept the audience safe from the wild animals? Nothing! The audiences at the Circus Maximus and Forum put their lives on the line. There wasn't a barrier keeping the wild animals from attacking them. Usually, the wild animal hunts took place in the morning, with gladiator contests following in the afternoon. Thousands of animals died in a day, although they sometimes killed their hunters first. At the Colosseum's dedication, nine thousand wild animals died in the cruel hunts.

What kind of animals did the Romans use for these hunts? Most animals came from Rome's new lands in Africa and the Middle East. Some of the animals that entertained the crowds with their bloody deaths were rhinos, giraffes, zebras, ostriches, camels, crocodiles, leopards, bears, elephants, hippos, and lions.

Execution by Animals

Sometimes, instead of hunters killing animals, the tables were turned. The animals hunted and killed humans. This kind of execution was called **damnatio ad bestias** or "damnation from beasts." Rome's audiences couldn't get enough of the twisted practice. In the early empire, some emperors, like Nero and Trajan, killed Christians this way. They forced the Christians to sacrifice to the Roman gods or get eaten by animals.

Chariot Racing

Ancient Rome had four chariot-racing teams called Red, Blue, White, and Green. Each team had their own stables with trainers, groomers, blacksmiths, and veterinarians (yes, Rome had vets). Chariot racing was huge in Rome. There could be up to twenty-four races every day. As many as eight hundred horses raced each day in the Circus Maximus. On the straight part of the track, the horses reached forty-five miles (seventy-two kilometers) an hour.

This panel from the Circus Maximus shows a chariot team approaching a curve.[156]

Who drove the chariots? The team managers bought young slave boys and trained them in the art of charioteering. Chariot racing was a dangerous business. Even though the charioteers wore helmets and padding, the crashes killed many boys. A driver wrapped the reins around his left wrist and held the whip in his right hand. He would get dragged if he fell from the chariot, so he carried a knife to cut the reins. He would have to roll himself off the track and out of the way of the horses charging around the track. Sometimes, massive accidents involved multiple chariots as they charged around a turn. The Romans called these "shipwrecks."

A staggering number of drivers died in their teens. One famous charioteer named Scorpus won 2,048 races and many bags of gold before being killed in a crash at age 26. Another famous driver, Gaius Appuleius Diocles, raced for 24 years and won 1,462 races. He survived and retired as a fabulously wealthy man.

Dancers, Jugglers, and Acrobats

When the Romans conquered new lands, they were always on the lookout for professional dancers, jugglers, acrobats, and other entertainers. They would take these performers back to Italy as enslaved people to entertain in parades, chariot races, and gladiator fights. Dancing in ancient Rome was usually a performance. It wasn't something that people just did for fun, except in some religious festivals. The dances could be funny, scary, or sexy. The female Spanish dancers gained fame by kicking their feet higher than their shoulders.

Pantomimus was a dancing performance that acted out a story using body movements, hand gestures, and masks. The dancers did not speak. It was similar to a mime, except it told a story, usually of a divine nature, rather than just to amuse people. Also, the dancers did not use facial expressions since they wore masks.

Jugglers provided entertainment before or between competitions in the Colosseum or Circus Maximus. Some jugglers used their hands and feet to keep the balls in the air. Others used various parts of their body to keep a glass ball in the air. An incredibly skilled juggler named Agathinus juggled a shield, catching it with his feet and bouncing it with his back and head to keep it in constant motion. Some experts even juggled knives! While the jugglers entertained the crowd on the ground, acrobats danced on tightropes overhead.

A mural from Pompeii of acrobats dancing on a tightrope.[187]

Mock Naval Battles

Julius Caesar wanted to celebrate his triumphs in France and Egypt. So, he threw an enormous mock naval battle in 46 BCE. He had a lake dug next to the Tiber River. The manmade lake was filled with water from the river. Caesar's workers built marble seats for the patrician spectators. The mock battle had twelve Roman warships.

Emperor Claudius put on an even grander fake naval battle in 52 CE at Fucine Lake in northern Italy. This battle had one hundred ships and nineteen thousand condemned prisoners as the marines. One may wonder why he had so many men sentenced to die! Before the battle, the prisoners expected to either drown or die in the fighting greeted the emperor, saying, "Those who are about to die salute you!"

Emperor Titus ordered one hundred days of games to celebrate the grand opening of the Colosseum in 80 CE. One of the extravagant shows included a naval battle. He had the Colosseum flooded, and the sailors used flat-bottomed ships since the water was only about 5 feet (1.5 meters) deep. An artificial island in the middle of the manmade lake gave a place for the sailors to jump onto land to fight.

Dramas

The ancient Romans loved to copy the Greeks. One thing they copied was theater. Roman drama focused on tragedies and comedies. After a plague struck Rome in the 4th century BCE, the Romans felt that performing drama as part of worshiping the gods would help end the epidemic. Livius Andronicus, Rome's first schoolmaster, got involved a century later. He had been a Greek scholar before being captured and knew Greek drama well. He translated Greek plays into Latin and also wrote plays of his own.

A mosaic showing masks worn for tragedies and comedies.[158]

Roman Baths and Toilets

The Roman baths were much more than just a place to get clean. People gathered at the baths to relax, read, visit with their friends, and make business or political deals. The baths were similar to a fancy spa today. They had multiple rooms beautifully decorated with arches, statues, and mosaics. The public baths had places to exercise, changing rooms, outside swimming pools, inside baths of various temperatures, steam rooms, and places to get a massage. Towns and cities throughout Italy and the Roman provinces had public baths.

The Romans built the Temple of Mercury near Naples in the 1st century BCE. It has the oldest surviving concrete dome. At seventy-one feet (twenty-two meters) in diameter, it was the largest dome built up to that point. The dome covered the baths. Baths were often built in or next to temples. Wealthy Romans had private baths in their homes but also used the public baths for socializing.

Plebians didn't have toilets in their apartments. They had to either use a chamber pot or run down the street to the nearest public restroom. They would toss the urine and feces in the chamber pots out the window, so folks on the street had to stay out of the line of fire. They also had to tread carefully around the messes on Rome's smelly streets. Rome's plebian neighborhoods had public toilets attached to the public baths. When the baths emptied, the water flowed through pipes to the toilet room. It swept through the troughs under the latrines and washed them clean.

A public toilet room.[169]

A public restroom was one large room with a bench against the walls. It had multiple holes where people could sit down to relieve themselves. Privacy when using the toilet wasn't a concept. The holes were so close that a person's thighs could brush against the person sitting at the next hole. A little gutter with running water ran around the room just in front of where people's feet would be when sitting on the toilet. At each toilet was a stick with a sea sponge on the end. People used these sponges to clean their bottoms and then rinsed them in the running stream of water.

What Happened in Rome's Forum?

Rome's Forum was the town hub. It was a market, an entertainment center, and a place to worship. The Forum was a rectangular outdoor meeting place in the middle of Rome. People gathered to listen to political speeches and attend elections. They made business deals and met with their friends. Parades, gladiator contests, and acrobatic performances always drew a crowd. Much of the architecture surrounding the Forum followed Greek styles. However, the Romans put their own stamp on the Forum with domes and triumphal arches.

The Arch of Septimus Severus at the Forum.[160]

What Drove Rome's Economy?

Rome traded with lands around the Mediterranean Sea. Syria acted as an eastern trade hub, receiving silk, perfumes, ginseng, and other treasures from China and India, which it shipped to Rome. Syria also bred racing camels and racehorses and shipped those to Rome, along with its native lions and leopards. The craftspeople in Sidon, Lebanon, used a blowpipe to produce mold-blown glass vessels. The Romans couldn't get enough of these exquisite glasses. The Phoenicians made a wildly popular purple dye from the Murex sea snail, and the Romans bought this for more than 1,000 denarii (around $1,150 USD) a pound. When Rome warred against the Parthian Empire, the Persians cut off the *Silk Road*, the land and sea routes that brought silk and other items from eastern Asia to the Mediterranean. The price of silk went sky-high in Rome. When the government tried to set fixed prices on silk, the merchants couldn't survive.

Rome imported copper and gold from Spain, olive oil from Libya, and wine from France. Ships brought tin, silver, and wool from Britain and ivory from Africa. Rome used a standard form of money—gold and silver coins—to make trade on three continents easier. Once Rome gained control of almost every country around the Mediterranean Sea, it could provide reasonably safe sea trade. Pirates were not the threat to ships they had once been.

Egypt was Rome's breadbasket. Italy did not have enough agricultural land to support the growing population. However, Egypt produced three times more wheat and barley than it needed to feed its own people. The Nile River flooded every year, leaving the moist soil full of nutrients. The Egyptians also had a sophisticated irrigation system to water their crops even in times of no rain. Egypt shipped twenty-six million tons of grain to Rome annually during the Roman Empire.

However, with the grain came death. From 249 to 263 CE, the Plague of Cyprian spread from Alexandria, Egypt, to Rome. People suddenly fell ill with diarrhea, vomiting, and fever. Their eyes bled, and their arms and legs turned black with tissue death. No one had seen such a terrifying plague. Even healthy teens and young adults dropped dead. It was probably a filovirus, like Ebola. Thousands of people died every day in Rome, and the disease devastated the military.

Roundup Activity

Ancient Romans hung up posters to advertise gladiator contests, chariot races, dramas, and other events. Choose an event, and make your own promotional poster. You can get creative with color and illustrations. Remember to list the date and time, the names of the show's stars, and what snacks will be on sale.

Chapter 7: Key Achievements of Ancient Rome

Where would we be today without Rome's achievements? Rome built excellent roads and aqueducts. Ancient Roman technology and political thought changed how things were done and how governments were run. Rome's imprint on the world survived its collapse. It shaped civilizations and governments through the millennia. It's hard to grasp all the parts of our lives that echo ancient Rome.

Concrete

Think of all the things made of concrete. We walk on concrete sidewalks, drive over concrete bridges, and leave our cars in concrete parking lots. Did you know that over 70 percent of buildings where we live, work, or attend school are built using concrete? Who do we have to thank for this? The ancient Romans gave us this incredibly strong building material.

The Romans used concrete to build their roads, aqueducts, and domed buildings. They even used concrete to heat their houses. How did they make concrete? They started with lime, which was created by burning limestone rocks and mixing it with water. Then, they mixed lime with volcanic ash, sand, brick rubble, and tiny chunks of limestone. Many buildings, bridges, and aqueducts the Romans built two thousand years ago still stand today. In fact, Roman concrete was better than today's concrete.

What was their secret? In 2022, scientists at the Massachusetts Institute of Technology and Harvard University decided to find out. One readily available ingredient (thanks to Mount Vesuvius) was volcanic ash, which helped with strength. However, the researchers found that those tiny limestone chunks were even more important. They could self-heal. The Romans used high heat when mixing concrete, which produced a chemical reaction. We all know that concrete can get cracks in it. But when cracks formed in the Roman concrete, and water seeped into the cracks, guess what happened? Those tiny limestone pieces reacted with the water. They crystallized and filled in the cracks. How amazing is that?

A thermopolium or fast food eatery.[161]

Thermopolium: Takeaway Food

How often do you swing through your favorite fast-food restaurant to grab a quick bite? Did you know Rome had fast food? The plebians who lived in the insulae didn't have kitchens in their apartments. So, they had *thermopolia*. A thermopolium, a place that sells hot food, was a one-room kitchen with a stone counter in the front. The counter had holes. Large clay jars fit in the holes and held hot food, nuts, and dried fruit. Some of the thermopolia were only for takeaway food. Others had tables and chairs where customers could sit.

Underfloor Heating

Wouldn't you love waking up on a chilly morning and putting your feet on a warm floor? The Romans thought so too! A *hypocaust* is a heating system that is under a floor. As we know, heat rises. So, a heated floor not only keeps a person's toes warm but also efficiently warms a room. The

Romans built hypocausts to warm their public bathhouses. Some wealthy Romans used this heating system in their townhouses and villas.

How did the underfloor heating work? First, the building had a shallow basement about three feet (one meter) deep. It was filled with short pillars made from brick or concrete. The pillars had flat tops on which the first floor of a building rested. A furnace constantly burned and sent heat into the basement area. It also heated water for the baths. Ducts or tubes in the walls lifted the cool air out of the basement.

Aqueducts and Sewers

The Minoan people of Crete and the ancient Iraqis developed an early system of moving water through short channels or clay pipes. However, the Romans literally took aqueduct technology to new heights. They moved water through miles of pipes traveling over mountains and on high structures going over valleys. France's Pont du Gard aqueduct soared 161 feet (49 meters) in the air.

How did the Romans keep the water moving through the pipes when it had to go over mountains? They used inverted siphons in a U-shape going down and then back up. The force of the water running downhill pushed it back up through the pipe. Rome had eleven aqueducts that carried water to large tanks in the city. From there, pipes ran the water through Rome for baths, drinking, cooking, and toilets.

The Pont du Gard aqueduct in France.[162]

The dirty water had to go somewhere, so the Romans built the ***Cloaca Maxima*** when Rome was still a kingdom. It was one of the world's earliest sewers. It was built to remove wastewater and drain Rome's marshy land.

It was large enough for a hay wagon to pass through! Did you know that parts of this ancient sewer are still used today?

All Roads Lead to Rome!

The *viae Romanae* or Roman roads traveled through Europe, North Africa, and western Asia. This road network ultimately covered 750,000 miles (1,200,000 kilometers). The primary function of the roads was to enable quick travel. The military could quickly march twenty miles a day to deal with uprisings or other emergencies. These roads also greatly improved trade on three continents. The Roman roads were so well built that some still have their original cobblestones today, two thousand years later. Others formed the base for modern roads.

How did the Romans build their roads? They started by digging out a wide trench, which they filled with four layers. At the bottom was dirt, then gravel, and then bricks. Rock slabs or cobblestones formed the pavement at the top. The Romans made their roads to last! They could withstand floods and earthquakes. The middle of the road was slightly higher, so rainwater would drain to the sides. Signposts provided mile markers and told how far it was to the next town.

Rome began building its outstanding road system in the early Roman Republic. In 450 BCE, the Law of Twelve Tables, the first written laws in ancient Rome, said the roads had to be eight feet wide. Rome's government paid to build the roads, but the provinces had to maintain and repair the roads that went through their lands. The Romans dug tunnels through mountains and built bridges over rivers and deep valleys. The Pons Fabricius bridge, built in 62 BCE, still stands over the Tiber River in Rome today.

The Pon Fabricius bridge in Rome.[168]

Feeding the Poor: Rome's Early Welfare System

In the late republic and empire, Rome imported grain, mainly from Egypt. The government sold it at a discount to the poorest citizens in times of emergency. By the beginning of the empire, the government provided free bread to about one-fifth of the population. It also offered cheap entertainment to keep the poor population happy. The emperors hoped that if the poorest people were fed and entertained, they would be less likely to lead protests. The people experiencing poverty received enough to feed two people. If they had large families, they had to figure out a way to feed everyone.

The Roman Calendar and Roman Numerals

Rome's founder, Romulus, supposedly developed the first Roman calendar. It had ten months and started in March. The next king made it twelve months following the solar year. In the Roman Republic, the year ran for 355 days. However, this didn't work with the solar year. Julius Caesar revised it in 45 BCE. He used the Egyptian calendar as a model. Now, a year had 365 days, and all the months except February had 30 or 31 days. February had twenty-eight days, except for the leap year, which occurred every four years, when it got twenty-nine days.

Rome began using **Roman numerals** in its earliest days, copying its Etruscan neighbors. Letters represented numbers. The letter "I" was one, "V" was five, "X" was ten, and "L" was fifty. "C" stood for one hundred, "D" for five hundred, and "M" for one thousand. Combinations of these letters formed other numbers. What about large numbers? The year 2024 is MMXXIV. Roman numerals are used today for kings and queens like King Charles III. One also sees them in outlines, book chapters, film sequels, and page numbers at the beginning of a book. Some clocks and watches still use Roman numbers.

Engineering, Math, Astronomy, and Medicine

Heron's steam engine. The fire heated water into steam, which turned the ball. [164]

Egypt was a Roman colony in the early empire. The Egyptian city of Alexandria was the intellectual hub of the Western world. Heron of Alexandria lived in the 1st century CE and invented the first steam engine and a wind-powered wheel. Heron's formula calculated the area of a triangle based on the lengths of its sides. In the 2nd century CE, Claudius Ptolemy of Alexandria wrote the *Almagest* on astronomy. It listed forty-eight of the eighty-eight constellations that the International Astronomical Union recognizes today. Diophantus, the Father of Algebra, taught in Alexandria in the 3rd century CE. He wrote *Arithmetica*, which shows how to use algebra to solve arithmetic problems.

Galen was a Greek doctor who lived in Rome. He dissected apes to understand the human body. After a while, he found their faces too much like humans and decided to dissect pigs instead. When the Antonine Plague (probably smallpox) struck the empire from 166 to 169 CE, it killed at least 10 percent of the people. The estimates go as high as half the population. Galen recorded the people's symptoms and experimented with ways to treat them.

Mosaic Art

Rome perfected the mosaic art form and produced it on a grander scale than any other culture. Pebbles formed early mosaics, but the Romans used small pieces of ceramic, glass, or stone held together with mortar to create a picture or pattern. It usually covered a section of floor or wall. Many ancient Roman mosaics are still in reasonably good condition today. They give us insight into everyday Roman life, mythology, and history.

Teen athletes in a 4th-century CE mosaic from Sicily.[165]

Innocent until Proven Guilty!

Most ancient cultures followed the idea that one was guilty until proven innocent. If someone was accused of a crime, they would have to find some evidence or testimony to prove their innocence. That might be hard to do. Let's say, for instance, that the crime happened at night when you were home asleep in bed. How could you prove you were there if no one else was at home? You would have no witnesses.

With innocence until proven guilty, the other party would have to find evidence to prove you weren't at home asleep. They needed a witness or some proof placing you at the crime scene. Today, most countries follow "innocent until proven guilty," and this is thanks to ancient Rome.

Roman courts also had a preliminary hearing to decide if a case had "just cause" or enough evidence to go to trial. If so, the next step was a formal indictment that named the charges. This was followed by a trial by jury with witnesses and evidence. Today, the majority of courts around the world follow this pattern.

Political Ideas

Rome led the way with political concepts that are common today in democratic governments. Rome had the first large-scale government with a constitution. It had a system of ***checks and balances*** that prevented one person or one group of people from making all the decisions. One example during the Roman Republic was having two consuls. They could balance each other. If one started getting a little extreme on something, the other consul could "check" him. They usually did this through a veto, which was another Roman innovation.

Rome's three branches of government were another example of checks and balances. The Senate and the assemblies did the lawmaking in ancient Rome. Usually, the Senate proposed laws, and the assemblies voted to accept or reject them. Rome's consul was similar to a president today. The consuls and, later, the emperor were the executive branch. Rome also had a judicial system with eight primary judges, which would be similar to today's Supreme Court.

By the late republic, Rome's legislative branch represented both the patricians and the plebians. Not every citizen could vote, but the assemblies represented both the working class and the upper class. Rome introduced term limits. The consuls and other important positions only had a one-year term. Rome also introduced impeachment. The senators served for life, but the censor could impeach them if they got too far out of line. Rome introduced quorum requirements, where a certain number of senators had to be present before voting on something. The votes were public. Anybody could listen in on discussions of new proposals and voting.

Roundup Activity

Think about the list of Roman achievements below. Which do you think are the most important? List them below, with #1 being the most important. Give a brief reason for why you think that.

1. Concrete
2. Thermopolium: takeaway food
3. Underfloor heating
4. Aqueducts and sewers
5. Roads that lasted
6. Cheap or free food for the poor
7. Roman calendar and numerals
8. Heron's steam engine and wind-powered wheel
9. Advances in algebra and geometry
10. Mosaic art
11. Innocent until proven guilty
12. Political ideas: checks and balances, term limits, constitution, impeachment, etc.

Chapter 8: Colossal Figures

Many exceptional individuals left their mark on Rome. Some were heroes who saved Rome from disaster or lifted it to new levels. Others struggled with mental health issues and led Rome into disorder. Many of Rome's colossal figures were both brilliant and brutal, courageous yet corrupt. However, they all molded ancient Rome into the world-changing force it grew to be.

Camillus

Camillus came to the rescue in 390 BCE after the Celtic Senone people defeated the Roman troops in a battle a few miles from Rome. The Celts killed half of Rome's army. Part of the survivors escaped to the town of Veii. The rest raced back to Rome. As the Celts headed their way, Rome's townspeople ran for the hills. The army and senators holed up on Rome's high Capitoline Hill with a stockpile of weapons and food.

The Celts looted and burned Rome but could not get past the barriers protecting Capitoline Hill. The Senones began raiding the nearby villages for food. Camillus, who was once a dictator of Rome, lived in a rural area outside the city. He had fallen out of favor and been exiled. Camillus spied on the Celts and saw they got drunk at night. So, he led a small force at night and killed the Senone unit raiding his town. Encouraged, the Roman soldiers in Veii asked Camillus to lead them in a counterattack on the Celts in Rome.

"Of course!" Camillus agreed. "But the Senate needs to let me out of exile and appoint me as dictator again."

How could they get a message to the senators? A brave young man snuck into Rome at night and scaled a secret path up Capitoline Hill. The senators happily appointed Camillus as dictator. They had run out of food and were desperate. Camillus allied with the Etruscans and descended on Rome with twelve thousand soldiers just as the Celts were negotiating with the senators.

Brennus, the Senone chieftain, as the figurehead of a French warship.[166]

"Give us one thousand pounds of gold, and we'll leave!" the Senone chieftain Brennus promised.

Camillas arrived at that point and bellowed, "Gold won't deliver Rome! Our iron swords will!"

Camillus obliterated the Senones. The Romans rebuilt their city and took control of central and southern Italy.

Marcus Licinius Crassus

Crassus was the richest man in Rome in Julius Caesar's day. His fortune was the equivalent of almost fourteen billion dollars today. How did he get all his money? He came from a wealthy patrician family who supported Senator Sulla in a civil war against Consul Marius. When Marius had the upper hand, he took the Crassus family's property. Sulla won the war, and the Crassus family got their property back.

Rome's government then took land belonging to Marius's supporters. Crassus bought up that land at rock-bottom prices. Another way Crassus got land was by setting up Rome's first fire brigade. It had five hundred firefighters. His firemen would only put out a fire if the owners sold their property to Crassus at below-market prices. Through his shady land deals, Crassus owned more land than anyone in Rome. He also owned silver mines and was a slave trafficker.

Crassus was Rome's hero for finally ending the slave revolt led by Spartacus. Yet, he was so cruel toward his troops that the Roman historian Appian said, "He was more dangerous to them than the enemy." Crassus joined with Julius Caesar and Pompey in the First Triumvirate. When Caesar became the governor of Gaul (France), Crassus served as his general. He conquered Normandy in northern France.

In 53 BCE, Crassus marched to Turkey to fight the Parthian Empire without the Senate's approval. He ignored warnings to stay away from the desert. He lost a battle to the Parthians. He also lost his head.

Julius Caesar

Julius Caesar's father died when he was sixteen. He had to make some tough decisions as the new head of the family. He needed to choose a career immediately. He used his influential connections to get himself appointed as the high priest of Rome's chief god, Jupiter. Julius was engaged to Cossutia, a girl from a plebian family. However, a priest of Jupiter had to be married to a patrician woman. So, Julius broke off his relationship with Cossutia and married Cornelia when she was thirteen. Julius was only sixteen. Their daughter Julia was Julius Caesar's only legitimate child.

Julius Caesar.[167]

After forming the First Triumvirate, Julius Caesar served as Rome's consul for a year. He then became the governor of northern Italy and southern France in 58 BCE. Caesar attacked the Helvetii and Suebi tribes pouring into France from Germany. Caesar even crossed the English Channel. Although he did not conquer Britain, he gained valuable knowledge of the island. He wrote his eight-volume book, *Commentaries of the Gallic Wars*, about his stunning conquests. Each time he finished a section, he would send it back to Rome. He made sure the people back home didn't forget about him and knew what a great hero he was.

When Julius Caesar returned to Rome, he was elected as consul again and later dictator. He began to promote himself more as a king than an appointed leader. He wore a purple toga and had statues made showing him wearing a crown. The Senate usually had between one hundred and three hundred men, but he packed it with one thousand men to get a majority of senators who would support his wishes.

On the morning of March 15th, 44 BCE, his third wife, Calpurnia, woke up shrieking in horror. "Stay home!" she begged Caesar. "I had a nightmare of your body flowing with blood!"

Caesar thought about dismissing the Senate for the day, but then his friend Decimus Brutus came over. "You're listening to a woman?" Embarrassed, Caesar walked with Brutus to the Senate and to his doom.

Marcus Cicero

Cicero was a scholar, a writer, and a consul of Rome in the 1st century BCE. He was also a skeptic. This philosophy questioned whether one could really know anything, especially about what is right and wrong. Cicero said he could argue both for and against the same thing and make equally convincing points. He encouraged people to think for themselves rather than just accept what the "experts" said.

Cicero desperately wanted to solve the crisis that was destroying Rome. He wrote many papers pleading for a return to law and order. He said this could only happen if everyone cooperated. Cicero called for freedom but not the kind of lawless freedom that ignored the rights of others. "Law is liberty's foundation, and we are all slaves of the law that we might be free." Cicero believed in an unchanging natural law that applied to everyone. He thought doing this was the key to justice.

When Mark Antony locked horns with Octavian, Cicero defended Octavian with fiery speeches. "Antony is an outlaw!" Cicero roared. However, when the Senate plotted to kill Octavian, he grew desperate. Octavian united with Antony and Lepidus in the Second Triumvirate. Antony put Cicero on the list of enemies of the state despite Octavian's protests. Cicero was hunted down and caught while trying to escape to Macedonia. He bared his neck to his captors, allowing them to cut off his head.

Cleopatra in 46 BCE with her son Caesarion as a cupid.[168]

Mark Antony and Cleopatra VII

As a teenager, Mark Antony was involved in a street gang in Rome. He eventually joined the military, where he rose through the ranks until he became Caesar's right-hand man. While Caesar was fighting in Egypt, Antony attempted to restore order in Rome as consul. However, Antony was better at war than leading a city. Caesar had to come back to Rome to calm things down. Later, at Caesar's funeral, Antony held up Caesar's blood-stained toga, and the crowd went wild with rage. The senators involved in the murder escaped Rome, leaving Antony in charge.

In 41 BCE, Antony asked Cleopatra to meet with him. They needed to settle matters between Rome and Egypt. Cleopatra and Julius Caesar's son, Caesarion, was her co-pharaoh. Cleopatra sailed up the river to meet Antony in a beautiful boat with purple sails and silver oars. When Antony saw her dressed as Aphrodite, the goddess of love, he fell under her spell. He moved to Alexandria, Egypt, and they had twins together. Back in

Rome, Antony's wife, Fulvia, was warring with the Senate against Octavian's land grants, which she knew Antony opposed.

She stirred up a war against Octavian with the help of Antony's brother, Lucius. They lost, and Fulvia escaped to Greece, where she met with Antony. Instead of congratulating her for defending his cause, he lit into her for inciting a war. She conveniently died a few days later. She might have been poisoned. Antony hurried to Rome. He mended things with Octavian and married Octavian's sister, Octavia, just weeks after his wife died.

Antony needed to fight the Parthian Empire, but he didn't have a big enough army. He renewed his affair with Cleopatra to get control of Egypt's army. They had another son. Back in Rome, Octavian was hearing rumors about his brother-in-law. He went to the Vestal Virgin's temple and found Antony's secret will. Octavian discovered that Antony planned to give some of Rome's provinces to his sons by Cleopatra. Antony also declared Caesarion to be Caesar's heir. Octavian took this information to the Senate. The senators declared war on Antony and Cleopatra.

A coin issued in 32 BCE with Cleopatra on one side and Antony on the other.[169]

After losing the war, Antony stabbed himself with his sword. Cleopatra knew the Romans would force her to march through Rome in chains. What would her ultimate fate be? She allowed a poisonous snake to bite her. She died of its venom. Octavian buried the couple together but killed Caesarion. He spared Cleopatra's children by Antony and gave them to his sister Octavia to raise. This was a bit weird, given that they were the children of her husband's lover, but Octavia was known as a kind woman.

Marcus Vipsanius Agrippa

Agrippa and Octavian (later Caesar Augustus) were close friends as teens. They were both nineteen and in the army when they heard about Caesar's death. Octavian, Agrippa, and another friend, Rufus, met together. Octavian had to decide what to do. Julius Caesar was his uncle, and he was Caesar's heir.

"Going to Rome will be dangerous! Caesar's assassins will be out to get you too," Rufus warned.

"True," Agrippa replied. "But I think the best thing to do is meet the challenge head-on."

Agrippa and Octavian fought Caesar's assassins in the Battle of Philippi in 42 BCE. Their victory ended the civil war, placing Octavian firmly in charge of Rome. Shortly after, Agrippa was elected as tribune of the plebs. He led the People's Assembly, proposed new laws, and helped the plebians with legal problems. Agrippa became consul in 37 BCE. This was remarkable because he was a pleb. He was also only twenty-six at the time. A consul was supposed to be at least forty-three.

As Caesar Augustus transformed Rome from a republic to an empire, Agrippa remained his closest friend and second in command. Agrippa was the general who defeated Antony and Cleopatra in the Battle of Actium in 31 BCE. He was a great military commander, but he was also an architect and engineer. He built the Pantheon on his own land as a temple dedicated to all Rome's gods. In 609 CE, it became a Catholic church.

Agrippa built aqueducts, baths, and gardens in Rome and made a complete survey of the entire Roman Empire. He married Augustus's daughter, Julia. Augustus adopted their two sons, Gaius and Lucius. He planned to make one of them the next emperor, but they both died before he did. Their daughter Agrippina was Emperor Caligula's sister and mother to Emperor Nero.

Nero

In 54 CE, Nero became the emperor at the age of sixteen. His mother forced him to marry his stepsister, Octavia. The Romans loved Octavia, but Nero didn't. Nero came from a bizarre and violent family. However, when he was a teenager, his tutor, Seneca, and his advisor, Burrus, guided him. He made good reforms and achieved military conquests in western

Europe.

Nero and his mother, Agrippina.[170]

Nero was more interested in playing his lyre, dancing, writing poetry, and racing chariots. He competed in the Olympic Games and won every competition he joined, even when his chariot tipped over. As Nero grew older, he had a mental illness that made him violent. When his mistress, Poppaea, got pregnant, he divorced Octavia and married Poppaea. Later, Poppaea and Nero quarreled. "You're spending too much time at the races!" she cried. Nero kicked her in the belly, causing her to have a miscarriage. She died from complications. Overcome with grief, he married a boy who looked like his dead wife.

Rome burned for a week in 64 CE, and the people blamed Nero, saying he set the fire to make room for his new building project. Nero laid the blame on the Christians. Many Christians died at his hands. He had Paul the Apostle's head cut off, and he crucified Peter the Apostle.

Trajan

Emperor Nerva had a problem. He was elderly and sick. He wouldn't live long, and he was childless. Who would follow him? Trajan was not related to Nerva. However, he had a stellar military career and came from a leading family. Yes, he was born in Spain, but he had Roman parents. Nerva adopted Trajan as his heir and died six months later in 98 CE.

Trajan and his wife Pompeia had no children. However, Trajan adopted his young cousins, Hadrian and Paulina, when their parents died. Trajan had grown up in Rome's provinces. His father had been the governor of Syria, Cappadocia, and Spain. As a result, he was sensitive to the needs of Roman citizens living outside Italy. He felt the Senate should include men from the provinces to support their needs adequately. He appointed fourteen Greeks to Rome's Senate.

The Roman Empire grew to its largest size under Trajan. He conquered Dacia (Romania), the Nabataean Kingdom (Jordan), Armenia, and Babylon (southern Iraq). Trajan collected a lot of plunder in these conquests, which he brought back to Rome. Some of the wealth went to a welfare program that provided schooling and food to Italy's orphans and impoverished children. He also threw games at the Colosseum. For three months straight, five million Romans packed the Colosseum to watch chariot races and gladiator contests. Eleven thousand fighters died.

Hadrian

Hadrian became emperor in 117 CE after his cousin Trajan died. He ruled for twenty-one years. He spent half of his time traveling throughout Rome's provinces, ensuring all was well. He checked that his governors followed his orders and that the military was disciplined. He built Hadrian's Wall in Britain in 122 CE. This wall was close to the border of today's England and Scotland. It was 70 miles long (113 kilometers) and stretched across Britain from the North Sea to the Irish Sea. Hadrian built the wall to keep the Picts in the north. The Picts covered their bodies with blue tattoos.

Hadrian.[171]

Hadrian decided to rebuild Jerusalem, which Titus had destroyed in 70 CE. He gave Jerusalem the new name of Aelia Capitolina. The Jews thought he was going to let them rebuild their temple. They were horrified when he built a temple to Jupiter on the Temple Mount, where the Jewish Temple once stood.

The Jews led the Bar Kokhba Revolt against the Romans in Judaea. They suffered a devastating loss. The Romans killed a half million Jews, enslaved 100,000, and tore down hundreds of Jewish towns and villages. Hadrian changed the name of Judaea to Palaestina. Jerusalem had been the Jews' holy city for a millennium. Hadrian banned them from their ancient capital.

Roundup Activity

Mark each statement T for true or F for false. Check your answers in the back of the book.

( ) 1. Camillus was a one-time Roman dictator who had been exiled.
( ) 2. Crassus got rich from silver mines, slave trafficking, and shady land deals.
( ) 3. Julius Caesar wrote *Commentaries of the Gallic Wars* about his conquests in Galilee.
( ) 4. Cicero told people to believe what the experts said and not try to think for themselves.
( ) 5. Cleopatra seduced Mark Antony by dressing as Aphrodite.
( ) 6. Mark Antony's wife Fulvia went to war against Octavian.
( ) 7. Agrippa was the mortal enemy of Octavian (Caesar Augustus).
( ) 8. Nero blamed the Christians when Rome burned.
( ) 9. The Roman Empire shrank during Trajan's reign.
( ) 10. Hadrian built Hadrian's Wall in Judaea.

Chapter 9: Constantine and Christianity

Lots of things changed when Constantine became emperor. He built the new capital of Constantinople, where Europe and Asia meet. He wasn't baptized until just before he died, but he was the first Christian emperor.

What led to these changes? We must step back to the Severen dynasty, the Crisis of the Third Century, and Diocletian's persecution of Christians. They set the stage for Constanine's rise to power and his transformation of the empire.

The Severan Dynasty

Septimus Severus was born in Libya. He was the first African emperor of the Roman Empire. How did he become emperor? Severus started in the military and worked his way up to become the tribune of the plebs. Next, he became governor of Upper Pannonia in central Europe.

Meanwhile, Emperor Commodus was having delusions of being Hercules, the son of Zeus. When the Senate refused to go along with this, he murdered most of them. Everyone breathed a sigh of relief when his wrestling partner killed him. Severus clawed his way to the top in the violent Year of the Five Emperors. He killed most of his rivals until he was the only emperor standing.

Emperor Severus, Julia Domna, and their sons, Geta and Caracalla. Caracalla murdered Geta and blotted his face off the painting.[173]

During the Severen dynasty, Jews and Christians sometimes faced unfair treatment. The Romans required all their conquered people to recognize the Roman gods. Most people didn't mind because they were polytheistic. They just added the Roman gods in with their own. However, the Jews and Christians were **monotheistic**, which means they worshiped only one god. They refused to offer sacrifices to the Roman gods.

Sometimes, the Romans let the Jews get by with it because they had a long history of worshiping one god. But Christianity was a new religion. The Romans didn't understand the sacraments, like taking communion. Some Romans thought Christians were cannibals because they said the wine and bread were the "body and blood of Christ."

However, Severus liked Christians. He had a Christian doctor who had saved him from death. He never issued any decrees condemning Christians. During his reign, local leaders acted on their own against Christians. They threw them into boiling water, cut off their heads, and fed them to wild animals. Other Severen emperors persecuted Christians. For instance, two bishops of Rome were executed.

Alexander became the last Severan emperor at the age of fifteen. He and his mother were interested in the teachings of Jesus and took lessons from the Christian scholar Origen. Alexander prayed to Jesus every morning, but he also prayed to the Roman gods and his ancestors. He didn't want to leave anyone out. When the Alemanni of Germany attacked France, he tried to bribe them to leave. His soldiers thought this was cowardly. They killed Alexander and his mother, ending the Severen dynasty.

The Crisis of the Third Century

A series of disasters from 235 to 284 CE sent shockwaves through the Roman Empire. Invasions of the Alamanni, Goths, and Vandals struck terror in the Romans' hearts. The value of money plummeted. Many died in the terrifying Plague of Cyprian. Chaos rocked Rome as fifty-two warlords tried to steal Rome's throne.

Emperor Valerian was afraid of the growing Christian faith. He knew the Roman gods weren't happy about it. In his opinion, that was why so many bad things were happening. In 257 CE, he ordered that all Christian senators and pastors should lose their heads or be burned at the stake. Pope Sixtus II and Bishop Cyprian were beheaded. Two years later, the Persians captured Valerian. His son, Gallienus, issued the Decree of Toleration. The Christians got their churches and cemeteries back.

Cyprian was an African bishop who told Christians to take care of the sick and bury the dead during the pandemic.[178]

During this leadership crisis, the Roman Empire split into three. France, Spain, and Britain broke off, becoming the Gallic Empire. Queen Zenobia ruled the Palmyrene Empire of Syria, Palestine, and Egypt. The tide began to turn when Emperor Claudius II got Spain back. After Claudius died in the plague, Aurelian put the broken Roman Empire back together. Yet, Rome's former glory and wealth were a distant memory.

Diocletian Divides the Empire

Diocletian became emperor in 284 CE. The empire was too big for one man to rule, so he split it. He ruled the east, and General Maximian ruled the west. In 293 CE, Diocletian made a new plan with four emperors. He and Maximian were the lead emperors. Galerius and Constantius were the junior emperors. Galerius would take Diocletian's place when he died or retired. Constantius would take Maximian's place. Constantius's son, Constantine, would become a junior emperor when Constantius became the lead emperor. Maximian's son, Maxentius, would take Galerius's place.

"I hope it all works," Diocletian told Maximian. "I'm trying to avoid all the drama that usually happens when an emperor dies."

The Great Persecution

Diocletian and Galerius scored a thrilling victory over the Persians of the Sassanid Empire. However, a problem popped up. They were joyfully offering sacrifices to the gods. Usually, the priests inspected the intestines of the sacrificed animals to predict the future. But they couldn't read the omens this time. Something blocked their divinations.

"Sire." The priests turned to Diocletian. "We believe the Christians in your palace are silencing our gods."

"These Christians are everywhere!" Galerius sputtered. "And now our gods won't speak to us! We've got to do something."

"I agree," said Diocletian. "But I don't want bloodshed. I'll call all my soldiers and everyone in my court to sacrifice to our Roman gods. If they don't, they lose their jobs. That should solve the problem."

It didn't. The Christians refused to sacrifice to the Roman gods. Diocletian ejected all Christians from the military and government. He burned Bibles and destroyed churches. He put the priests in prison and told the Christians not to meet together.

"It's not doing any good! We've got to kill them," Galerius pressed. "Otherwise, they'll take over!"

The Great Persecution began. Thousands of Christians were killed on Diocletian's orders. The Romans began to feel sorry for the Christians. In Britain, Constantius mostly ignored the orders. His first wife, Helena, was a Christian. King Tiridates of Armenia received a miracle healing and became a Christian in 301 CE. He declared Armenia, which was part of the Roman Empire, a Christian state. Christianity was growing faster than ever. As Tertullian had written a century earlier, "The blood of the martyrs is the seed of the church."

Constantine Fights His Way to Power

Diocletian was getting old and sick. Galerius bullied him and Maximian into retiring. Galerius was now the top emperor, while Constantius was the other lead emperor. Galerius pushed Constantine and Maxentius out of the picture. He brought in his drinking buddy, Severus, and his nephew, Maximinus, as the new junior emperors. At this time, Constantine was living in the palace, getting trained to be a junior emperor. However, the plan for him to become junior emperor had ended. The palace now belonged to Galerius.

"Constantine, you need to get out of there now!" Constantius wrote to his son. "It's not safe. Come to Britain!"

That night, after getting Galerius drunk, Constantine asked permission to leave.

"Yes, that's fine," Galerius muttered.

Constantine escaped that night before Galerius sobered up. He traveled to Britain and fought the Picts with Constantius. Constantius died a year later. Before his death, he declared Constantine the new emperor in his place. He had the support of the armies of France and Britain.

Constantine wrote to Galerius. "Sire, I'm sad to tell you my father has died. His army forced me to become the new emperor in his place. I apologize. I know this is highly irregular. But sire, it is natural for a son to become his father's successor."

Galerius turned purple with rage when he read the letter. "I'll burn this letter and then burn Constantine!"

"Oh, please reconsider, sire," his counselors urged. "Take the middle path! We must avoid open war. He's got the legions of France and Britain behind him! Anyway, we need a new junior emperor since Severus is stepping into the lead emperor position."

So, they negotiated a compromise. Instead of becoming a lead emperor, Constantine would become the junior emperor, which had been Diocletian's plan. He ruled his father's former territories of Britain, France, and Spain.

Maximian	Lead emperor with Diocletian, forced into retirement
Maxentius	Son of Maximian, meant to be the next junior emperor but passed over
Maximinus	Galerius's nephew and current junior emperor

In Italy, Maxentius seethed with jealousy. "Diocletian meant me to be the other junior emperor! I'm declaring myself emperor of Italy!"

Severus marched to Italy to arrest Maxentius. However, he led an army that had been under Maximian's command. The men were still loyal to Maximian, so they defected to his son and killed Severus.

"It's time to come out of retirement!" Maximian gloated. He became co-emperor with his son Maxentius. Then, he wrote to Constantine, offering his daughter, Fausta, in marriage.

"I will help you become lead emperor if you help me fight Galerius."

Constantine wanted to see how things played out before fighting Galerius. It was a wise move because Maxentius and his father couldn't get along. Maximian betrayed his son by meeting with Galerius and Diocletian to revise the plan. The new lead emperor alongside Galerius was his old friend, Licinius. Constantine was still a junior emperor, and Galerius's nephew Maximinus was the other. Maximian and Diocletian went back into retirement. Maxentius was left without anything.

Soon after, Galerius fell horribly ill. He had gangrene in his lower abdomen. On his deathbed, Galerius issued the Edict of Toleration in 311 CE. "We now recognize and accept the Christian religion in the empire. We ask them to pray to their god for our safety and the peace of the empire."

Galerius's death left Licinius as a lead emperor. Constantine was under him. Maxentius immediately proclaimed himself Maximinus's junior emperor. But Constantine crossed the Alps and marched to Rome to fight Maxentius. On his way, he had a vision. He saw a cross in the sky and the words, "In this sign, you will conquer." That night, he dreamed Jesus said the same thing to him. Constantine wasn't yet a Christian, but he had a new official emblem made. It had an X over a P. These were the first two letters in the Greek word ΧΡΙΣΤΟΣ, which means "Christ." He put this emblem on his helmet, soldiers' shields, and the battle standard.

X (chi) and P (rho), Constantine's new emblem.[174]

Maxentius met Constantine with his army at the Tiber River. Constantine's men quickly overcame their opponents. Maxentius drowned in the river. Constantine entered Rome to the cheers of the people. He broke custom by not sacrificing to Jupiter, but he pacified the Senate by promising them they would regain their power. The following year, Maximinus fought Licinius. He wanted to be the only lead emperor. He lost and fled to Turkey, where he died.

The Edict of Milan

Now, there were just two emperors: Licinius and Constantine. Constantine gave his sister Constantia in marriage to Licinius. While celebrating the wedding in Milan, the emperors formed the Edict of Milan in 313 CE. This edict gave every Roman the opportunity to worship as they pleased. The edict applied to all religions. Christianity now had legal status, which meant Christians could no longer be persecuted. They were released from prisons and slavery. They got their churches back.

Was Constantine a Christian by this time? He didn't publicly worship the Roman gods, but the sun god Sol Invictus appeared on his coins for a few years. Constantine didn't get baptized, but he had Christian ministers teach and advise him. He read the Bible and gave money to build new churches.

Constantinople

Licinius and Constantine were co-emperors for the next ten years. However, Licinius was angry when Constantine crossed into his territory while chasing a group of Goths. They went to war, and Licinius finally surrendered. Constantine's sister, Constantia, begged him to spare her husband. At first, Constantine did. But then Licinius tried to raise troops for another challenge. Constantine hanged him.

Constantine.[175]

Constantine became the sole emperor of the Roman Empire. He wanted a new capital to represent the empire's fusion of East and West. Byzantium was an ancient Greek colony built in the 7th century BCE. It was on a strip of land reaching out to the Bosphorus Strait that connected the Black Sea with the Sea of Marmara. The strait divided Europe and Asia. It was in a perfect spot to control sea trade.

Surrounded on three sides by water, the city was easy to defend. In 324, Constantine began transforming Byzantium into a brilliant trade and cultural center. He renamed it Constantinople. It quickly grew into the world's richest and largest city. Constantinople continued as the capital of the Eastern Roman Empire (or the Byzantine Empire) for eleven centuries. Today, it is called Istanbul.

The Council of Nicaea

In 325, Constantine called for a conference of the Christian bishops. A controversy was dividing the church, and Constantine wanted it dealt with quickly. The bishops met in Nicaea, a city across the Bosphorus Strait from where Constantine was building his new capital. What was the controversy? It concerned the Trinity: the Father (God), the Son (Jesus), and the Holy Spirit.

Arius was a priest in Alexandria. He was teaching something different from most other churches. He said, "Jesus can't be equal with God. We know that God the Father has always existed. He is eternal without any beginning or ending. But Jesus had a beginning. Jesus isn't eternal."

Constantine called the bishops to sort it out. Over three hundred bishops arrived. As the church leaders entered the hall, the first thing they saw was the open Bible lying on the table. It reminded everyone this wasn't a battle of wits. It was a battle for what was written in the book.

Constantine swept into the room. Everyone fell silent as he spoke.

"We are here to decide an important question. I beg everyone here! Work in unity. Lay whatever personal issues you have about someone else aside. We need to focus on the matter at hand. Christ tells us to forgive our brothers. I insist on peace in this room. Division in the church is worse than war!"

The bishops began to discuss Arius's teaching. Did it line up with the Scripture?

"Look! Arius says Jesus had a beginning. But the Apostle John says something different. 'In the beginning was the Word, and the Word was with God, and the Word was God. He was with God in the beginning. Through him, all things were made, and without him, nothing was made that has been made.'"

"Jesus wasn't created; he was the creator. Yes, Jesus's physical body had a beginning, but he existed as God from infinity."

Arius argued, "The Scripture says in Colossians 1:15 that Jesus is 'the firstborn of all creation.' If he was born, then he had a beginning. He is God's oldest and most beloved creation. He is God's direct offspring. But Jesus can't be equal with God."

Yet, some other bishops pointed out, "The next verse, Colossians 1:16, says, 'All things were created through him and for him.' How could

Jesus *be* created if he created *all* things? Jesus said, 'I and the Father are one' in John 10:30."

The majority of the bishops decided that Jesus the Son was equal to God the Father and the Holy Spirit. They wrote the Nicene Creed that spelled out the doctrine of the Trinity.

In 337, Constantine became seriously ill. He realized he wouldn't live. He called the bishops to his bedside. "I always wanted to be baptized in the Jordan River. That's where John baptized Jesus. But I'm afraid I've waited too long. I need baptism right away, as I will die soon." Bishop Eusebius of Nicomedia baptized Constantine shortly before he passed away.

Roundup Activity

Fill in the blanks below with the correct answer. Remember, the answers are at back of the book if you get stuck.

Constantine	Constantinople	Council of Nicaea
Crisis of the Third Century	Diocletian	Edict of Toleration
Galerius	Great Persecution	Severus

Septimus _____ was the first African emperor of the Roman Empire. He started the Severen dynasty. During this period, persecution of Christians happened in the provinces. The Severen dynasty ended in the _____ ____ _____ _____, when invasions, a horrible plague, economic disaster, and political chaos almost destroyed the empire. As the empire recovered, _____ divided it into four sections led by two lead emperors and two junior emperors. He and _____ started the _____ _____ of Christians. Thousands died. As he was dying, Galerius issued the _____ ____ _____ in 311, which ended the state-mandated persecution of Christians. _____ eventually became the only emperor of the Roman Empire. He built his new capital of _____ on the Bosphorus Strait. He called the _____ ____ _____ for the bishops to discuss the Trinity.

Chapter 10: The Fall of an Empire

Constantine united the empire and ended the persecution of Christians. However, Constantine's death spelled the beginning of the end for the empire, at least for the Western part. Within 140 years, the Western Roman Empire fell apart, never to rise again.

Meanwhile, the Eastern Empire continued to thrive for centuries. Historians later named it the Byzantine Empire. Its citizens still called it the Roman Empire. It didn't matter that Rome was outside its boundaries. The Eastern Empire separated from the Roman Catholic Church. It also exchanged the Latin language for Greek. Still, in their minds, it was the Roman Empire continuing its legacy.

Why Did the Roman Empire Fall?

Although many factors caused the Roman Empire's fall, five stand out. Rome had little control over the first three. It suffered from invasions, climate change, and pandemics. The other two factors were inept government officials and economic disaster. All five formed a lethal combination that brought Rome to its knees.

1. Invasions

The Persian-Sassanid Empire was a constant thorn in the side of the Eastern Roman Empire. The Sassanids ruled the Middle East for four centuries, beginning in 224 CE. They swallowed up Rome's Asian provinces. Meanwhile, Rome had to fend off barbarian hordes. It went bankrupt to pay the military.

Who were these barbarians who wreaked havoc? And what is a barbarian? The name came from a Greek word that meant anyone who wasn't Greek. The Romans used the word to refer to most people outside the empire. It especially applied to anyone they considered "uncivilized."

One of Rome's greatest threats was the Goths. They came from Scandinavia but migrated to Germany. In 268 CE, the Goths invaded Macedonia and Greece. Emperor Claudius II chased them off, earning the nickname "Gothicus." His victory was a turning point in the Crisis of the Third Century.

Claudius II Gothicus.[176]

Aurelian was the next emperor. He chased the Goths across the Danube but decided that evicting them from Romania was too hard. Ongoing conflict with the Goths in the Balkans destabilized the empire.

The Goths in western Europe were called Visigoths. Those in eastern Europe were called Ostrogoths. They eventually swept through all of southern Europe.

The Vandals came from southern Poland and migrated to Germany and the Czech Republic. Constantine permitted them to settle in central Europe. Later, the Huns pushed them out, so they headed to western Europe. They moved south to Spain and finally settled in North Africa.

From their new headquarters, they launched raids on Italy and the islands of the Mediterranean Sea.

During the Severan dynasty, the Alemanni from Germany and Switzerland moved into the Roman Empire. Emperor Caracalla chased them off. They threatened the empire again in the Crisis of the Third Century. Emperor Claudius ran them back to Germany. They stayed there for about a century and then crossed the frozen Rhine to invade the empire again.

The Saxons unsuccessfully attacked Britain in 367. Another invading tribe from Germany was the Franks, who attacked France with the Saxons. When the Romans withdrew from Britain, the Angles and Saxons (the Anglo-Saxons) settled on the island.

The Huns were from today's southern Russia and Kazakhstan. In 370 CE, they appeared in the areas bordering the Roman Empire. They displaced the Goths and other tribes, who migrated into the Roman Empire. This created disorder and destruction. Eventually, the Huns began invading the empire. The emperors were powerless to run them off, so they bribed the Huns to behave themselves.

2. Climate change

Climate change probably isn't the first thing that leaps to mind when thinking about the fall of Rome. However, centuries of warm weather followed by cool weather helped drive the empire's collapse. Beginning around 200 BCE, Rome had a *Climatic Optimum*, a time of stable, warm weather with lots of rain. The weather was great for Rome and its provinces. Despite wars and political upheavals, Rome thrived. The farms produced plenty of food.

Around 150 CE, the weather got cooler around the Mediterranean. Cooler air meant less rain and more crop failure. The Romans began to have trouble finding enough food to feed the people. Hungry people were unhappy people. They were more likely to cause problems. They might revolt or even kill the emperor. Rome had to ship in grain, but that brought new problems.

3. Pandemics

The weather change coincided with two terrible pandemics. The Antonine Plague struck in 165 CE, and it was followed by the Plague of Cyprian in 215. Did the cooler weather cause the pandemics? No, it didn't make people sick. However, it caused disruptions that led to the spread of disease. For instance, less rain meant smaller harvests. People tended to move to areas with more food. More migrations meant the disease spread more.

Rome had to ship grain from North Africa and other areas less affected by drought. Rats were on the ships that carried the grain. They probably spread the viruses around the Mediterranean. These deadly pandemics killed millions of people.

The pandemics meant fewer soldiers to fight off the invaders. They also caused economic crises. The crippled population was unable to produce food and goods at the same rate as before.

4. The economy tanked

Invasions, epidemics, and climate change all impacted the economy. Rome's constant overspending and oppressive taxes also impacted it. Where was the money going? The games held at the Colosseum were free for everyone. Rome's wealthy elite paid for some of the games to win favor. The government sponsored a lot of them to celebrate special events.

Having to constantly defend the borders against invasion by the barbarians and Persians drained the budget. Meanwhile, Rome's income sources were drying up. Most of the income in the late republic and early empire came from the wealth captured from conquered lands. The government also taxed farms, workshops, and trade.

By the 3rd century CE, Rome had stopped conquering new lands. It was desperately trying not to become a conquered land. Without the money flowing from military conquests, the government's leading source of income was taxes. Taxes soared higher and higher to pay the enormous cost of defending the empire from the Huns, Vandals, and other invaders.

Another issue was pirates. The empire had always depended on its sea trade. But now, pirates were everywhere on the seas. At one time, the Romans had kept the pirates at bay. Now, their navy was engaged in fighting the invasions. The water highways were no longer safe for merchant ships. Trade broke down, further crumbling the empire's economy.

5. The leadership fell flat

Diocletian knew the empire was too big for one emperor to manage. So, he started the trend of having two or more emperors in strategic locations. Constantine divided the empire among his sons and nephews.

However, Constantine's family killed each other rather than work together. Eventually, the empire permanently split into the Eastern Roman Empire and the Western Roman Empire.

The government was corrupt and unstable. The Roman military liked an emperor who was smart on the battlefield. A man who could win battles could run the government. If an emperor's poor decisions cost too many lives or lost battles, the military sometimes killed him. Cowardly emperors were even worse. It reached the point where the military chose most of the emperors.

How Did the Fall of the West Play Out?

Before he died, Constantine appointed his three sons—Constantine II, Constantius II, and Constans—as the lead emperors. His nephews—Dalmatius and Hannibalianus—were the junior emperors. However, after Constantine died, his sons killed the junior emperors. Constantine II ruled Britain, France, and Spain. Constans was still a boy, so Constantine II ruled as his regent over Italy, Libya, and central Europe. Constantius took Egypt, Greece, Bulgaria, and western Asia.

When Constans became old enough to be emperor, Constantine II refused to hand over his provinces. They went to war. Constans killed his older brother and got his land and Constantine's land. However, he was not cut out for leadership. His military killed him. They made General Magnentius emperor. He lasted three years. Constantius killed him, becoming the empire's only emperor.

Constantius and Persian King Shapur II warred against each other for years. In 350, Shapur attacked Nisibis on Syria's northern border. He diverted the Mygdonius River and flooded the valley surrounding the city. He then sailed his ships right up to the city walls, breaking part of them down. However, his war elephants got stuck in the mud. Then, he had to quickly leave to defend Persia against an attack by the Huns.

In 361, Constantius fell ill. He declared his cousin, Julian, the next emperor on his deathbed. Julian had left the Christian faith as a young man to embrace the Eleusinian Mysteries, a cult of the goddesses Demeter and Persephone. He only ruled for two years until a spear impaled him while fighting the Persians. His legions promptly made their general, Jovian, the next emperor. He died mysteriously eight months later.

Valentinian.[177]

Valentinian, a former tribune, became emperor in 364. He made his brother, Valens, his co-emperor. Valens ruled the Eastern Roman Empire from Constantinople, and Valentinian ruled the Western Roman Empire from Milan. Valentinian successfully fought off an invasion of the Alemanni in France. Meanwhile, Valens fought and killed Procopius, the only male descendent of the Constantinian dynasty, who had tried to claim the empire.

In Britain, the Roman troops guarding Hadrian's Wall had lost many soldiers. They eventually deserted their posts. In the Great Conspiracy, multiple tribes worked together to take Britain. The Picts poured over the wall, and the Scots and Saxons attacked by sea. Almost all the Roman cities in Britain fell.

General Flavius Theodosius the Elder and his son Theodosius I came to the rescue in 369. They crossed the English Channel and sneaked into Londinium (London), surprising the barbarian tribes. They ran them out of Britain and reinforced Hadrian's Wall with fresh troops.

Five years later, Emperor Valentinian butted heads with the Quadi people of Moravia. "Why are you building Roman forts on our land?" they complained. "We've made treaties with you!"

"Some of your people have been crossing the border and attacking my land," Valentinian retorted. During a heated argument, Valentinian dropped dead of a stroke. His brother, Valens, continued to rule the Eastern Roman Empire. Valentinian's sons, Gratian and Valentinian II, became co-emperors of the Western Roman Empire.

Valens was not a good military commander. Nevertheless, he led his armies to fight the Goths in Bulgaria. "My troops are on the way!" Gratian messaged him. "Wait for us to get there!"

However, Valens wanted the glory for himself. He led his troops against the Goths, and the result was catastrophic. The Goths killed Valens and two-thirds of the Eastern Roman Empire's military. Gratian made Theodosius I the new emperor of the East. He was the general who had scored the astounding victory in Britain with his father.

In 383, a Celt named Magnus Maximus invaded France. He killed Gratian and usurped power over France, Britain, and Spain. Theodosius marched west in 388. He killed Maximus and took back the western provinces. Gratian's brother, Valentinian II, was now the only emperor of the Western Roman Empire. However, he either hung himself or was murdered in 392. Theodosius died the following year. His two sons, Honorius and Arcadius, were small children.

Stilicho the Vandal was married to Theodosius's niece. He became the regent for Honorius over the Western Roman Empire. Praetor Prefect Rufinus essentially ruled the Eastern Roman Empire until the Goths killed him in 398. Arcadius died in 408, leaving his seven-year-old son, Theodosius II, as the emperor of the Eastern Roman Empire. Theodosius's sister, Pulcheria, became empress of the East until her brother was old enough to rule.

In 410, a famine struck Italy. Visigothic King Alaric's rag-tag army of runaway slaves and Goths stormed Rome. Its people were too weak to defend themselves. He killed or enslaved most of the population. He stole all the valuables his men could carry and burned the historic buildings around the Forum. He left the cathedrals of Peter and Paul unharmed. A few months later, Alaric died. His army went to southwest France and set up the Visigothic Kingdom.

Meanwhile, Britain was in chaos. It was ruled by usurpers. The Roman citizens in Britain begged Honorius to restore order, but he didn't have the resources. Britain was on its own.

In the Eastern Roman Empire, the Huns attacked Constantinople. Theodosius struck a deal with them. "Here's 350 pounds of gold. Leave Constantinople alone, and you can live in the empire as long as you are peaceful." The Huns agreed, but they demanded 350 pounds of gold every year. When Attila became their leader, he doubled the bribe money.

Honorius died in 423. Theodosius II put his seven-year-old cousin, Valentinian III, on the Western Roman Empire's throne. Valentinian's mother, Galla Placidia, ruled until her son was old enough to be emperor. The Western Roman Empire had already lost Britain. The Visigoths and Franks now controlled most of France. In 428, the Vandals took North Africa, the empire's main grain source. The two emperors united to attack the Vandals, but the Persians attacked the Eastern Roman Empire. Attila the Hun attacked the West. The Western Roman Empire suffered a humiliating loss to Attila. He forced them to pay him 2,100 pounds of gold each year.

Based on coins from his day, Attila might have looked like this depiction in a museum in Hungary, which was probably his birthplace.[178]

In 450, Theodosius II fell off his horse and died. He had no sons. His sister Pulcheria married a palace administrator named Marcian. They ruled the Eastern Roman Empire together. By this point, the East and West were no longer a united empire. They were more like two separate empires that occasionally allied to fight enemies. When Marcian became emperor, he stopped the payments to Attila the Hun from the Eastern Roman Empire.

Assassins killed Valentinian III in 455. One of the plotters in his murder, Petronius Maximus, stole the Western Roman Empire's throne. In the chaos, the Vandals sailed from North Africa and attacked Italy. They knocked down Rome's aqueducts leading into the city, but Pope Leo I met them at the city gates. "We won't open the gates until you promise not to harm any people or property in Rome." The Vandals promised the pope. They stole the city's treasures and enslaved some of the people, but they did not burn the city or kill many citizens. However, in the confusion, the Romans killed Maximus.

The following two decades were a time of murder and mayhem in the Western Roman Empire. Barbarian warlords ran rampant, and the puppet emperors could do nothing to stop them. General Orestes, an envoy for Attila the Hun, made his ten-year-old son, Romulus Augustus, the emperor of the Western Roman Empire in 475. He only lasted a few weeks. King Odoacer led a horde of Germanic tribes into Italy, forcing the child-king Romulus to abdicate on September 4th, 476. The Western Roman Empire had collapsed.

What Were the Impacts of the Roman Empire's Fall?

The fall of the Western Roman Empire plunged western Europe into the Dark Ages. Instead of a strong central government, western Europe was divided into small kingdoms, each with its own ruler. A hierarchal system called feudalism developed. The population plummeted due to plagues, warfare, and instability. Rome had once been a city of about a half-million people; it declined to about thirty thousand. Almost all the people in Milan were killed or enslaved in 539 when the Ostrogoths attacked. Western Europe lost many of its large cities and became a rural society.

The Roman Catholic Church now dominated politics, education, and culture. Europe lost its technical knowledge in areas like civil engineering. With no central government protecting the roads and seas, trade and the exchange of ideas in the Western world broke down. The economy collapsed, and people left the cities. They became serfs under wealthy landowners, who gave them protection in exchange for labor. Communities were isolated. Intellectual thought and the classical Greco-Roman culture faded away.

Nevertheless, Rome's legacy will continue to endure. During the Renaissance, classical ideas from ancient Greece and Rome resurfaced, allowing people to once again celebrate Rome's past achievements.

Roundup Activity

Look at the list of key events in ancient Roman history. Number them (to the right of each sentence) in the order they happened. Check your answers in the back of the book.

1. Caesar, Crassus, and Pompey formed the First Triumvirate.
2. Constantine and Licinius passed the Edict of Milan.
3. Hadrian built the wall across Britain.
4. Romulus built the new city of Rome.
5. Spartacus led the Great Slave Revolt.
6. Tarquinius built the Circus Maximus and Cloaca Maxima.
7. The Celtic Senones sacked and burned Rome.
8. The child king Romulus Augustus abdicated the throne.
9. The Colosseum opened.
10. The Great Conspiracy almost drove the Romans out of Britain.
11. The plebs got their Plebian Assembly.
12. The Romans overthrew the monarchy and established the republic.

Roundup Activities Answer Key

Chapter 1: Crossword Puzzle
Who or what am I?

Chapter 2: Quiz

1. Who built the *Circus Maximus* stadium and the *Cloaca Maxima* sewer system?

    d. Tarquinius Priscus

2. Who spearheaded the overthrow of the monarchy?

    a. Brutus

3. Who elected the consuls, censors, and praetors?

    b. Centuriate Assembly

4. What was one of the largest naval battles in history?

    b. Battle of Cape Ecnomus

5. Who threw his sacred chickens overboard?

    b. Pulcher

Chapter 3: Define the Word or Phrase

1. **Transalpine Gaul:** Southern France
2. **"Crossing the Rubicon:"** Reaching a point of no return or committing to revolution
3. **Julian Calendar:** Julius Caesar's calendar with 365 days and an extra day in February every four years
4. **The Second Triumvirate:** An alliance made in 43 BCE consisting of Octavian, Antony, and Lepidus
5. *Princeps Senatus/Princeps Civitatis*: "First in the Senate, first among the citizens" Originally the Senate's leader title, it later meant "emperor," beginning with Caesar Augustus.
6. **Polytheistic:** Worshiping many gods and goddesses
7. **Colosseum:** The largest amphitheater of ancient history where Romans gathered for chariot races, gladiator fights, and animal hunts
8. **Antonine Plague:** An epidemic that began in 165 CE, apparently measles or smallpox. It killed five million in the empire.
9. **Pax Romana:** "Roman Peace." Two centuries of relative peace from 27 BCE to 180 CE. The Roman legions enforced law and order throughout the empire, allowing trade, engineering, and culture to flourish. It promoted the spread of Christianity.
10. **Ides of March:** March 15th, when the senators killed Julius Caesar

Chapter 4: Word Search

D	R	A	U	G	N	A	I	R	O	T	E	A	R	P
										L				U
		M	A	R	I	U	S			U				G
										P				I
										A				O
										T				
				N						A				L
				O		T	R	O	H	O	C			I
H				I										A
P				G						P	I	L	U	M
M				E										N
U				L										I
I														A
R														H
T							Y	R	U	T	N	E	C	

1. A Roman army unit with eighty to one hundred soldiers (century)
2. Six centuries with 480 to 600 men (cohort)
3. Ten cohorts or about four thousand to six thousand men (legion)
4. An elite unit that protected the emperor (Praetorian Guard)
5. A Roman dagger (pugio)
6. A Roman spear (pilum)
7. A siege engine used to fling rocks or fiery pots of oil at the enemy (catapult)
8. A parade and ceremony celebrating a Roman war victory (triumph)
9. A Roman consul who reformed Rome's army (Marius)
10. Small circles of iron linked together to form armor (chain mail)

Chapter 8: True or False?

Mark each statement T (true) or F (false). Check your answers in the back of the book.

(T)1. Camillus was a one-time Roman dictator who had been exiled.

(T)2. Crassus got rich from silver mines, slave trafficking, and shady land deals.

(F) 3. Julius Caesar wrote *Commentaries of the Gallic Wars* about his conquests in ~~Galilee~~ (Gaul/France).

(F) 4. Cicero told people to believe what the experts said and not try to think for themselves.

(T)5. Cleopatra seduced Mark Antony by dressing as Aphrodite.

(T)6. Mark Antony's wife Fulvia went to war against Octavian.

(F) 7. Agrippa was the ~~mortal enemy~~ (best friend) of Octavian (Caesar Augustus).

(T)8. Nero blamed the Christians when Rome burned.

(F) 9. The Roman Empire ~~shrank~~ (reached its largest size) during Trajan's reign.

(F) 10. Hadrian built Hadrian's Wall in ~~Judaea~~ (Britain).

Chapter 9: Fill in the Blank

Septimus <u>Severus</u> was the first African emperor of the Roman Empire. He started the Severen dynasty. During this period, persecution of Christians happened in the provinces. The Severen dynasty ended in the <u>Crisis of the Third Century</u>, when invasions, a horrible plague, economic disaster, and political chaos almost destroyed the empire. As the empire recovered, <u>Diocletian</u> divided it into four sections led by two lead emperors and two junior emperors. He and <u>Galerius</u> started the <u>Great Persecution</u> of Christians. Thousands died. As he was dying, Galerius issued the <u>Edict of Toleration</u> in 311, which ended the state-mandated persecution of Christians. <u>Constantine</u> eventually became the only emperor of the Roman Empire. He built his new capital of <u>Constantinople</u> on the Bosphorus Strait. He called the <u>Council of Nicaea</u> for the bishops to discuss the Trinity.

Chapter 10: What Happened When?

Caesar, Crassus, and Pompey formed the First Triumvirate. (7)
    Constantine and Licinius passed the Edict of Milan. (10)
    Hadrian built the wall across Britain. (9)
    Romulus built the new city of Rome. (1)
    Spartacus led the Great Slave Revolt. (6)
    Tarquinius built the Circus Maximus and Cloaca Maxima. (2)
    The Celtic Senones sacked and burned Rome. (5)
    The child king Romulus Augustus abdicated his throne. (12)
    The Colosseum opened. (8)
    The Great Conspiracy almost drove the Romans out of Britain. (11)
    The plebs got their Plebian Assembly. (4)
    The Romans overthrew the monarchy and established the republic. (3)

Here's another book by Enthralling History that you might like

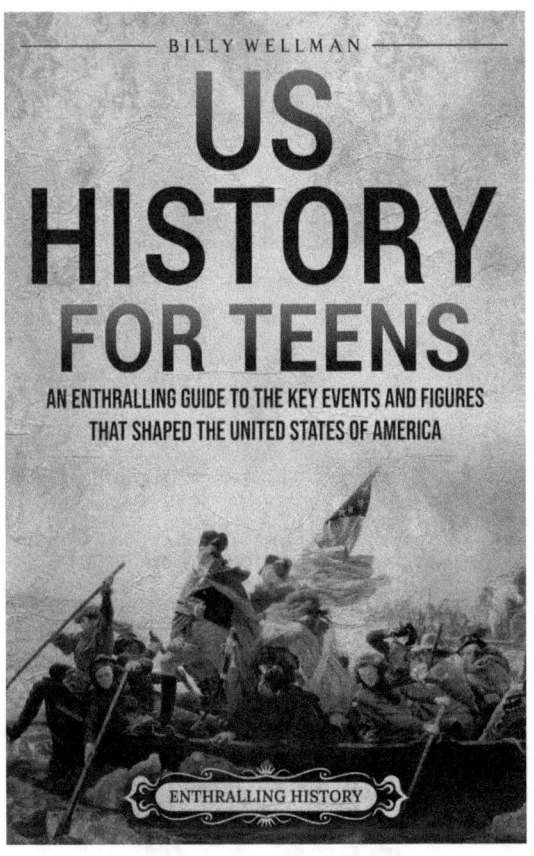

Free limited time bonus

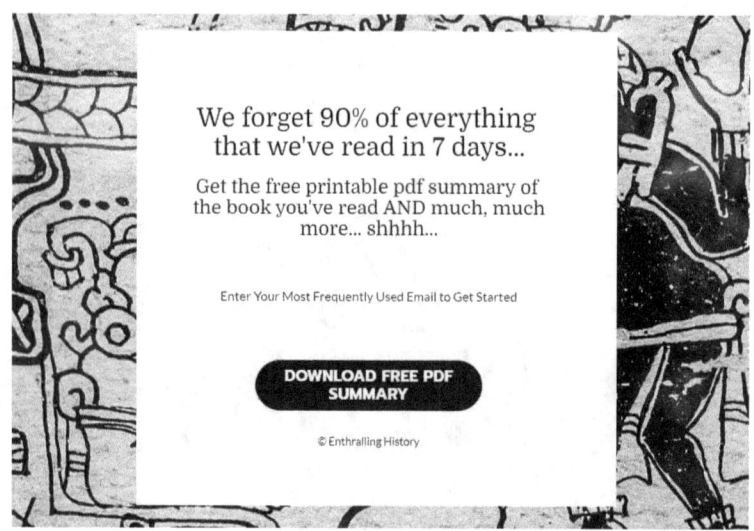

Stop for a moment. We have a free bonus set up for you. The problem is this: we forget 90% of everything that we read after 7 days. Crazy fact, right? Here's the solution: we've created a printable, 1-page pdf summary for this book that you're reading now. All you have to do to get your free pdf summary is to go to the following website:
https://livetolearn.lpages.co/enthrallinghistory/

Or, Scan the QR code!

Once you do, it will be intuitive. Enjoy, and thank you!

Bibliography

Part 1

Agence France-Presse. "New Quest Aims to Settle Debate over Which River Is Longest - Amazon or Nile." *Voice of America*, June 27, 2023. https://www.voanews.com/a/new-quest-aims-to-settle-debate-over-which-river-is-longest-amazon-or-nile-/7154329.html.

"Ahmose, Son of Ebana. "The Expulsion of the Hyksos," San Jose State University. Accessed February 17, 2025. https://www.sjsu.edu/people/d.mesher/hum1a/Lecture-2-Egypt-Reading.pdf.

Arnold, Dorothea. "Image and Identity: Egypt's Eastern Neighbors, East Delta People, and the Hyksos." In *The Second Intermediate Period (Thirteenth-Seventeenth Dynasties). Current Research, Future Prospects*, edited by Marcel Marée. Leuven: Peeters, 2010.

Bietak, Manfred. "From Where Came the Hyksos and Where Did They Go?" In *The Second Intermediate Period (Thirteenth - Seventeenth Dynasties): Current Research, Future Prospects*, edited by Marcel Marée. Leuven: Peeters, 2010. https://www.academia.edu/10074987/_From_where_came_the_Hyksos_and_where_did_they_go_in_M_Mar%C3%A9e_ed_The_Second_Intermediate_Period_Thirteenth_Seventeenth_Dynasties_Current_Research_Future_Prospects_OLA_192_Leuven_2010_Peeters_139_181.

"Byblos," Articles on Ancient History, Livius.org, updated November 9, 2020. https://www.livius.org/articles/place/byblos/.

Enmarch, Roland. "Some Literary Aspects of the Kamose Inscriptions." *The Journal of Egyptian Archaeology* 99 (2013): 253-63. http://www.jstor.org/stable/24644936.

Eusebius. *Egyptian Chronicle*. Translated by Robert Bedrosian. Robert Bedrosian, 2008. http://www.attalus.org/armenian/euseb.html.

Gardiner, Sir Alan H. *Egypt of the Pharaohs*. Oxford University Press, 1979.

Goncalves, Isabelle. "Exploiting and Crossing the Egyptian Eastern Desert during the Pharaonic Era." In *Networked Spaces*, edited by Caroline Durand, Julie Marchand, Bérangère Redon, and Pierre Schneider. MOM Éditions, 2022. https://doi.org/10.4000/books.momeditions.16431.

Hernández, Roberto A. Díaz. "The Role of the War Chariot in the Formation of the Egyptian Empire in the Early 18th Dynasty." *Studien Zur Altägyptischen Kultur* 43 (2014): 109-22. http://www.jstor.org/stable/44160271.

Josephus, Flavius. *Of the Antiquity of the Jews Against Apion: Book One*. The University of Chicago. Accessed February 17, 2025. https://penelope.uchicago.edu/josephus/apion-1.html.

Kamrin, Janice. "The Procession of "Asiatics" at Beni Hasan." *The Metropolitan Museum of Art Symposia: Cultures in Contact from Mesopotamia to the Mediterranean in the Second Millennium*, edited by Joan Aruz, Sarah B. Graff, and Yelena Rakic. Yale University Press, 2013. https://www.academia.edu/30529730/The_Procession_of_Asiatics_at_Beni_Hasan_in_Cultures_in_Contact?auto=download.

Levy, Thomas E, Edwin C. M. van den Brink, Yuval Goren, and David Alon. "New Light on King Narmer and the Protodynastic Egyptian Presence in Canaan." *The Biblical Archaeologist* 58, no. 1 (March 1995): 26-35. https://doi.org/10.2307/3210465.

Lundström, Peter. "The king lists of Africanus." Pharaoh.se. Accessed February 17, 2025. https://pharaoh.se/africanus-king-list.

Morenz, Ludwig D. and Lutz Popko. "The Second Intermediate Period and the New Kingdom." In *A Companion to Ancient Egypt: Vol. I*, edited by Alan B. Lloyd. Wiley-Blackwell, 2010.

Redford, Donald B. "Egypt and Western Asia in the Old Kingdom." *Journal of the American Research Center in Egypt* 23 (1986): 125-43. https://doi.org/10.2307/40001094.

Ryholt, Kim. "The Turin King-List." *Ägypten und Levante / Egypt and the Levant* 14 (2004): 135-55. http://www.jstor.org/stable/23788139.

Shaw, Garry J. "The Death of King Seqenenre Tao." *Journal of the American Research Center in Egypt* 45 (2009): 159-76. http://www.jstor.org/stable/25735452.

Shortland, Andrew J., ed. *The Social Context of Technological Change: Egypt and the Near East, 1650-1150 BC*. Oxbow Books, 2016.

Silverman, David P., Josef W. Wegner, and Jennifer Houser Wegner. *Akhenaten and Tutankhamun: Revolution and Restoration*. University of

Pennsylvania Museum of Archaeology and Anthropology, 2006.

"Who Built the Pyramids?" NOVA, 1997. https://www.pbs.org/wgbh/nova/pyramid/explore/builders.html.

Wiener, Malcolm H. "Egypt & Time." *Ägypten und Levante / Egypt and the Levant* 16 (2006): 325-39. http://www.jstor.org/stable/23790293.

You, Jia. "Origin of Mummies Pushed Back 1500 Years: Study on Embalming in Ancient Graves 'Rewrites' Chapter in Egyptian History." *Science*, August 13, 2014. https://www.science.org/content/article/origin-mummies-pushed-back-1500-years.

Part 2

Arrian. "Alexander the Great." In *The Anabasis and the Indica*. Translated by Martin Hammond. Oxford: Oxford University Press, 2013.

Austin, M. M. "Greek Tyrants and the Persians, 546-479 B. C." *The Classical Quarterly* 40, no. 2 (1990): 289-306. http://www.jstor.org/stable/639090.

Bennett, Bob, and Mike Roberts. *The Wars of Alexander's Successors, 323-281 BC (Commanders and Campaigns Book 1)*. South Yorkshire: Pen & Sword Military, 2013.

Bennett, Bob, and Mike Roberts. *The Wars of Alexander's Successors 323 - 281 BC. Volume 2: Battles and Tactics*. South Yorkshire: Pen & Sword Military, 2009.

Cartledge, Paul. *The Spartans: The World of the Warrior-Heroes of Ancient Greece*. New York: The Overlook Press, 2003.

Clogg, Richard. *A Concise History of Greece*. Cambridge: Cambridge University Press, 2021.

Guthrie, W. K. C. *A History of Greek Philosophy*. Cambridge: Cambridge University Press, 1979.

Guthrie, W. K. C. *The Sophists*. Cambridge: Cambridge University Press, 1977.

Herodotus, *The Histories*. Translated by George Rawlinson. New York: Dutton & Co, 1862. http://classics.mit.edu/Herodotus/history.html

Hippocrates' Oath. Translated by Amelia Arenas. Boston University. https://www.bu.edu/arion/files/2010/03/Arenas_05Feb2010_Layout-3.pdf

Homer. *The Iliad*. Translated by Samuel Butler. Internet Classics Archive. http://classics.mit.edu/Homer/iliad.html

Homer. *The Odyssey*. Translated by Samuel Butler. Internet Classics Archive. http://classics.mit.edu/Homer/odyssey.html

Isocrates. *Letters*. Perseus Digital Library. Tufts University. http://www.perseus.tufts.edu/hopper/text?doc=Perseus:text:1999.01.0246:letter=3.

Martin, Thomas R. *Ancient Greece: From Prehistoric to Hellenistic Times.* New Haven: Yale University Press, 1996.

Matyszak, Philip. *Greece Against Rome: The Fall of the Hellenistic Kingdoms 250-31 BC.* South Yorkshire: Pen & Sword Military, 2020.

Matyszak, Philip. *The Rise of the Hellenistic Kingdoms, 336-250 BC.* South Yorkshire: Pen & Sword Military, 2019.

Napoli, Donna Jo. *Treasury of Greek Mythology: Classic Stories of Gods, Goddesses, Heroes & Monsters.* Washington, D.C.: National Geographic Kids, 2011.

Nur, A., & E. H. Cline. "Poseidon's Horses: Plate Tectonics and Earthquake Storms in the Late Bronze Age Aegean and Eastern Mediterranean." *Journal of Archaeological Science,* 27(1), (2000): 43-63. https://doi.org/10.1006/jasc.1999.0431

Plato. *The Republic.* Translated by Benjamin Jowett. Internet Classics Archive. http://classics.mit.edu/Plato/republic.9.viii.html

Polybius. *Histories.* http://www.perseus.tufts.edu/hopper/text?doc=Perseus:text:1999.01.0234

Plutarch. *Cimon.* Translated by John Dryden. Internet Classics Archive. http://classics.mit.edu/Plutarch/cimon.html

Pomeroy, Sarah B., Stanley M. Burstein, Walter Donlan, Jennifer Tolbert Roberts, David W. Tandy, and Georgia Tsouvala. *Ancient Greece: Politics, Society, and Culture.* New York: Oxford University Press, 2020.

Rhodes, P. J. *Athenian Democracy* (Edinburgh Readings on the Ancient World). Oxford: Oxford University Press, 2004.

Rodgers, Nigel. *Ancient Greece: An Illustrated History: The Illustrated Encyclopedia; A Comprehensive History With 1000 Images.* Dayton, Ohio: Lorenz Books, 2017.

Stein, Daniel. "Plague, Climate Change, and the End of Ancient Civilizations." *Discentes.* June 25:2023. https://web.sas.upenn.edu/discentes/2023/06/25/plague-climate-change-and-the-end-of-ancient-civilizations/

Thucydides. *History of the Peloponnesian War.* Translated by Rex Warner. New York: Penguin Classics, 1972.

Worthington, Ian. *By the Spear: Philip II, Alexander the Great, and the Rise and Fall of the Macedonian Empire (Ancient Warfare and Civilization).* Oxford: Oxford University Press, 2016.

Xenophon. *The Landmark Xenophon's Hellenika.* Translated by John Marincola. New York: Anchor, 2010.

Part 3

Appian. *Punic Wars.* http://www.perseus.tufts.edu/hopper/text?doc=Perseus%3Atext%3A1999.01.0230%3Atext%3DPun.%3Achapter%3D16%3Asection%3D111

Barchiesi, Alessandro and Walter Scheidel. *The Oxford Handbook of Roman Studies.* Oxford: Oxford University Press, 2010.

Boatwright, Mary T., Daniel J. Gargola, Noel Lenski, Richard J. A. Talbert. *The Romans: From Village to Empire: A History of Rome from Earliest Times to the End of the Western Empire.* Oxford: Oxford University Press, 2011.

Caesar, Julius. *The Gallic Wars.* Translated by W. A. McDevitte and W. S. Bohn. The Internet Classics Archive. http://classics.mit.edu/Caesar/gallic.1.1.html

Casson, Lionel. *Everyday Life in Ancient Rome.* Baltimore: Johns Hopkins University Press, 1998.

Chandler, David L. "Riddle Solved: Why Was Roman Concrete So Durable?" *MIT News Office* (January 6, 2023). https://news.mit.edu/2023/roman-concrete-durability-lime-casts-0106

Cicero. *Pro Cluentio.* http://www.thelatinlibrary.com/cicero/cluentio.shtml

Davies, Penelope J. E. *Architecture and Politics in Republican Rome.* Cambridge: Cambridge University Press, 2017.

DiBacco, Cory R. "The Position of Freedmen in Roman Society." *MAD-RUSH Undergraduate Research Conference,* (Spring 2017), JMU Scholarly Commons. https://commons.lib.jmu.edu/cgi/viewcontent.cgi?article=1069&context=madrush

Dio, Cassius. *Roman History.* Translated by H. B. Foster. Volume I of the Loeb Classical Library edition, New York: Macmillan Publishers, 1914. https://penelope.uchicago.edu/Thayer/E/Roman/Texts/Cassius_Dio/1*.html.

Gwynn, David M. *The Roman Republic: A Very Short Introduction.* Oxford: Oxford University Press, 2012.

Jones, Christopher. "The Emperor and the Giant." *Classical Philology* 95, no. 4 (2000): 476-81. http://www.jstor.org/stable/270519.

Josephus, Flavius. *The Jewish War.* http://penelope.uchicago.edu/josephus/war-3.html

Lintott, Andrew. *The Constitution of the Roman Republic.* Oxford: Oxford University Press, 2003.

Livy. *The Rise of Rome: Books One to Five.* Oxford: Oxford University Press, July 1, 2009.

Martin, Thomas R. *Ancient Rome: From Romulus to Justinian.* New Haven: Yale University Press, September 10, 2013.

Mitchell, Thomas N. "Roman Republicanism: The Underrated Legacy." *Proceedings of the American Philosophical Society* 145, no. 2 (2001): 127–37. http://www.jstor.org/stable/1558267.

Nicolaus of Damascus. *Life of Augustus*. Translated by Clayton M. Hall. https://web.archive.org/web/20070714144802/http://www.csun.edu/~hcfll004/nicolaus.html

Ovid. *Metamorphoses*. Translated by Sir Samuel Garth, John Dryden, et al. http://classics.mit.edu/Ovid/metam.1.first.html

Plutarch. *Fall of the Roman Republic*. London: Penguin Classics, 2006.

Plutarch. *De Fortuna Romanorum*. Translated by F. C. Babbitt. Vol. IV of the Loeb Classical Library edition, Cambridge: Harvard University Press, 1936. https://penelope.uchicago.edu/Thayer/E/Roman/Texts/Plutarch/Moralia/Fortuna_Romanorum*.html#T320c.

Plutarch. *The Parallel Lives*. Loeb Classical Library edition, 1914. https://penelope.uchicago.edu/Thayer/e/roman/texts/plutarch/lives/home.html

Polybius. *The Rise of the Roman Empire*. London: Penguin Classics, February 28, 1980.

Ricciotti, Giuseppe. *The Age Of Martyrs: Christianity from Diocletian (284) to Constantine (337)*. Gastonia, North Carolina: TAN Books, January 1, 2009.

Sheridan, Paul. "The Sacred Chickens of Rome." *Anecdotes from Antiquity*. November 8, 2015. http://www.anecdotesfromantiquity.net/the-sacred-chickens-of-rome/

Urbanus, Jason. "A Shrine to Romulus." *Archaeology Magazine*. Archaeological Institute of America, February 2021. https://www.archaeology.org/issues/406-2101/features/9269-rome-romulus-shrine.

Virgil. *The Aeneid Book IV*. Translated by A. S. Kline. Poetry in Translation, 2002. https://www.poetryintranslation.com/PITBR/Latin/VirgilAeneidIV.php

Image Sources

1 Created by author
2 Jeff Dahl, CC BY-SA 4.0 <https://creativecommons.org/licenses/by-sa/4.0>, via Wikimedia Commons: https://commons.wikimedia.org/wiki/File:Ancient_Egypt_map-en.svg
3 Jeff Dahl, CC BY-SA 4.0 <https://creativecommons.org/licenses/by-sa/4.0>, via Wikimedia Commons: https://commons.wikimedia.org/wiki/File:Khnum.svg
4 https://commons.wikimedia.org/wiki/File:Design_of_the_Abydos_token_glyphs_dated_to_3400-3200_BCE.jpg
5 Photo zoomed in. Quibell,1898, pl. 13, CC BY-SA 4.0 <https://creativecommons.org/licenses/by-sa/4.0>, via Wikimedia Commons: https://commons.wikimedia.org/wiki/File:Narmer_Palette_recto.svg
6 Photo zoomed in. Quibell,1898, pl. 13, CC BY-SA 4.0 <https://creativecommons.org/licenses/by-sa/4.0>, via Wikimedia Commons: https://commons.wikimedia.org/wiki/File:Narmer_Palette_verso.svg
7 Captmondo, GFDL <http://www.gnu.org/copyleft/fdl.html>, via Wikimedia Commons; https://commons.wikimedia.org/wiki/File:MacGregor_Plate_(with_background).jpg
8 Mastaba.jpg: Unknown. Originally uploaded by Oesermaatra0069 at 2006-03-12.derivative work: Master Uegly, CC BY-SA 3.0 <http://creativecommons.org/licenses/by-sa/3.0/>, via Wikimedia Commons: https://commons.wikimedia.org/wiki/File:Mastaba_schematics.svg
9 Charles J. Sharp, CC BY-SA 3.0 <https://creativecommons.org/licenses/by-sa/3.0>, via Wikimedia Commons: https://commons.wikimedia.org/wiki/File:Saqqara_pyramid_ver_2.jpg

10 Photo zoomed in. lienyuan lee, CC BY 3.0 <https://creativecommons.org/licenses/by/3.0/>, via Wikimedia Commons: https://commons.wikimedia.org/wiki/File:Bent_Pyramid_%E6%9B%B2%E6%8A%98%E9%87%91%E5%AD%97%E5%A1%94_-_panoramio.jpg

11 Iry-Hor, CC BY-SA 3.0 <https://creativecommons.org/licenses/by-sa/3.0>, via Wikimedia Commons: https://commons.wikimedia.org/wiki/File:Mentuhotep_Closeup.jpg

12 Photo Modified: zoomed in, labels added. Ancient_Egypt_map-en.svg: Jeff Dahlderivative work: MinisterForBadTimes, CC BY-SA 3.0 <https://creativecommons.org/licenses/by-sa/3.0>, via Wikimedia Commons: https://commons.wikimedia.org/wiki/File:Lower_Egypt-en.png

13 Photo zoomed in. NebMaatRa, CC BY-SA 3.0 <http://creativecommons.org/licenses/by-sa/3.0/>, via Wikimedia Commons: https://commons.wikimedia.org/wiki/File:Drawing_of_the_procession_of_the_Aamu_group_tomb_of_Khnumhotep_II_at_Beni_Hassan.jpg

14 Rozemarijn vanL, CC BY-SA 4.0 <https://creativecommons.org/licenses/by-sa/4.0>, via Wikimedia Commons; https://commons.wikimedia.org/wiki/File:Proto-sinaitic-phoenician-latin-alphabet.jpg

15 https://commons.wikimedia.org/wiki/File:Lepsi_Hyks.JPG

16 Metropolitan Museum of Art, CC0, via Wikimedia Commons: https://commons.wikimedia.org/wiki/File:Standing_Hippopotamus_MET_DP248993.jpg

17 https://commons.wikimedia.org/wiki/File:Pharaoh_Ahmose_I_slaying_a_Hyksos_(axe_of_Ahmose_I,_from_the_Treasure_of_Queen_Aahhotep_II)_Colorized_per_source.jpg

18 Photo zoomed in. https://commons.wikimedia.org/wiki/File:Beni_Hassan_(Lepsius,_BH_3)_04.jpg

19 Vassil, CC0, via Wikimedia Commons: https://commons.wikimedia.org/wiki/File:St%C3%A8le_Mercenaire_syrien_18%C3%A8me_dynastie_Neues_Museum_image_%C3%A9claircie_et_perspective_corrig%C3%A9e.jpg

20 https://commons.wikimedia.org/wiki/File:Egyptian_lute_players_001.jpg

21 Jon BodsworthZerida at en.wikipedia, Copyrighted free use, via Wikimedia Commons: https://commons.wikimedia.org/wiki/File:EgyptianScribe.jpg

22 Photo zoomed in. https://commons.wikimedia.org/wiki/File:Egyptian_harvest.jpg

23 Jeff Dahl, CC BY-SA 4.0 <https://creativecommons.org/licenses/by-sa/4.0>, via Wikimedia Commons: https://commons.wikimedia.org/wiki/File:Mut.svg

24 Brooklyn Museum, CC BY-SA 2.0 <https://creativecommons.org/licenses/by-sa/2.0>, via Wikimedia Commons: https://commons.wikimedia.org/wiki/File:Dynasty_12_Egyptian_model_boat_(Amenemhet_I).jpg

25 Boston Museum of Fine Arts, CC BY-SA 4.0 <https://creativecommons.org/licenses/by-sa/4.0>, via Wikimedia Commons: https://commons.wikimedia.org/wiki/File:Nefu_and_his_wife,_official_at_5th_dynasty,_Giza,_Old_Kingdom,_ancient_Egypt.jpg

26 Metropolitan Museum of Art, CC0, via Wikimedia Commons: https://commons.wikimedia.org/wiki/File:Scarab_finger_rign_with_the_name_of_Maatkare_MET_25.3.193_EGDP021780.jpg

27 Metropolitan Museum of Art, CC0, via Wikimedia Commons: https://commons.wikimedia.org/wiki/File:Scarab_finger_rign_with_the_name_of_Maatkare_MET_25.3.193_EGDP021779.jpg

28 Photo zoomed in. Olaf Tausch, CC BY 3.0 <https://creativecommons.org/licenses/by/3.0>, via Wikimedia Commons: https://commons.wikimedia.org/wiki/File:Giseh_Sonnenbarke_07.jpg

29 Althiphika, CC BY-SA 3.0 <https://creativecommons.org/licenses/by-sa/3.0>, via Wikimedia Commons: https://commons.wikimedia.org/wiki/File:Other_ramps1b.svg

30 Photo zoomed in. Walkerssk, CC0, via Wikimedia Commons: https://commons.wikimedia.org/wiki/File:Pyramids_in_Giza_-_Egypt.jpg

31 Eternal Space, CC BY-SA 4.0 <https://creativecommons.org/licenses/by-sa/4.0>, via Wikimedia Commons: https://commons.wikimedia.org/wiki/File:Ba-bird.png

32 Petar Milošević, CC BY-SA 4.0 <https://creativecommons.org/licenses/by-sa/4.0>, via Wikimedia Commons: https://commons.wikimedia.org/wiki/File:Great_Sphinx_of_Giza_(%D8%A3%D8%A8%D9%88_%D8%A7%D9%84%D9%87%D9%88%D9%84).jpg.

33 kairoinfo4u, CC BY-SA 2.0 <https://creativecommons.org/licenses/by-sa/2.0>, via Wikimedia Commons: https://commons.wikimedia.org/wiki/File:Column_of_Akhmenu_Hall_(Luxor).jpg

34 Diego Delso, CC BY-SA 4.0 <https://creativecommons.org/licenses/by-sa/4.0>, via Wikimedia Commons: https://commons.wikimedia.org/wiki/File:Templo_de_Luxor,_Luxor,_Egipto,_2022-04-01,_DD_02.jpg

35 Jeff Dahl, CC BY-SA 4.0 <https://creativecommons.org/licenses/by-sa/4.0>, via Wikimedia Commons: https://commons.wikimedia.org/wiki/File:Taweret.svg

36 Metropolitan Museum of Art, CC0, via Wikimedia Commons: https://commons.wikimedia.org/wiki/File:The_King_with_Isis,_Tomb_of_Haremhab_MET_DP276167.jpg

37 https://commons.wikimedia.org/wiki/File:BD_Hunefer_cropped_1.jpg

38 https://commons.wikimedia.org/wiki/File:Apep_1.jpg

39 Photo zoomed in. Metropolitan Museum of Art, CC0, via Wikimedia Commons: https://commons.wikimedia.org/wiki/File:The_Singer_of_Amun_Nany%27s_Funerary_Papyrus_MET_DT11633.jpg

40 https://commons.wikimedia.org/wiki/File:Anubis_attending_the_mummy_of_Sennedjem.jpg

41 Photo zoomed in. https://commons.wikimedia.org/wiki/File:Opening_of_the_mouth_ceremony.jpg

42 Osama Shukir Muhammed Amin FRCP(Glasg), CC BY-SA 4.0 <https://creativecommons.org/licenses/by-sa/4.0>, via Wikimedia Commons: https://commons.wikimedia.org/wiki/File:Representation_of_the_deified_Amenhotep_I._From_Tomb_TT359_at_Deir_el-Medina,_Egypt._Neues_Museum,_Berlin.jpg

43 Paul James Cowie (Pjamescowie), CC BY 2.0 <https://creativecommons.org/licenses/by/2.0>, via Wikimedia Commons: https://commons.wikimedia.org/wiki/File:Thutmose_I,_copy_of_relief,_Deir_el-Bahari_(MMA_30.4.137).jpg

44 Metropolitan Museum of Art, CC0, via Wikimedia Commons: https://commons.wikimedia.org/wiki/File:Head_of_an_Osiride_Statue_of_Hatshepsut_MET_21II_FIG3A3_1R1.jpg

45 Metropolitan Museum of Art, CC0, via Wikimedia Commons: https://commons.wikimedia.org/wiki/File:Large_Kneeling_Statue_of_Hatshepsut_MET_21V_CAT092R3.jpg

46 British Museum, CC BY-SA 3.0 <http://creativecommons.org/licenses/by-sa/3.0/>, via Wikimedia Commons: https://commons.wikimedia.org/wiki/File:BlockStatueOfSenenmutAndNeferura-LeftProfile-BritishMuseum-August19-08.jpg

47 Charlie Phillips, CC BY 2.0 <https://creativecommons.org/licenses/by/2.0>, via Wikimedia Commons: https://commons.wikimedia.org/wiki/File:Deserted_temple_of_Hatshepsut,_Deir_El_Bahri,_Egypt.jpg

48 Metropolitan Museum of Art, CC0, via Wikimedia Commons: https://commons.wikimedia.org/wiki/File:Upper_part_of_a_statue_of_Thutmose_III_MET_07.230.3_10.jpg

49 https://crosswordlabs.com/view/who-or-where

50 https://commons.wikimedia.org/wiki/File:Menphtah_II_(Merneptah),_figlio_e_successore_di_Ramses_III_(Ramesses_II),_sta_dinnanzi_a_Phr%C3%AA_(Ra)-_due_figure_gigantesche_scolpite_e_dipinte_nell%27ingresso_della_tomba_di_quel_re_a_(NYPL_b14291206-425610).jpg

51 https://commons.wikimedia.org/wiki/File:Amenhotep_II_Uraeus.jpg

52 Jon Bodsworth, Copyrighted free use, via Wikimedia Commons: https://commons.wikimedia.org/wiki/File:Akhenaten_statue.jpg

53 Keith Schengili-Roberts, CC BY-SA 3.0 <http://creativecommons.org/licenses/by-sa/3.0/>, via Wikimedia Commons:

https://commons.wikimedia.org/wiki/File:ReliefFragmentOfAkhenatenWithSunDiskOfAten.png

54 Photo zoomed in. Olaf Tausch, CC BY 3.0 <https://creativecommons.org/licenses/by/3.0>, via Wikimedia Commons: https://commons.wikimedia.org/wiki/File:Luxor_Museum_Statuenkopf_Echnaton_01.jpg

55 Philip Pikart, CC BY-SA 3.0 <https://creativecommons.org/licenses/by-sa/3.0>, via Wikimedia Commons: https://commons.wikimedia.org/wiki/File:Nofretete_Neues_Museum.jpg

56 https://commons.wikimedia.org/wiki/File:Maia_and_tut.gif

57 Jean-Pierre Dalbéra from Paris, France, CC BY 2.0 <https://creativecommons.org/licenses/by/2.0>, via Wikimedia Commons: https://commons.wikimedia.org/wiki/File:Couple_royal_dans_un_jardin_(Neues_Museum,_Berlin)_(11545827426).jpg

58 Djehouty, CC BY-SA 4.0 <https://creativecommons.org/licenses/by-sa/4.0>, via Wikimedia Commons: https://commons.wikimedia.org/wiki/File:Respaldo_del_trono_de_oro_de_Tutankam%C3%B3n.jpg

59 Jean-Pierre Dalbéra, CC BY 2.0 <https://creativecommons.org/licenses/by/2.0>, via Wikimedia Commons: https://commons.wikimedia.org/wiki/File:T%C3%AAte_de_Tout%C3%A2nkhamon_enfant_(mus%C3%A9e_du_Caire_Egypte).jpg

60 https://commons.wikimedia.org/wiki/File:Tutankhamun_tomb_photographs_4_326.jpg

61 EditorfromMars, CC BY-SA 4.0 <https://creativecommons.org/licenses/by-sa/4.0>, via Wikimedia Commons: https://commons.wikimedia.org/wiki/File:King_Tut_over_enemies,_18th_dynasty,_Cairo_Museum.jpg

62 : https://commons.wikimedia.org/wiki/File:Opening_of_the_Mouth_-_Tutankhamun_and_Aja-2.jpg

63 Credit: Dosseman, CC BY-SA 4.0 <https://creativecommons.org/licenses/by-sa/4.0>, via Wikimedia Commons; https://commons.wikimedia.org/wiki/File:Antakya_Archaeological_Museum_Statue_of_Suppiluliuma_sept_2019_5792.jpg

64 en:User:MykReeve, CC BY-SA 3.0 <http://creativecommons.org/licenses/by-sa/3.0/>, via Wikimedia Commons: https://commons.wikimedia.org/wiki/File:Tutanchamun_Maske.jpg

65 ddenisen (D. Denisenkov), CC BY-SA 2.0 <https://creativecommons.org/licenses/by-sa/2.0>, via Wikimedia Commons: https://commons.wikimedia.org/wiki/File:Ushabti_of_Tutankhamun_(KV62).jpg

66 https://commons.wikimedia.org/wiki/File:Ramses_III_(Ramses_II)_lanciato_col_suo_carro,_e_seguito_da_tre_figli_ugualmente_sul_carro,_assale_una_f

ortezza_piantata_sopra_una_rupe,_saettandone_gli_atterriti_difensori_(NYPL_b142 91206-425634).jpg:

67 Osama Shukir Muhammed Amin FRCP(Glasg), CC BY-SA 4.0 <https://creativecommons.org/licenses/by-sa/4.0>, via Wikimedia Commons: https://commons.wikimedia.org/wiki/File:Pharaoh_Seti_I,_detail_of_a_wall_painting_from_the_Tomb_of_Seti_I_at_the_Valley_of_the_Kings,_Western_Thebes,_Egypt._Neues_Museum.jpg

68 Pbuergler, CC BY-SA 3.0 <https://creativecommons.org/licenses/by-sa/3.0>, via Wikimedia Commons: https://commons.wikimedia.org/wiki/File:Ramses_II_British_Museum.jpg

69 https://commons.wikimedia.org/wiki/File:Tavole_che_ritraggono_il_partimento_inferiore_della_medesima_tavola_87,_fin_dove_comincia_la_battaglia_dei_carri-_(le_tre_ultime_colorate)_(NYPL_b14291206-425654).jpg

70 Photo modified: zoomed in, labels added. O.Mustafin, CC0, via Wikimedia Commons: https://commons.wikimedia.org/wiki/File:F_Crescent.png

71 https://commons.wikimedia.org/wiki/File:Hittite_Chariot.jpg

72 Photo zoomed in. https://commons.wikimedia.org/wiki/File:Tavole_che_ritraggono_il_partimento_inferiore_della_medesima_tavola_87,_fin_dove_comincia_la_battaglia_dei_carri-_(le_tre_ultime_colorate)_(NYPL_b14291206-425654).jpg

73 https://commons.wikimedia.org/wiki/File:Modern_loose_interpretation_at_the_The_Pharaonic_Village_in_Cairo_of_a_Battle_scene_from_the_Great_Kadesh_reliefs_of_Ramses_II_on_the_Walls_of_the_Ramesseum.jpg

74 https://commons.wikimedia.org/wiki/File:Penmaat_Priest_Book_of_the_Dead.jpg

75 Émile Prisse d'Avennes (1807-1879), CC BY 4.0 <https://creativecommons.org/licenses/by/4.0>, via Wikimedia Commons: https://commons.wikimedia.org/wiki/File:Queen_Tausret_%C3%89mile_Prisse_d%27Avennes.jpg

76 https://commons.wikimedia.org/wiki/File:Cambyses_II_capturing_Psamtik_III.png

77 https://commons.wikimedia.org/wiki/File:Venus_and_Cupid_from_the_House_of_Marcus_Fabius_Rufus_at_Pompeii,_most_likely_a_depiction_of_Cleopatra_VII_(2).jpg

78 Roman Eisele, CC BY-SA 4.0 <https://creativecommons.org/licenses/by-sa/4.0>, via Wikimedia Commons; https://commons.wikimedia.org/wiki/File:Mundelsheim_-_M%C3%BChlbachweinberge_-_Weinbergmauern_beim_Steinbruch_(1).jpg

79 Photo Modified: labels added. Source: Peterfitzgerald (Peter Fitzgerald), Shaundd, CC BY-SA 4.0 <https://creativecommons.org/licenses/by-sa/4.0>, via Wikimedia Commons: https://commons.wikimedia.org/wiki/File:Greece_WV_regions_map_2016.svg

80 RickyBennison, CC0, via Wikimedia Commons; https://commons.wikimedia.org/wiki/File:Panathenaic_Amphora_Sprinters.jpg

81 https://commons.wikimedia.org/wiki/File:A_muse_with_a_harp,_and_two_others_with_Lyres_from_a_Greek_vase_in_the_Munich_Museum.jpg

82 William Neuheisel from DC, US, CC BY 2.0 <https://creativecommons.org/licenses/by/2.0>, via Wikimedia Commons; https://commons.wikimedia.org/wiki/File:Lions_Gate_at_Mycenae_(5228010382).jpg

83 Zde, CC BY-SA 4.0 <https://creativecommons.org/licenses/by-sa/4.0>, via Wikimedia Commons: https://commons.wikimedia.org/wiki/File:Middle_Corinthian_pottery_amphora,_Geledakis_Painter,_590-570_BC,_AM_Corinth,_Korm421.jpg

84 Yair Haklai, CC BY-SA 3.0 <https://creativecommons.org/licenses/by-sa/3.0>, via Wikimedia Commons; https://commons.wikimedia.org/wiki/File:Antonio_Canova-Helen_of_Troy-Victoria_and_Albert_Museum.jpg

85 Photo zoomed in. Source: Ricardo André Frantz (User:Tetraktys), CC BY-SA 3.0 <https://creativecommons.org/licenses/by-sa/3.0>, via Wikimedia Commons: https://commons.wikimedia.org/wiki/File:Netuno16b.jpg

86 ArchaiOptix, CC BY-SA 4.0 <https://creativecommons.org/licenses/by-sa/4.0>, via Wikimedia Commons: https://commons.wikimedia.org/wiki/File:Group_of_Polygnotos_ARV_1057_98_return_of_Hephaistos_-_three_maenads_(05).jpg

87 https://commons.wikimedia.org/wiki/File:Mattei_Athena_Louvre_Ma530_n2.jpg

88 Zde, CC BY-SA 4.0 <https://creativecommons.org/licenses/by-sa/4.0>, via Wikimedia Commons: https://commons.wikimedia.org/wiki/File:Oracle_of_Delphi,_red-figure_kylix,_440-430_BC,_Kodros_Painter,_Berlin_F_2538,_141668.jpg

89 Mary Harrsch, CC BY-SA 4.0 <https://creativecommons.org/licenses/by-sa/4.0>, via Wikimedia Commons: https://commons.wikimedia.org/wiki/File:Menelaus_bearing_the_corpse_of_Patroclus._Marble,_Flavian_Era_(1st_century_CE)_Roman_copy_after_a_Hellenistic_original_of_the_3rd_century_BCE_MH_04.jpg

90 Photo Modified: zoomed in, labels added. Source: Peripheries_of_Greece_numbered.svg:
*Greek_Macedonia_map_with_subdivisions.svg:
*Greece_2011_Periferiakes_Enotites.svg: Pitichinaccioderivative work: Philly boy92 (talk)derivative work: Fulvio314, CC BY-SA 3.0 <https://creativecommons.org/licenses/by-sa/3.0>, via Wikimedia Commons: https://commons.wikimedia.org/wiki/File:Greece_(ancient)_Epirus.svg

91 Photo zoomed in. Source: George E. Koronaios, CC0, via Wikimedia Commons; https://commons.wikimedia.org/wiki/File:The_Temple_of_Athena_Nike_on_the_Acropolis_of_Athens_on_13_February_2019.jpg

92 https://commons.wikimedia.org/wiki/File:Solon.jpg

93 https://commons.wikimedia.org/wiki/File:Return_of_Peisistratus_to_Athens_with_the_false_Minerva.jpg

94 Mary Harrsch, CC BY-SA 4.0 <https://creativecommons.org/licenses/by-sa/4.0>, via Wikimedia Commons: https://commons.wikimedia.org/wiki/File:Bronze_banqueter_from_the_tripod_support_of_a_bronze_bowl_Laconian_530-500_BCE_from_Dodona_British_Museum.jpg

95 user:Megistias background cleaned by Chabacano, CC BY-SA 3.0 <http://creativecommons.org/licenses/by-sa/3.0/>, via Wikimedia Commons: https://commons.wikimedia.org/wiki/File:Hoplites.jpg

96 Caeciliusinhorto, CC BY-SA 4.0 <https://creativecommons.org/licenses/by-sa/4.0>, via Wikimedia Commons; https://commons.wikimedia.org/wiki/File:Spartan_running_girl_(cropped).jpg

97 Mary Harrsch, CC BY-SA 4.0 <https://creativecommons.org/licenses/by-sa/4.0>, via Wikimedia Commons: https://commons.wikimedia.org/wiki/File:Statue_of_a_hoplite_known_as_Leonidas_480-470_BCE_Sparta_Acropolis_Sanctuary_of_Athena_Chalkioikos_01.jpg

98 https://commons.wikimedia.org/wiki/File:Greek_Galleys.jpg

99 https://commons.wikimedia.org/wiki/File:The_Battle_of_Marathon.jpg

100 https://commons.wikimedia.org/wiki/File:Construction_of_Xerxes_Bridge_of_boats_by_Phoenician_sailors.jpg

101 Photo modified: zoomed in, labels added. Source: Greece_location_map.svg: Lencer / derivative work: Uwe Dedering, CC BY-SA 3.0 <https://creativecommons.org/licenses/by-sa/3.0>, via Wikimedia Commons: https://commons.wikimedia.org/wiki/File:Greece_relief_location_map.jpg

102 https://commons.wikimedia.org/wiki/File:Ship_dashed_against_ship,_till_the_Persian_Army_dead_strewed_the_deep_like_flowers.jpg

103 lensnmatter, CC BY 2.0 https://creativecommons.org/licenses/by/2.0>, via Wikimedia Commons: https://commons.wikimedia.org/wiki/File:Caryatids_of_Erechtheion_(20419658495).jpg

104 Metropolitan Museum of Art, CC0, via Wikimedia Commons: https://commons.wikimedia.org/wiki/File:Terracotta_Nolan_amphora_(jar)_MET_DT229457.jpg

105 Photo zoomed in. Source: ArchaiOptix, CC BY-SA 4.0 <https://creativecommons.org/licenses/by-sa/4.0>, via Wikimedia Commons: https://commons.wikimedia.org/wiki/File:Attic_red_figure_kylix_-_ARV_extra_-_symposion_-_Athens_NAM_1357.jpg

106 ArchaiOptix, CC BY-SA 4.0 <https://creativecommons.org/licenses/by-sa/4.0>, via Wikimedia Commons: https://commons.wikimedia.org/wiki/File:Very_early_red_figure_pot_ARV_11_1_Dionysos_with_maenads_-_Achilles_and_Ajax_playing_(06).jpg

107 Photograph by Dean Dixon, Sculpture by Alan LeQuire, FAL, via Wikimedia Commons: https://commons.wikimedia.org/wiki/File:Athena_Parthenos_LeQuire.jpg

108 Photo zoomed in. Source: Jacques-Louis David, CC0, via Wikimedia Commons; https://commons.wikimedia.org/wiki/File:The_Death_of_Socrates_MET_DT40.jpg

109 Vatican Museums, CC BY 3.0 <https://creativecommons.org/licenses/by/3.0>, via Wikimedia Commons: https://commons.wikimedia.org/wiki/File:Pericles_Pio-Clementino_Inv269_n4.jpg

110 Photo Modified: zoomed in, labels added. https://commons.wikimedia.org/wiki/File:Pineios_river_(Peloponnese).jpg

111 Yair Haklai, CC BY-SA 4.0 <https://creativecommons.org/licenses/by-sa/4.0>, via Wikimedia Commons: https://commons.wikimedia.org/wiki/File:Thucydides_at_Exterior_of_the_Austrian_Parliament_Building.jpg

112 Photo zoomed in. Source: Morn, CC BY-SA 4.0 <https://creativecommons.org/licenses/by-sa/4.0>, via Wikimedia Commons: https://commons.wikimedia.org/wiki/File:Sicilian_Expedition_map_en.svg

113 https://commons.wikimedia.org/wiki/File:Bust_Alcibiades_Musei_Capitolini_MC1160_(cropped).jpg

114 Jona Lendering, CC0, via Wikimedia Commons: https://commons.wikimedia.org/wiki/File:Philip_II_statue_350-400_CE.jpg

115 Photo modified: zoomed in and labels added. Source: ArnoldPlaton, CC BY-SA 3.0 <https://creativecommons.org/licenses/by-sa/3.0>, via Wikimedia Common: https://commons.wikimedia.org/wiki/File:Balkan_Peninsula.svg

116 https://commons.wikimedia.org/wiki/File:Alexander_The_Great_statue_-_estatua_de_Alejandro_Magno.jpg

117 https://commons.wikimedia.org/wiki/File:Meister_der_Alexanderschlacht_003.jpg

118 https://commons.wikimedia.org/wiki/File:The_charge_of_the_Persian_scythed_chariots_at_the_battle_of_Gaugamela_by_Andre_Castaigne_(1898-1899).jpg

119 Massimo Finizio, CC BY-SA 2.0 via Wikimedia Commons: https://commons.wikimedia.org/wiki/File:Seleuco_I_Nicatore.JPG

120 Fotogeniss, CC BY-SA 3.0 <https://creativecommons.org/licenses/by-sa/3.0>, via Wikimedia Commons: https://commons.wikimedia.org/wiki/File:Coin_olympias_mus_theski.JPG

121 Naples National Archaeological Museum, CC BY 2.5 <https://creativecommons.org/licenses/by/2.5>, via Wikimedia Commons: https://commons.wikimedia.org/wiki/File:Ptolemy_II_MAN_Napoli_Inv5600.jpg

122 https://commons.wikimedia.org/wiki/File:Pyrrhus.JPG

123 Photo zoomed in. https://commons.wikimedia.org/wiki/File:Alma-tadema-antony-cleopatra.jpeg

124 Original: Andre Engels Vector: Wimmel, CC BY-SA 3.0 <http://creativecommons.org/licenses/by-sa/3.0/>, via Wikimedia Commons; https://commons.wikimedia.org/wiki/File:Pythagorean_theorem_abc.svg

125 Source: user:shakko, CC BY-SA 3.0 <https://creativecommons.org/licenses/by-sa/3.0>, via Wikimedia Commons: https://commons.wikimedia.org/wiki/File:Hippocrates_pushkin02.jpg

126 Photo zoomed in. Source: Steve Swayne, CC BY 2.0 <https://creativecommons.org/licenses/by/2.0>, via Wikimedia Common: https://commons.wikimedia.org/wiki/File:The_Parthenon_in_Athens.jpg

127 Drummyfish, CC0, via Wikimedia Commons: https://commons.wikimedia.org/wiki/File:Platonic_Solids_Transparent.svg

128 Photo zoomed in. Source: ZDF/Terra X/Gruppe 5/ Susanne Utzt, Cristina Trebbi/ Jens Boeck, Dieter Stürmer / Fabian Wienke / Sebastian Martinez/ xkopp, polloq, CC BY 4.0 <https://creativecommons.org/licenses/by/4.0>, via Wikimedia Commons: https://commons.wikimedia.org/wiki/File:Archimedes%27-Lever.png

129 https://commons.wikimedia.org/wiki/File:Pi_eq_C_over_d.svg

130 https://commons.wikimedia.org/wiki/File:Batoni,_Pompeo_%E2%80%94_Aeneas_fleeing_from_Troy_%E2%80%94_1750.jpg

131 https://commons.wikimedia.org/wiki/File:Tiepolo_-_Latinus_Offering_his_Daughter_Lavinia_to_Aeneas_in_Matrimony,_1753_%E2%80%93_1754,_KMS4201.jpg

132 Trougnouf, CC BY 4.0 <https://creativecommons.org/licenses/by/4.0>, via Wikimedia Commons: https://commons.wikimedia.org/wiki/File:Maison_de_la_Louve_(DSC_0377).jpg

133 Photo zoomed in, labels added.: Cassius Ahenobarbus, CC BY-SA 3.0 <https://creativecommons.org/licenses/by-sa/3.0>, via Wikimedia Commons: https://commons.wikimedia.org/wiki/File:Ligue-latine-carte.png

134 Zoomed in.: https://commons.wikimedia.org/wiki/File:Nicolas_Poussin_-_L%27Enl%C3%A8vement_des_Sabines_(1634-5).jpg

135 https://commons.wikimedia.org/wiki/File:Servius_Tullius_by_Frans_Huys.jpg

136 https://commons.wikimedia.org/wiki/File:Fran%C3%A7ois-Joseph_Navez001.jpg

137 Photo zoomed in.: https://commons.wikimedia.org/wiki/File:Cicer%C3%B3n_denuncia_a_Catilina,_por_Cesare_Maccari.jpg

138 Mathiasrex, CC BY-SA 3.0 <http://creativecommons.org/licenses/by-sa/3.0/>, via Wikimedia Commons; https://commons.wikimedia.org/wiki/File:Romtrireme.jpg

139 https://commons.wikimedia.org/wiki/File:Schlacht_bei_Zama_Gem%C3%A4lde_H_P_Motte.jpg

140 Alphanidon, CC BY-SA 4.0 <https://creativecommons.org/licenses/by-sa/4.0>, via Wikimedia Commons; https://commons.wikimedia.org/wiki/File:Pompey_the_Great.jpg

141 https://commons.wikimedia.org/wiki/File:Death_of_Julius_Caesar_2.png

142 Stephencdickson, CC BY-SA 4.0 <https://creativecommons.org/licenses/by-sa/4.0>, via Wikimedia Commons: https://commons.wikimedia.org/wiki/File:Augustus_Caesar.png

143 Homoatrox, CC BY-SA 4.0 <https://creativecommons.org/licenses/by-sa/4.0>, via Wikimedia Commons: https://commons.wikimedia.org/wiki/File:Roman_empire_14_AD_(provinces)_en.png

144 Photo zoomed in. Avidius, CC BY-SA 4.0 <https://creativecommons.org/licenses/by-sa/4.0>, via Wikimedia Commons: https://commons.wikimedia.org/wiki/File:ClaudiusJupiter.jpg

145 Diliff, CC BY-SA 2.5 <https://creativecommons.org/licenses/by-sa/2.5>, via Wikimedia Commons: https://commons.wikimedia.org/wiki/File:Colosseum_in_Rome-April_2007-1-_copie_2B.jpg

146 Photo zoomed in.: Sparrow (麻雀), CC BY-SA 4.0 <https://creativecommons.org/licenses/by-sa/4.0>, via Wikimedia Commons: https://commons.wikimedia.org/wiki/File:Pompeii_casts_18.jpg

147 Photo zoomed in.: Sergey Sosnovskiy, CC BY-SA 4.0 <https://creativecommons.org/licenses/by-sa/4.0>, via Wikimedia Commons: https://commons.wikimedia.org/wiki/File:Roman_warrior,_ca._80%E2%80%9420_BC.jpg

148 Vatican Museums, CC BY 3.0 <https://creativecommons.org/licenses/by/3.0>, via Wikimedia Commons: https://commons.wikimedia.org/wiki/File:Marius_Chiaramonti_Inv1488.jpg

149 Toledo Museum of Art, CC0, via Wikimedia Commons: https://commons.wikimedia.org/wiki/File:Toledo_Museum_of_Art_-_Portrait_of_a_Young_Man_in_Armor_(2).jpg

150 Rpanjwani3, CC BY-SA 3.0 <https://creativecommons.org/licenses/by-sa/3.0>, via Wikimedia Commons: https://commons.wikimedia.org/wiki/File:Mang2.png

151 https://commons.wikimedia.org/wiki/File:Pompeii_-_Casa_del_Poeta_Tragico_-_Theater_3.jpg

152 https://commons.wikimedia.org/wiki/File:OstianInsulae.JPG

153 Dennis Jarvis, CC BY-SA 2.0 <https://creativecommons.org/licenses/by-sa/2.0>, via Wikimedia Commons: https://commons.wikimedia.org/wiki/File:Dougga_cup-bearers_mosa%C3%AFc.jpg

154 https://commons.wikimedia.org/wiki/File:Borghese_villa_gladiator_mosaic.jpg

155 TimeTravelRome, CC BY 2.0 <https://creativecommons.org/licenses/by/2.0>, via Wikimedia Commons: https://commons.wikimedia.org/wiki/File:Nennig_Roman_Villa_and_Mosaics_-_51134391753.jpg

156 Jamie Heath, CC BY-SA 2.0 <https://creativecommons.org/licenses/by-sa/2.0>, via Wikimedia Commons: https://commons.wikimedia.org/wiki/File:Circus_Maximus_Panel_(51220278177).jpg

157 Photo zoomed in.: ArchaiOptix, CC BY-SA 4.0 <https://creativecommons.org/licenses/by-sa/4.0>, via Wikimedia Commons: https://commons.wikimedia.org/wiki/File:Wall_painting_-_satyrs_as_tightrope_acrobats_-_Pompeii_(villa_of_Cicero)_-_Napoli_MAN_9118.jpg

158 https://commons.wikimedia.org/wiki/File:Mosaic_depicting_theatrical_masks_of_Tragedy_and_Comedy_(Thermae_Decianae).jpg

159 Fubar Obfusco, CC0, via Wikimedia Commons: https://commons.wikimedia.org/wiki/File:Latrines_romaine_%C3%A0_Ostie.JPG

160 A. Hunter Wright, CC BY-SA 3.0 <http://creativecommons.org/licenses/by-sa/3.0/>, via Wikimedia Commons: https://commons.wikimedia.org/wiki/File:Arch_of_Septimius_Severus_East.jpg

161 Dave & Margie Hill / Kleerup from Centennial, CO, USA, CC BY-SA 2.0 <https://creativecommons.org/licenses/by-sa/2.0>, via Wikimedia Commons: https://commons.wikimedia.org/wiki/File:Thermopolium_(7254049600).jpg

162 Roberto Ferrari, CC BY-SA 2.0 <https://creativecommons.org/licenses/by-sa/2.0>, via Wikimedia Commons: https://commons.wikimedia.org/wiki/File:Pont_du_Gard_3.jpg

163 Pascal Reusch, CC BY-SA 3.0 <https://creativecommons.org/licenses/by-sa/3.0>, via Wikimedia Commons; https://commons.wikimedia.org/wiki/File:Ponte_Quattro_Capi.jpg

164 https://commons.wikimedia.org/wiki/File:Aeolipile_illustration.png

165 https://commons.wikimedia.org/wiki/File:Mosa%C3%AFque_des_bikinis,_Piazza_Armerina.jpg

166 https://commons.wikimedia.org/wiki/File:Brennus_mg_9724.jpg

167 Andrea Ferrucci, CC0, via Wikimedia Commons: https://commons.wikimedia.org/wiki/File:Julius_Caesar_MET_267739.jpg

168 https://commons.wikimedia.org/wiki/File:Venus_and_Cupid_from_the_House_of_Marcus_Fabius_Rufus_at_Pompeii,_most_likely_a_depiction_of_Cleopatra_VII_(2).jpg

169 https://commons.wikimedia.org/wiki/File:011-Mark_Antony,_with_Cleopatra_VII_-3.jpg

170 Carlos Delgado, CC BY-SA 3.0 <https://creativecommons.org/licenses/by-sa/3.0>, via Wikimedia Commons https://commons.wikimedia.org/wiki/File:Ner%C3%B3n_y_Agripina.jpg

171 Carole Raddato from FRANKFURT, Germany, CC BY-SA 2.0 <https://creativecommons.org/licenses/by-sa/2.0>, via Wikimedia Commons:

https://commons.wikimedia.org/wiki/File:Hadrian-_An_Emperor_Cast_in_Bronze,_Israel_Museum_(27801269805).jpg

172 © José Luiz Bernardes Ribeiro: https://commons.wikimedia.org/wiki/File:Portrait_of_family_of_Septimius_Severus_-_Altes_Museum_-_Berlin_-_Germany_2017.jpg

173 https://commons.wikimedia.org/wiki/File:Cyprian_von_Karthago2.jpg

174 Immanuel Giel, CC BY-SA 4.0 <https://creativecommons.org/licenses/by-sa/4.0>, via Wikimedia Commons: https://commons.wikimedia.org/wiki/File:Schlosskirche_(Blieskastel)_Chi-Rho.jpg

175 York Minster, CC BY-SA 2.0 <https://creativecommons.org/licenses/by-sa/2.0>, via Wikimedia Commons: https://commons.wikimedia.org/wiki/File:Constantine_York_Minster.jpg

176 Museum of Fine Arts, Boston, CC0, via Wikimedia Commons: https://commons.wikimedia.org/wiki/File:ClaudiusGothicusSC265569.jpg

177 Classical Numismatic Group, Inc. http://www.cngcoins.com, CC BY-SA 2.5 <https://creativecommons.org/licenses/by-sa/2.5>, via Wikimedia Commons: https://commons.wikimedia.org/wiki/File:Valentinian1cng1570366obverse.jpg

178 A.Berger, CC BY-SA 3.0 <https://creativecommons.org/licenses/by-sa/3.0>, via Wikimedia Commons: https://commons.wikimedia.org/wiki/File:Attila_Museum.JPG

www.ingramcontent.com/pod-product-compliance
Lightning Source LLC
Chambersburg PA
CBHW070323010526
44107CB00004B/398